The Muslim OCD Recovery Guide

Overcoming Waswas and Religious Anxiety with Faith
and Evidence-Based Treatment

Kirill Esau Hafidi

Copyright © 2026 by Kirill Esau Hafidi

All rights reserved. No part of this publication may be reproduced, distributed, or transmitted in any form or by any means, including photocopying, recording, or other electronic or mechanical methods, without the prior written permission of the author, except in the case of brief quotations embodied in critical reviews and certain other noncommercial uses permitted by copyright law.

ISBN: 978-1-923646-77-3

First Edition: 2026

This book is intended for educational and informational purposes only and is not a substitute for professional medical advice, diagnosis, or treatment. The information provided represents the author's research and understanding but should not be considered definitive religious rulings or clinical recommendations for any individual situation.

Readers experiencing mental health concerns should consult qualified mental health professionals. Readers with religious questions should consult knowledgeable Islamic scholars. The combination of both professional psychological treatment and sound Islamic guidance is recommended for those struggling with OCD. This book does not create a therapist-patient or counselor-client relationship.

While this book references Islamic sources including Quranic verses, hadith, and scholarly opinions, readers should verify religious information with qualified scholars from their chosen school of thought. The author has made every effort to ensure accuracy of Islamic references and psychological information, but interpretations may vary among scholars and schools of jurisprudence. No warranty is made regarding the completeness or accuracy of the information provided.

Case examples in this book are composite illustrations created for educational purposes. Any resemblance to actual persons, living or deceased, or actual events is purely coincidental. Names, situations, and details have been modified to protect privacy while illustrating common OCD presentations in Muslim populations.

The treatment approaches described, particularly Exposure and Response Prevention (ERP), should ideally be practiced under the guidance of a qualified mental health professional specializing in OCD treatment. Self-directed treatment may be helpful but professional support is recommended, especially for moderate to severe cases.

Medication information is provided for educational purposes only. Any decisions regarding psychiatric medication should be made in consultation with qualified prescribing physicians. Do not start, stop, or adjust medications without medical supervision.

The author and publisher disclaim any liability for any adverse effects or consequences resulting from the use or application of the information contained in this book. Readers assume all responsibility for their use of this material.

If you are experiencing a mental health crisis or having thoughts of self-harm, please contact emergency services or a crisis hotline immediately. In the United States, call 988 for the Suicide and Crisis Lifeline.

Table of Contents

Preface 1
Chapter 1: What is OCD? Recognizing the Disorder Beyond "Just Being Religious" 4
    What OCD Actually Means 4
    The Four Components That Define OCD 5
    OCD vs. Healthy Religious Devotion 7
    OCD vs. Waswas (Understanding the Relationship) 8
    Why OCD Is NOT a Spiritual Failing 9
    Prevalence in Muslim Communities 10
    Case Studies: Profiles of Muslim OCD Sufferers 11
    What All These Cases Share 13
    What You Need to Know Going Forward 13
Chapter 2: Waswas in Islamic Tradition: Theology Meets Psychology 15
    Quranic References to Waswas and Shaytan 15
    Hadith Literature on Intrusive Thoughts 16
    Classical Islamic Scholars on Waswas 17
    The Concept of "Al-Waswas Al-Khannas" (The Whisperer) 19
    Islamic Perspective: When Do Thoughts Become Sinful? 20
    The Mercy of Allah: "Allah Does Not Burden a Soul Beyond What It Can Bear" 21
    Understanding That Allah Knows the Difference Between Waswas and Intention 22
    How OCD Exploits Religious Devotion 23
    The OCD-Waswas Connection: Where Theology and Psychology Meet 25
    What This Means for Your Recovery 26
Chapter 3: Muslim-Specific OCD Presentations 28
    Religious/Scrupulosity OCD 28
    Contamination OCD with Islamic Themes 33
    Harm OCD 35

- Relationship OCD (ROCD) 38
- Moral Scrupulosity 39
- Recognizing the Pattern 41

Chapter 4: How OCD Hijacks Your Faith 42
- The OCD Cycle Explained 42
- How Certainty-Seeking Feeds OCD 44
- Why Reassurance Doesn't Work 46
- The Role of Anxiety vs. Actual Sin 48
- OCD's Exploitation of Islamic Values 49
- The Difference Between Taqwa (God-Consciousness) and OCD 51
- How OCD Creates "False Prophets" of Doubt 52
- Breaking Free from the Hijacking 54

Chapter 5: Is Seeking Treatment Permissible? The Islamic Case for Therapy 56
- Prophetic Tradition of Seeking Treatment 56
- Scholarly Consensus on Mental Health Treatment 57
- Addressing Common Concerns 58
- The Concept of Tawakkul (Trust in Allah) Alongside Action 60
- Mental Health as Physical Health 62
- Fatawa from Contemporary Scholars on OCD Treatment 63
- What Treatment Actually Looks Like 64
- What About Spiritual Alternatives? 65
- Take Aways 66

Chapter 6: Distinguishing Religious Obligation from OCD Compulsion 68
- Fiqh Principles for Minimum Requirements 68
- The Concept of "Al-Mash'aqqa Tajlib al-Taysir" (Hardship Brings Ease) 70
- Rulings on Excessive Wudu 71
- Rulings on Excessive Prayer Repetition 73
- When Uncertainty is Acceptable in Worship 74
- The Danger of Bid'ah (Innovation) Through OCD 75
- Consulting Qualified Scholars vs. OCD-Driven Research 76
- Setting Boundaries with Islamic Practices During Treatment 78

    When to Follow Fiqh vs. When to Follow Your Therapist 80

    What This Means for Your Recovery 81

Chapter 7: Exposure and Response Prevention (ERP) 83

    What is ERP and Why It Works 83

    The Neuroscience of OCD and Extinction Learning 84

    Islamic Compatibility: ERP as Trusting Allah's Plan 85

    Creating Your Fear Hierarchy 86

    Planning Exposures 88

    Response Prevention Strategies 89

    Working with Uncertainty in a Faith Context 91

    Case Examples: Muslim Individuals in ERP 92

    What All Three Cases Show 94

    The Path Forward 95

Chapter 8: Cognitive Approaches: Restructuring OCD Thoughts 96

    Cognitive Behavioral Therapy (CBT) for OCD 96

    Identifying Cognitive Distortions 97

    Thought Records from Islamic Perspective 99

    Challenging OCD "Fatwas" 101

    Islamic Cognitive Reframes 103

    Inference-Based Cognitive Behavioral Therapy (I-CBT) 105

    Distinguishing Imagined Possibility from Reality 105

    The Obsessional Story vs. What Actually Happened 106

    Trusting Your Senses (A Form of Tawakkul) 107

    Putting It All Together 108

Chapter 9: Acceptance and Commitment Therapy (ACT): Living with Uncertainty 109

    ACT Principles and Islamic Compatibility 109

    Psychological Flexibility and Surrender to Allah 111

    Defusion from Intrusive Thoughts 112

    Values Clarification: What Kind of Muslim Do You Want to Be? 113

    Committed Action Despite Discomfort 115

    Mindfulness Practices Compatible with Dhikr 116

    The Concept of Sabr (Patience) in ACT Context 118

    Acceptance Is Not Resignation 119

    ACT and ERP Together 119

    The Willingness to Struggle 120

    What This Means for Your Recovery 121

Chapter 10: Islamic Spiritual Practices as Support (Not Compulsions) 123

    Healthy Use of Dhikr and Dua 123

    Ruqyah: When Is It Appropriate? 125

    The Role of Quran Recitation 126

    Distinguishing Spiritual Practice from Reassurance-Seeking 127

    Creating a Balanced Spiritual Routine 127

    When to Seek Islamic Spiritual Counseling vs. Psychological Treatment 129

    Integration: Faith as Motivation, Not Compulsion 130

    The Beautiful Balance 131

Chapter 11: Assessment and Preparation 133

    Self-Assessment Tools (Y-BOCS Adaptation) 133

    Identifying Your OCD Subtypes 135

    Mapping Your Triggers and Compulsions 136

    Building Your Support Team 138

    Setting Realistic Recovery Goals 141

    Creating Safety Plans 142

    Practical Assessment Exercise 144

    Moving Forward 145

Chapter 12: Wudu and Prayer: Reclaiming Your Worship 146

    Wudu Protocol 146

    ERP Hierarchy for Ablution 147

    Time-Limited Wudu Practice 147

    Managing Doubt During Wudu 149

    Prayer Protocol 150

    Managing Intrusive Thoughts During Salah 151

    Perfection vs. Sincerity 152

    Prostration and Movement 153

    Practical Example: Bilal's Prayer Recovery 154

    Your Wudu and Prayer Protocol 155

    What to Expect 156

Chapter 13: Purity and Contamination Concerns 157

    Understanding Najis from Fiqh Perspective 157

    ERP for Contamination Fears 158

    Bathroom and Istinja Practices 159

    Menstruation-Related Exposures 161

    Clothing and Environment Contamination 162

    Gradual Reduction of Washing Rituals 163

    Scripts for Managing Uncertainty About Purity 164

    Aisha's Contamination Recovery 165

    Your Contamination Protocol 166

Chapter 14: Intrusive Thoughts: When Your Mind Whispers Blasphemy 168

    Understanding That Thoughts Are Not Sins 168

    The Islamic Position on Intrusive Thoughts 169

    Why Trying NOT to Think Something Doesn't Work 170

    Exposure to Blasphemous Thoughts (With Theological Grounding) 172

    Accepting Uncertainty About Your Faith 174

    Resisting Mental Rituals 175

    Not Seeking Forgiveness for Intrusive Thoughts 176

    Not Mentally "Correcting" Thoughts 177

    Not Testing Your Faith 178

    Case Study: Khalid's Recovery from Blasphemous Thought OCD 179

    Your Intrusive Thought Protocol 180

Chapter 15: Moral Scrupulosity and Excessive Repentance 182

    The Balance of Tawbah 182

    When Istighfar Becomes Compulsion 183

    ERP for Moral Uncertainty 184

    Accepting That You Might Have Sinned 185

- Trusting Allah's Mercy Without Guarantees 186
- Reducing Confession Behaviors 187
- Managing "What If I Forgot to Repent" Thoughts 189
- Your Moral Scrupulosity Protocol 190

Chapter 16: Building Your Personal Recovery Plan 192
- 12-Week Structured ERP Program 192
- Daily Practice Schedules 194
- Tracking Progress 196
- Managing Setbacks 197
- Adjusting Difficulty Levels 199
- Self-Compassion Practices 200
- When to Seek Professional Help 201
- Your 12-Week Plan Template 202
- Moving Forward 203

Chapter 17: For Family Members: How to Help Without Enabling 205
- Understanding Accommodation 205
- Why You Accommodate 206
- How Reassurance Feeds OCD 207
- Supporting Exposure Work 208
- What to Say and What Not to Say 210
- Managing Your Own Anxiety as a Loved One 210
- Cultural Considerations in Muslim Families 211
- When the Family Member Is Resistant to Treatment 213
- Resources for Families 214
- What Healthy Support Looks Like 215
- What You Need to Know 216

Chapter 18: For Islamic Counselors and Imams 217
- Recognizing OCD vs. Spiritual Struggle 217
- When to Refer to Mental Health Professionals 219
- How to Provide Islamic Guidance Without Feeding OCD 220
- Avoiding Reassurance Traps 221

    Fatwa Guidelines for OCD Sufferers 222

    Collaboration with Therapists 223

    Cultural Sensitivity in Muslim Communities 225

    What to Say in Your Khutbahs and Classes 225

    Handling Your Own Limitations 226

    The Profound Impact You Can Have 227

Chapter 19: Medication: Islamic Perspective and Practical Guidance 228

    Islamic Rulings on Psychiatric Medication 228

    How SSRIs Work for OCD 230

    Common Medications and Side Effects 230

    Combining Medication with Therapy 232

    Working with Prescribers 232

    Addressing Stigma in Muslim Communities 233

    When Medication Is Necessary 234

    Long-Term Use 235

    What Medication Can and Can't Do 236

    Practical Guidance 237

    What Success Looks Like 238

    Making the Decision 238

Chapter 20: Relapse Prevention and Lifelong Recovery 239

    Understanding That Recovery Is Not "Cured" 239

    Maintaining Exposure Practices 240

    Early Warning Signs 241

    Booster Sessions 242

    Building Resilience 243

    Keeping Faith and Treatment in Balance 244

    Your New Relationship with Uncertainty 245

    Living a Values-Driven Life as a Muslim in Recovery 246

    What Long-Term Recovery Looks Like 247

    The Freedom You've Gained 248

    Your Ongoing Commitment 248

Chapter 21: OCD in Muslim Youth and Children 250
- Recognizing OCD in Young Muslims 250
- Developmentally Appropriate Treatment 251
- Working with Parents 253
- School Accommodations 255
- Age-Appropriate Islamic Education Without Triggering OCD 257
- When to Seek Professional Help for Children 258
- Growing Up with OCD 259

Chapter 22: Women-Specific Issues 261
- Menstruation-Related OCD 261
- Pregnancy and Postpartum OCD 263
- Modesty-Related Compulsions 264
- Gender-Specific Treatment Considerations 265

Chapter 23: Marriage and Relationships with OCD 268
- Relationship OCD (ROCD) in Muslim Context 268
- Communication with Spouse 269
- Sexual Relationship Concerns 270
- When to Disclose OCD in Marriage Search 271
- Couples Therapy Considerations 272

Chapter 24: Hajj and Ramadan: Managing OCD During Sacred Times 275
- Planning for Ramadan with OCD 275
- Fasting and Medication 276
- Tarawih Prayers 277
- Hajj Preparation and Accommodations 278
- Managing Scrupulosity During Sacred Practices 280
- Working with Scholars for Accommodations 280
- What You've Learned 281

Appendix A: Resources 283
- Mental Health Professionals with Islamic Cultural Competence 283
- Online Support Groups 284
- Recommended Books and Websites 285

    Crisis Resources 286

    Islamic Counseling Services 286

    Making the Most of These Resources 287

Appendix B: Assessment Tools 288

    Y-BOCS Self-Assessment 288

    OCD Subtype Checklist 290

    Accommodation Scale for Family Members 291

    Progress Tracking Forms 292

Appendix C: Quick Reference Guides 294

    Wudu Minimum Requirements Chart 294

    Prayer Essential Actions 295

    Purity Rulings Quick Guide 296

    Crisis Management Scripts 296

    Thought Record Templates 297

Appendix D: Islamic Scholarly References 299

    Compilation of Relevant Fatwas on OCD 299

    Quranic Verses on Mercy and Ease 299

    Hadith on Mental Health and Treatment 300

    Scholarly Quotes on Waswas 301

Appendix E: ERP Practice Worksheets 303

    Fear Hierarchy Templates 303

    Exposure Planning Forms 304

    Daily Practice Logs 305

Appendix F: Glossary 306

Acknowledgments 311

About the Author 312

References and Bibliography 314

Preface

For years, Muslims with obsessive-compulsive disorder have been caught between two incomplete worlds. The mental health field offers effective treatments but often lacks understanding of Islamic practices and concerns. Islamic counseling provides spiritual guidance but sometimes fails to recognize OCD as a medical disorder requiring specialized treatment. Neither approach alone is sufficient—and Muslims with OCD deserve better.

This book exists because too many Muslims are suffering in silence, believing their religious anxiety is a test they must endure alone, or worse, evidence of weak faith. They spend hours trapped in rituals that should take minutes. They're tormented by intrusive thoughts that horrify them precisely because they love Allah. They're exhausted, isolated, and desperate for help that honors both their faith and their mental health.

The integration of Islamic scholarship and evidence-based psychology isn't just possible—it's necessary. Islam has addressed waswas (intrusive whispers) for over 1,400 years. The Prophet Muhammad, peace be upon him, taught the Companions how to handle disturbing thoughts. Classical scholars developed principles to help Muslims distinguish reasonable religious practice from excessive scrupulosity. Contemporary Islamic scholars affirm that seeking mental health treatment is not only permissible but often obligatory.

Meanwhile, psychological science has made enormous strides in understanding and treating OCD. Exposure and Response Prevention (ERP) is one of the most effective psychological treatments we have for any mental health condition. Cognitive-behavioral approaches, acceptance-based strategies, and when needed, psychiatric medications provide real relief for millions of people with OCD worldwide.

The question isn't which approach to choose. The question is: How do we bring these two bodies of wisdom together to serve Muslims struggling with OCD?

This book represents an attempt to answer that question. It's written for multiple audiences: Muslims experiencing religious OCD who need practical recovery tools; family members trying to support loved ones without enabling the disorder; mental health professionals treating Muslim clients; and Islamic counselors and imams fielding questions about religious anxiety and compulsive behaviors.

The approach is straightforward: Take Islam seriously as Muslims actually practice it, with all its requirements and nuances. Take psychology seriously as a science that has developed effective treatments through rigorous research. Then show how these work together rather than against each other.

Throughout these pages, you'll find Islamic sources—Quranic verses, authentic hadith, scholarly rulings, and fiqh principles—presented alongside psychological concepts and treatment protocols. You'll see how the Prophet's teachings on waswas align with modern understanding of intrusive thoughts. You'll learn how Islamic principles about certainty, mercy, and ease provide a theological foundation for response prevention. You'll discover that pursuing professional treatment while maintaining faith isn't compromise—it's following both Islamic guidance and common sense.

Some Muslims worry that psychological treatment will weaken their faith or ask them to violate Islamic principles. This concern is understandable but unfounded. Effective OCD treatment doesn't require abandoning religious practice. It requires distinguishing authentic Islamic requirements from OCD's distortions. When a therapist asks you to resist repeating prayers compulsively, they're not attacking Islam—they're helping you return to how the Prophet, peace be upon him, actually taught Muslims to pray: once, with sincerity, then moving forward with life.

Some mental health professionals worry that accommodating religious concerns will interfere with treatment. This concern is also understandable but overstated. You can teach ERP while respecting that your Muslim client actually needs to perform wudu and pray—you're just helping them do it according to Islamic requirements rather than OCD demands. Cultural competence isn't an obstacle to treatment; it's a prerequisite for effective treatment.

This book is long because OCD is complicated and Islam is detailed. You'll find 24 chapters covering everything from the neurobiology of OCD to managing symptoms during Hajj. You'll find appendices with assessment tools, reference guides, and resources. You'll find case examples illustrating common presentations and recovery journeys.

But the core message is simple: OCD is a treatable medical disorder. Islam is a religion of mercy and ease. Effective treatment exists. Recovery is possible. And you don't have to choose between your faith and your mental health.

You can reclaim your worship from OCD. You can practice Islam with peace instead of panic. You can experience prayer as connection with Allah rather than torture. Thousands of Muslims have walked this path before you—pursuing treatment, learning to distinguish waswas from genuine faith, rebuilding their relationship with Islamic practice, and emerging stronger and more spiritually grounded than before.

This journey requires courage. It requires challenging the anxiety that has controlled you, sitting with uncertainty that feels unbearable, and resisting compulsions that promise relief. It requires patience with yourself when progress feels slow. It requires help from professionals who understand OCD and from communities that support mental health.

But the freedom on the other side is worth every difficult step. The ability to pray five times daily without torture, to practice Islam with joy, to connect with Allah without constant fear—this is what Islam is meant to be. This is what recovery offers. This is what you deserve.

Bismillah - In the name of Allah, the Most Merciful, the Most Compassionate. May this work be of benefit to all who seek healing, and may Allah grant recovery to every Muslim struggling with OCD.

Chapter 1: What is OCD? Recognizing the Disorder Beyond "Just Being Religious"

Here's something that happens all the time: A young Muslim man spends three hours performing wudu before each prayer. He washes each body part exactly seven times, recounts his actions, and starts over if he loses track. His family tells him he's "just very dedicated to Islam." His friends admire his devotion. But inside, he's drowning in anxiety, missing work, and feeling like he's going insane.

This isn't dedication. This is Obsessive-Compulsive Disorder.

And it's one of the most misunderstood conditions in Muslim communities worldwide.

Let's clear something up right now: **OCD is a medical disorder, not a sign of strong faith**. It's not about being "too religious" or "overly careful about following Islam." OCD is a specific psychiatric condition with identifiable symptoms, a neurobiological basis, and evidence-based treatments that work.

But here's the tricky part. OCD loves to disguise itself as religious devotion, especially in communities where faith matters deeply. It whispers, "You're just being a good Muslim. Allah wants perfection, doesn't He?" And that's exactly how it traps you.

So we need to get crystal clear about what OCD actually is, how it works, and how it's completely different from healthy religious practice. Because until you can spot the difference, you'll keep feeding the disorder while thinking you're feeding your soul.

What OCD Actually Means

The American Psychiatric Association defines OCD in the Diagnostic and Statistical Manual of Mental Disorders, Fifth Edition (DSM-5) as a condition characterized by the presence of obsessions, compulsions, or both (American Psychiatric Association, 2013). But what does that really mean when you're living it?

Obsessions are intrusive thoughts, images, or urges that pop into your mind without permission and cause significant anxiety or distress. They're unwanted. They're repetitive. And they feel impossible to control.

Here's what makes them different from regular worries: You recognize that these thoughts are excessive or unreasonable, but you can't shake them. They stick like psychological glue.

Compulsions are repetitive behaviors or mental acts that you feel driven to perform in response to an obsession or according to rigid rules. You do these things to reduce anxiety or prevent some dreaded outcome. But here's the catch—the relief never lasts. You're back to square one within minutes or hours.

The International OCD Foundation estimates that OCD affects about 1-2% of the general population worldwide (International OCD Foundation, 2021). But research suggests the rates might be significantly higher in Muslim-majority countries, particularly when religious themes are involved.

A study published in the *Journal of Obsessive-Compulsive and Related Disorders* found that religious obsessions and compulsions are among the most common presentations in Middle Eastern populations (Yorulmaz, Gençöz, & Woody, 2010). Another study examining OCD in Turkish patients found that religious obsessions appeared in 31% of cases—far higher than typically seen in Western populations (Yorulmaz, Yılmaz, & Gençöz, 2004).

So if you're Muslim and struggling with these issues, you're not alone. Not even close.

The Four Components That Define OCD

To meet the diagnostic criteria for OCD, your experience needs to include four specific elements. Think of these as the four legs of a table—if any one is missing, it's probably not OCD (though it might be something else worth addressing).

Component 1: Obsessions That Won't Quit

These aren't casual worries about whether you locked the door. Obsessions are persistent, unwanted thoughts that intrude into your consciousness repeatedly throughout the day. They cause marked anxiety and feel almost impossible to dismiss.

For Muslim individuals, common obsessions include:

- Fears about whether wudu was performed correctly
- Doubts about whether prayers "counted" or were done with proper intention
- Terrifying thoughts about committing shirk (associating partners with Allah)
- Graphic, blasphemous images that horrify the person experiencing them
- Fears of being contaminated by najis (ritual impurity)

A young woman we'll call Maryam described it this way: "The thought would come—'What if I didn't really mean the prayer?'—and it was like an alarm going off in my brain. I couldn't think about anything else until I 'fixed' it."

Component 2: Compulsions That Promise Relief

Compulsions are what you do to make the obsessions stop—at least temporarily. They're behaviors or mental rituals that follow specific rules, often rules that make no logical sense to anyone else (and sometimes don't even make sense to you).

Common compulsions in Muslim OCD sufferers include:

- Repeating wudu multiple times until it "feels right"
- Redoing prayers over and over
- Excessive seeking of reassurance from imams or knowledgeable Muslims
- Mental reviewing of past actions to check for sins
- Excessive istighfar (seeking forgiveness) repeated in specific patterns

Here's the trap: Compulsions work. Sort of. They reduce anxiety for a few minutes. But then the obsession returns, often stronger than before, demanding another round of compulsions.

Component 3: Distress That Disrupts Your Life

This is where we separate OCD from quirky habits or preferences. The obsessions and compulsions cause significant distress. They're not just annoying—they're agonizing. They interfere with your ability to function normally.

Research using the Yale-Brown Obsessive Compulsive Scale (Y-BOCS), the gold standard assessment tool for OCD, shows that moderate to severe OCD can be as disabling as major depressive disorder (Eisen et al., 2006).

Ask yourself: Do these thoughts and behaviors:

- Make you late for work, school, or social obligations?
- Damage your relationships with family or friends?
- Prevent you from engaging in activities you used to enjoy?
- Cause physical exhaustion from repeated rituals?
- Make you feel hopeless or depressed?

If yes, then we're talking about a disorder, not just "being careful."

Component 4: Time Consumption That Steals Your Life

The DSM-5 specifies that obsessions and compulsions must take up more than one hour per day, though most people with moderate to severe OCD spend far more time than that (American Psychiatric Association, 2013).

Think about it. One hour every single day—that's 365 hours per year, or about 15 full days—lost to thoughts and rituals that accomplish nothing. And for many people, we're talking about 3, 4, 6 hours daily.

A study of OCD patients in Iran found that participants spent an average of 4.5 hours per day on obsessive-compulsive symptoms (Moradi et al., 2020). That's more than a part-time job dedicated to anxiety.

One young man, Ahmad, calculated that he spent approximately 25 hours per week on OCD-related behaviors—primarily repeating prayers and seeking reassurance online about Islamic rulings. That's nearly a full-time job's worth of time, producing zero spiritual benefit and maximum suffering.

OCD vs. Healthy Religious Devotion

This is where things get confusing, especially for Muslims who take their faith seriously. Islam encourages cleanliness, mindfulness in worship, and careful attention to religious obligations. So how do you tell the difference between *taqwa* (God-consciousness) and OCD?

Here's your litmus test:

Healthy religious devotion:

- Brings peace, tranquility, and connection to Allah
- Follows established Islamic guidelines without excessive elaboration
- Can be adjusted with flexibility when circumstances change
- Respects the principle of *yusur* (ease) that Islam teaches
- Doesn't interfere with other religious obligations or life responsibilities
- Involves trust (*tawakkul*) in Allah's mercy and acceptance

OCD:

- Creates anxiety, dread, and feelings of being trapped
- Demands certainty beyond what Islam requires
- Becomes more rigid and demanding over time
- Violates the Islamic principle that "the religion is ease, not hardship"
- Prevents you from fulfilling other obligations (like showing up for work or caring for family)
- Rests on doubt and fear rather than trust in Allah

The Prophet Muhammad (peace be upon him) was reported to have said, "This religion is easy. No one becomes harsh and strict in the religion without it overwhelming him" (Sahih Bukhari, Volume 1, Book 2, Number 38). OCD is the definition of harsh and strict—and it absolutely overwhelms people.

Dr. Jonathan Abramowitz, a leading OCD researcher, points out that the content of obsessions often reflects what matters most to the individual (Abramowitz, 2018). So if Islam is central to your identity, OCD will latch onto Islamic themes. If you're a loving parent, OCD might create fears about harming your children. The disorder targets what you value most.

This doesn't mean your faith caused your OCD. It means OCD exploits your faith.

OCD vs. Waswas (Understanding the Relationship)

Now we get to something really important for Muslim readers: How does the Islamic concept of *waswas* relate to what Western psychology calls OCD?

Waswas is an Arabic term that refers to the whispers of Shaytan (Satan)—intrusive, disturbing thoughts that create doubt and anxiety. The Quran mentions this concept directly:

"Who whispers [evil] into the breasts of mankind" (Quran 114:5)

Islamic scholars throughout history have recognized that these whispers are:

- Not the person's own thoughts
- Not sinful to experience
- Meant to disturb and distract from worship
- Best addressed by ignoring them and moving forward

Sound familiar? This is remarkably similar to how modern psychology describes obsessive thoughts.

Here's the relationship: Waswas describes the *experience* of intrusive thoughts from a theological perspective. OCD describes the *disorder* that results when these thoughts become chronic, distressing, and lead to compulsive behaviors.

Not everyone who experiences waswas has OCD. Occasional intrusive thoughts are normal and happen to everyone. But when waswas becomes:

- Persistent and daily
- Accompanied by compulsive rituals
- Time-consuming (more than an hour daily)
- Significantly distressing
- Interfering with normal functioning

...then you're dealing with OCD, not just ordinary waswas.

Think of it this way: Everyone experiences occasional headaches (like everyone experiences occasional waswas). But chronic, debilitating migraines that require medical treatment are a disorder (like OCD is a disorder).

Classical Islamic scholars like Imam Al-Ghazali and Ibn Taymiyyah wrote extensively about excessive waswas and how to manage it. Their advice—ignore the doubts and continue with your worship—aligns remarkably well with modern exposure and response prevention therapy, the gold standard treatment for OCD. We'll explore this connection more in Chapter 2.

Why OCD Is NOT a Spiritual Failing

Let's address the elephant in the room. In many Muslim communities, mental health struggles carry stigma. People might think:

- "If your faith was strong enough, you wouldn't have these problems"
- "Just make more dua and the thoughts will go away"
- "This is a test from Allah that you're failing"
- "Maybe you have jinn or need ruqyah"

Let me be absolutely clear: **OCD is a neurobiological disorder, not a character weakness or spiritual deficiency**.

Research using brain imaging has shown that people with OCD have distinct patterns of brain activity, particularly in circuits involving the orbitofrontal cortex, anterior cingulate cortex, and striatum (Saxena & Rauch, 2000). These are the brain regions involved in detecting errors, generating anxiety, and creating habitual behaviors.

In other words, your brain's alarm system is stuck in overdrive. This isn't something you can simply "pray away" any more than you could pray away diabetes or asthma.

A study published in *Depression and Anxiety* examined Muslim patients with OCD and found that increased religious involvement actually predicted *more severe* OCD symptoms when religious content was involved (Hussain & Cochrane, 2003). This doesn't mean religion causes OCD—it means OCD latches onto whatever matters most to you.

Here's what Islam actually teaches:

The Prophet Muhammad (peace be upon him) said, "Seek treatment, for Allah has not sent down a disease except that He has sent down a cure for it" (Sunan Abi Dawud,

Book 29, Hadith 3855). Notice—seek treatment. Not just make dua. Not just be patient. *Seek treatment*.

Think about it. If you broke your leg, would you refuse to see a doctor and just pray for healing? Of course not. You'd pray *and* go to the hospital. Mental health conditions deserve the same approach.

The Quran states: "Allah does not burden a soul beyond that it can bear" (Quran 2:286). OCD feels like an unbearable burden because, in a sense, it is. It's not a test of faith that you're supposed to white-knuckle through alone. It's a medical condition that requires proper treatment.

Prevalence in Muslim Communities

The research on OCD prevalence in Muslim communities reveals something striking: religious-themed OCD appears to be significantly more common in Muslim-majority countries than in Western populations.

A comprehensive review published in *Comprehensive Psychiatry* examined OCD presentations across different cultures and found that religious obsessions were reported in 50% or more of OCD patients in Middle Eastern countries, compared to about 10-15% in Western countries (Fontenelle et al., 2004).

A study specifically examining Turkish OCD patients found that 31% experienced religious obsessions, making it one of the most common symptom presentations (Yorulmaz et al., 2004). Research from Iran showed similar patterns, with religious obsessions affecting nearly half of OCD patients (Moradi et al., 2020).

But here's what's interesting—and important: The overall rates of OCD aren't necessarily higher in Muslim countries. What's different is the *content* of the obsessions. Muslims are more likely to experience religious-themed OCD because religion plays a central role in daily life.

A study comparing British Muslims with OCD to non-Muslim British individuals with OCD found that while the disorder's prevalence was similar, the symptom content differed dramatically (Mahgoub & Abdel-Hafeiz, 1991). Muslim participants were more likely to report contamination fears related to ritual purity and obsessions about prayer performance.

What does this tell us? **OCD is a universal human disorder that adapts to local culture**. In the United States, people might obsess about germs on doorknobs. In Muslim communities, people might obsess about najis on their clothing. The mechanism is identical; only the content changes.

Case Studies: Profiles of Muslim OCD Sufferers

Let's look at real patterns of how OCD presents in Muslim individuals. These are composite profiles based on common presentations, not specific individuals.

Case 1: Fatima, 28 – Purity Obsessions

Fatima's OCD began in her early twenties, shortly after she started practicing Islam more seriously. What started as careful attention to *tahara* (ritual purity) gradually spiraled into a nightmare.

Her morning routine looked like this: Wake up, go to the bathroom, shower for 45 minutes while obsessing about whether any urine droplets might have touched her body. Change clothes three times because she wasn't sure if the first two outfits were clean. Begin wudu, restart it seven times because she lost count or wasn't certain she washed properly. Finally start morning prayer—two hours after waking up, already exhausted.

Fatima knew her behavior was excessive. Her mother had performed wudu in two minutes her whole life and was a devoted Muslim. But Fatima couldn't shake the feeling: "What if my prayer doesn't count? What if Allah doesn't accept it because I missed a spot?"

She avoided certain areas of her home she'd deemed "contaminated." She changed her clothes multiple times daily. She spent hours researching Islamic rulings on purity online, seeking reassurance that only made her anxiety worse.

This is classic contamination OCD with an Islamic theme. The obsession: "I might be in a state of ritual impurity." The compulsion: Excessive washing and checking. The result: A life consumed by anxiety.

Case 2: Ahmed, 35 – Scrupulosity and Blasphemous Thoughts

Ahmed was a practicing Muslim with a successful career and young family. Then the thoughts started.

Horrifying, graphic blasphemous thoughts would intrude during prayer. Images of disrespecting the Quran. Thoughts that questioned Allah's existence or authority. Ahmed was mortified. He would never think such things—yet there they were, invading his mind dozens of times each day.

He started praying constantly for forgiveness. He'd repeat prayers up to 20 times, convinced he'd had a bad thought during the previous attempt and it didn't count. He researched obsessively online: "If you have a bad thought during prayer, is it invalid?" "Can you lose your faith by thinking something?"

The more he fought the thoughts, the more powerful they became. He started avoiding prayer altogether because the anxiety was unbearable. This created more guilt: "Now I'm not even praying! Maybe I really am losing my faith!"

Ahmed was experiencing *harm OCD* with religious content—specifically, fears of committing spiritual harm (shirk, blasphemy). The thoughts themselves were waswas, but his reaction to them (avoidance, excessive prayer, constant reassurance-seeking) turned it into OCD.

Case 3: Yasmin, 42 – Religious Perfectionism

Yasmin had always been detail-oriented. But after attending a particularly inspiring religious lecture series, something shifted. She became convinced that every aspect of her worship needed to be perfect.

She would recite Surah Al-Fatiha in prayer, then doubt whether she'd pronounced a letter correctly. She'd start over. And over. Her prayers stretched from five minutes to 45 minutes as she repeated verses to ensure perfection.

She began recording herself reciting Quran so she could review it later for errors. She spent hours researching the exact movements required in prayer—exactly how far to bow, exactly where hands should be placed.

Her husband tried to help: "Yasmin, this isn't normal. Islam teaches ease, not hardship." But Yasmin couldn't accept anything less than perfect. "How can I stand before Allah with sloppy prayer?" she'd ask.

Yasmin's case illustrates how OCD transforms legitimate Islamic values (excellence in worship) into tyrannical demands (absolute perfection or you're failing Allah). The line between *ihsan* (excellence) and OCD is this: *ihsan* brings peace and draws you closer to Allah; OCD brings anxiety and makes worship feel like torture.

Case 4: Hassan, 19 – Doubt About Intention (Niyyah)

Hassan's OCD focused entirely on *niyyah*—the intention behind actions. Islam teaches that actions are judged by intentions, and Hassan's mind latched onto this teaching with a death grip.

Before each prayer, he'd try to form the "correct" intention. But immediately, doubt would flood in: "Did I really intend to pray for Allah's sake? Or was there some ego involved? Was I showing off? Was I distracted?"

He'd try again. And again. Sometimes he'd stand for 20 minutes before prayer, trying to achieve the "right" mental state. He'd finish a prayer, then obsess for hours: "Did that prayer count? Was my intention pure enough?"

The same pattern infected every good deed. Giving charity? "Did I intend it for Allah, or did I want recognition?" Helping someone? "Was I being selfless, or seeking praise?"

Hassan's disorder transformed one of Islam's beautiful teachings—that sincere intention matters more than outward show—into a weapon of self-torture.

What All These Cases Share

Look at these four individuals. Different ages, different specific symptoms, different areas of struggle. But they all share the same underlying pattern:

1. **Intrusive thoughts or doubts** that create intense anxiety
2. **Compulsive behaviors or mental rituals** performed to reduce that anxiety
3. **Temporary relief** followed by return of obsessions
4. **Life interference**—relationships strained, time consumed, functioning impaired
5. **Recognition that the behavior is excessive** (at least sometimes)

This is OCD. Not weak faith. Not lack of Islamic knowledge. Not spiritual attack (though it certainly feels like one).

OCD is a pattern of anxiety and compulsive behavior that hijacks whatever matters most to you. And for Muslims, faith matters most—so OCD goes after faith.

What You Need to Know Going Forward

OCD is a specific psychiatric disorder with clear diagnostic criteria. It's not just being "really religious" or "very clean" or "careful about following Islam." It's a condition where intrusive thoughts create intense anxiety, leading to compulsive behaviors that provide only temporary relief.

For Muslim individuals, OCD often latches onto religious themes because religion is central to identity and daily life. This doesn't mean Islam causes OCD—it means OCD exploits what you value most.

The four components of OCD—obsessions, compulsions, distress, and time consumption—must all be present for an official diagnosis. But even if you don't meet full criteria, OCD-like symptoms can still cause significant suffering and deserve attention.

Research shows that religious-themed OCD is common in Muslim populations, with rates of religious obsessions ranging from 31% to over 50% in various studies. You're not alone, you're not weird, and you're not failing at Islam.

Most critically: **OCD is not a spiritual failing**. It's a neurobiological disorder that requires proper treatment. Islamic teachings support seeking treatment for illness, and countless Muslims have recovered from OCD using evidence-based therapy while maintaining or even strengthening their faith.

In the next chapter, we'll explore how Islamic theology has understood waswas for over 1,400 years—and you'll see that the wisdom of Islamic scholars aligns remarkably well with modern psychological treatment.

Chapter 2: Waswas in Islamic Tradition: Theology Meets Psychology

Something fascinating happens when you read classical Islamic scholars on the topic of waswas: They could be describing modern OCD treatment protocols.

Seriously. Scholars writing 800 years ago recommended approaches that mirror what cognitive-behavioral therapists prescribe today. They warned against excessive doubt, told people to ignore intrusive thoughts, emphasized that Allah judges intentions rather than fleeting mental content, and taught that certainty-seeking in matters of faith can become destructive.

This isn't coincidence. Islamic theology, developed over centuries of human experience, identified the same patterns that modern psychology has studied systematically. The language differs—one speaks of shaytan and waswas, the other of intrusive thoughts and compulsions—but they're describing the same human struggle.

So before we talk about exposure therapy, cognitive restructuring, or any other modern treatment, we need to understand what Islam itself teaches about these tormenting thoughts. Because when you're a Muslim with OCD, you need to know: **Your religion doesn't demand what your disorder demands**.

Quranic References to Waswas and Shaytan

The Quran addresses the phenomenon of waswas directly, particularly in Surah An-Nas, the 114th and final chapter:

"Say, 'I seek refuge in the Lord of mankind, The Sovereign of mankind, The God of mankind, From the evil of the retreating whisperer—Who whispers [evil] into the breasts of mankind—From among the jinn and mankind.'" (Quran 114:1-6)

The Arabic word *al-waswas* (الْوَسْوَاس) literally refers to the whisperer. The related verb *waswasa* means to whisper or to insinuate. The term *al-khannas* (الْخَنَّاس), translated as "the retreating whisperer," comes from a root meaning to withdraw or hide.

Here's what's significant: The waswas is described as something that *withdraws* when confronted or when someone seeks refuge in Allah. This detail becomes critically important for treatment, as we'll see.

The Quran also mentions shaytan's role in creating doubt and discord:

"Satan only wants to cause between you animosity and hatred through intoxicants and gambling and to avert you from the remembrance of Allah and from prayer. So will you not desist?" (Quran 5:91)

And in another verse:

"And if an evil suggestion comes to you from Satan, then seek refuge in Allah. Indeed, He is Hearing and Knowing." (Quran 7:200)

Notice the instruction: *seek refuge*, not "engage in extensive rituals to neutralize the thought." Not "pray 100 times to undo the suggestion." Just seek refuge and move on.

The Quran further clarifies that shaytan has no actual power over believers, only the power to whisper:

"Indeed, he has no authority over those who have believed and rely upon their Lord. His authority is only over those who take him as an ally and those who through him associate others with Allah." (Quran 16:99-100)

Think about what this means for OCD. The intrusive thought itself—the waswas—has no power over you. It doesn't make you a bad Muslim. It doesn't invalidate your worship. It doesn't put you in spiritual danger. It's a whisper that you can acknowledge and dismiss.

Hadith Literature on Intrusive Thoughts

The hadith literature provides even more specific guidance about dealing with intrusive, disturbing thoughts. Several narrations directly address the concerns that plague people with religious OCD.

One of the most relevant hadiths comes from Sahih Muslim:

Abu Huraira reported that some people from amongst the Companions of the Apostle (may peace be upon him) came to him and said: "Verily we perceive in our minds that which every one of us considers it too grave to express." He (the Holy Prophet) said: "Do you really perceive it?" They said: "Yes." Upon this he remarked: "That is the prominent manifestation of faith." (Sahih Muslim, Book 1, Hadith 209)

Read that again. The Companions—the best generation of Muslims—experienced thoughts so disturbing they were afraid to even speak them aloud. And the Prophet's response? This is actually evidence of strong faith, not weak faith.

Why? Because **only someone who truly cares about Islam would be distressed by blasphemous thoughts**. If you didn't care about Allah, a random blasphemous thought wouldn't bother you at all. The fact that you're horrified by such thoughts proves your faith, not the opposite.

Another narration makes this even clearer:

Some of the Companions came to the Prophet and asked him: "We find in our hearts thoughts that are too terrible to speak of." He said: "Are you really having such thoughts?" They said: "Yes." He said: "That is a clear sign of faith." (Sahih Muslim, Book 1, Hadith 210)

The Prophet (peace be upon him) also specifically addressed excessive doubt in worship:

Abu Huraira reported: The Messenger of Allah (peace be upon him) said, "Shaytan comes to one of you and says, 'Who created this and that?' until he says, 'Who created your Lord?' When it reaches that point, let him seek refuge in Allah and stop such thoughts." (Sahih Bukhari, Book 59, Hadith 336)

Notice the instruction: *seek refuge and stop*. Not "answer the doubts with theological arguments." Not "research extensively until you achieve certainty." Seek refuge and stop engaging.

This is precisely the response prevention component of modern OCD treatment—don't engage with the intrusive thought, don't perform mental compulsions to neutralize it, just let it be and move forward.

Classical Islamic Scholars on Waswas

The great Islamic scholars throughout history didn't just acknowledge waswas—they wrote extensively about it, often with remarkable psychological insight.

Imam Al-Ghazali (1058-1111 CE)

Al-Ghazali, one of the most influential Islamic theologians and philosophers, dedicated significant portions of his works to addressing religious anxiety and excessive scrupulosity.

In *Ihya Ulum al-Din* (Revival of the Religious Sciences), Al-Ghazali wrote about people who become paralyzed by doubts about the validity of their ritual purity and prayers. He argued that such doubts come from shaytan and should be dismissed, not indulged (Al-Ghazali, 1989).

Al-Ghazali specifically addressed the person who repeats wudu excessively or redoes prayers constantly due to doubt. His advice? **Follow the principle of certainty**. If you're certain you completed wudu properly, then later doubt does not override that certainty. Continue with your worship and ignore the doubt.

This is cognitive therapy in medieval language. Al-Ghazali is teaching people to trust their initial assessment and resist the compulsion to check and re-check.

He also warned that excessive attention to minor details in worship while neglecting major spiritual qualities (like sincerity, humility, and kindness to others) represents a deception from shaytan. In other words, OCD makes you focus obsessively on ritual perfection while your actual spiritual development stagnates.

Ibn Taymiyyah (1263-1328 CE)

Ibn Taymiyyah, the influential Hanbali scholar, was even more direct about dealing with waswas. He encountered many people suffering from religious doubts and compulsions, and his advice was consistent: **Don't engage with the doubts. Dismiss them and move on**.

Ibn Taymiyyah wrote that if a person doubts whether they completed an action in worship—like whether they said "Allahu Akbar" correctly or whether they bowed properly—they should assume they did it correctly and continue. Repeatedly going back to check or redo actions is following the whisperings of shaytan, not following Islam (Ibn Taymiyyah, 2001).

He explained that shaytan's strategy is to make you doubt what you've already done correctly, forcing you into endless cycles of repetition. This keeps you from actual worship and creates hardship, which contradicts Islam's core principle that "the religion is ease."

Ibn Taymiyyah also addressed people who experience blasphemous intrusive thoughts. He taught that such thoughts, when unwanted and distressing to the person, are not sinful and do not affect one's faith. They are waswas from shaytan, and the person should ignore them rather than dwelling on them or seeking to "undo" them through rituals.

Contemporary Scholars

Modern Islamic scholars have continued addressing these issues with increasing awareness of clinical OCD.

Dr. Yasir Qadhi, a contemporary Islamic scholar, has spoken about religious OCD in lectures and online content, clarifying that Islam does not require the excessive behaviors characteristic of OCD. He emphasizes that perfection is not demanded in worship—sincerity and genuine effort are what matter.

Mufti Abdur-Rahman ibn Yusuf Mangera has issued fatwas specifically addressing OCD-related questions. His guidance consistently emphasizes that people experiencing excessive waswas should:

1. Set reasonable time limits for acts of worship (like 5 minutes for wudu)
2. Perform the action once, properly, and then move on regardless of subsequent doubts
3. Not seek repeated reassurance about whether actions were valid
4. Trust that Allah knows the difference between waswas and actual negligence

Sheikh Haytham al-Haddad has similarly addressed OCD in religious practice, noting that when someone's worship becomes a source of extreme distress rather than peace and connection with Allah, something has gone wrong—and that "something" is usually waswas that has been indulged rather than dismissed.

The Concept of "Al-Waswas Al-Khannas" (The Whisperer)

The phrase *al-waswas al-khannas* from Surah An-Nas deserves special attention because it reveals something important about the nature of these intrusive thoughts.

Al-waswas refers to the entity doing the whispering—often understood as shaytan, though some scholars note this can include both jinn-shaytan and human suggestions that lead us away from good.

Al-khannas means "the one who withdraws" or "the sneaking one." The root *kh-n-s* implies something that appears, then hides when confronted.

This linguistic detail captures something that people with OCD know intimately: **The intrusive thoughts intensify when you engage with them and weaken when you dismiss them**.

When you try to argue with an OCD thought ("But I *did* wash my hands properly!"), when you perform compulsions to neutralize it, when you seek reassurance—the thought gets louder and more persistent. But when you acknowledge it without engaging ("There's that thought again") and move on—it eventually retreats.

This is *al-khannas*. It whispers powerfully when you fight it, but withdraws when you simply seek refuge in Allah and continue your activity.

The Quran's instruction to "seek refuge in the Lord of mankind" is not telling you to perform elaborate rituals. It's telling you to acknowledge Allah's protection, then get on with your life. The waswas has no power to harm you unless you give it power through engagement.

Islamic Perspective: When Do Thoughts Become Sinful?

This might be the most important theological question for someone suffering from OCD with religious themes: **When does a thought become a sin?**

The Islamic answer is clear and remarkably compassionate: **Unwanted thoughts are never sins**.

A fundamental hadith establishes this principle:

Allah has forgiven my ummah for what crosses their minds so long as they do not act upon it or speak of it. (Sahih Bukhari, Book 92, Hadith 391)

Let's break this down. Three things matter:

1. What crosses your mind (thoughts)—forgiven, not counted as sin

2. What you speak (verbal expression)—may be counted, depending on intention

3. What you act upon (actions)—counted according to intention

Notice what's missing from the "sin" category: **involuntary thoughts**.

Islamic theology makes a distinction between thoughts that you intentionally cultivate versus thoughts that simply appear. If you sit around deliberately imagining sinful scenarios, enjoying forbidden things in your mind, that's problematic—not because the thoughts themselves are sins, but because you're deliberately moving your heart toward something wrong.

But intrusive, unwanted thoughts that horrify you? Thoughts you're trying to push away? Those don't count at all.

Another hadith reinforces this:

The Prophet (peace be upon him) said: "A person will not be held accountable for what merely crosses his mind unless he speaks of it or acts upon it." (Sahih Muslim, Book 1, Hadith 201)

For someone with OCD, this means:

- That blasphemous thought that popped into your head during prayer? Not a sin.
- That doubt about Allah's existence that intruded while you were making wudu? Not a sin.

- That inappropriate image that flashed through your mind? Not a sin.
- That fear that you might have committed shirk accidentally? The fear itself isn't shirk.

Intent is what matters. And if your intent is to worship Allah properly, but waswas creates doubts and disturbing thoughts, Allah knows your intent. The thoughts don't change it.

The scholar Ibn Qayyim al-Jawziyya explained this beautifully. He wrote that the heart is like a courtyard—birds (thoughts) will fly over it, and you can't prevent that. But you can prevent them from building nests there. The passing of the bird is not your fault; giving it a place to nest is the choice (Ibn Qayyim al-Jawziyya, 2003).

In OCD terms: You can't prevent intrusive thoughts from occurring. But you can choose not to engage with them, not to perform compulsions in response to them, and not to let them determine your behavior.

The Mercy of Allah: "Allah Does Not Burden a Soul Beyond What It Can Bear"

One of the most frequently cited Quranic verses in Islamic theology is:

"Allah does not burden a soul beyond that it can bear." (Quran 2:286)

But here's where OCD creates a cruel paradox. People with OCD feel incredibly burdened—like they're drowning in religious obligations that feel impossible to fulfill correctly. So they think, "If Allah doesn't burden me beyond what I can bear, and I can't handle this, maybe I'm just not trying hard enough. Maybe I'm failing."

This is exactly backwards.

The burden you're experiencing—the endless compulsions, the paralyzing doubt, the time-consuming rituals—is *not from Allah*. That burden is from OCD. It's from waswas that you've been taught to engage with rather than dismiss.

Allah's actual religious requirements are described consistently in the Quran and Sunnah as merciful, manageable, and meant to bring ease:

"Allah intends for you ease and does not intend for you hardship." (Quran 2:185)

"He has chosen you and has not placed upon you in the religion any difficulty." (Quran 22:78)

The Prophet (peace be upon him) emphasized this repeatedly:

"Make things easy and do not make them difficult, give glad tidings and do not repel people." (Sahih Bukhari, Book 3, Hadith 125)

When someone came to the Prophet with excessive religious practices—spending entire nights in prayer, fasting every day—the Prophet corrected them. He told them to be moderate, to take care of their bodies, to maintain balance. He said:

"This religion is easy. No one becomes harsh and strict in the religion without it overwhelming him." (Sahih Bukhari, Book 2, Hadith 38)

So if your religious practice is overwhelming you, if it's consuming hours daily, if it's making you miserable—that's a sign that something is wrong. It's not a sign of proper Islam.

The actual requirements of Islam—five daily prayers performed in a few minutes each, wudu done properly in 1-2 minutes, normal attention to cleanliness—these are manageable burdens. Spending three hours on one wudu? Repeating prayers 20 times? That's not the burden Allah placed on you. That's OCD.

Understanding That Allah Knows the Difference Between Waswas and Intention

Here's something people with OCD desperately need to understand: **Allah knows what's in your heart**.

The Quran states:

"And We have already created man and know what his soul whispers to him, and We are closer to him than [his] jugular vein." (Quran 50:16)

Allah knows the difference between:

- A thought you chose versus a thought that intruded unbidden
- An intention you formed versus a doubt that waswas created
- Genuine negligence versus paralyzing fear of being negligent
- A sin you committed versus a fear of having possibly committed a sin

You might not be able to tell the difference in the moment—that's part of what makes OCD so tormenting. But Allah can tell. And here's the critical point: **Allah judges based on what He knows is in your heart, not based on the chaos OCD creates in your mind**.

A hadith makes this explicit:

"Verily, Allah does not look at your appearance or wealth, but rather He looks at your hearts and actions." (Sahih Muslim, Book 32, Hadith 6543)

Your *heart*—your actual intention, your genuine desire to worship Allah properly—that's what counts. Not whether you had a blasphemous intrusive thought. Not whether you can achieve 100% certainty that your wudu was perfect. Not whether waswas created doubts about your prayer.

When Fatima (the young woman from Chapter 1) spends 45 minutes in the shower obsessing about droplets of urine, does Allah think she's being lazy about purification? No. Allah knows her heart is desperate to be pure, so desperate that shaytan is exploiting that very desire through waswas.

When Ahmed experiences horrifying blasphemous thoughts during prayer and then prays 20 times for forgiveness, does Allah think Ahmed is blaspheming? No. Allah knows Ahmed loves Him and is being tormented by thoughts he doesn't want.

The Islamic tradition teaches that Allah is *Al-Aleem* (The All-Knowing), *Al-Khabeer* (The All-Aware), and *Ar-Rahman* (The Most Merciful). He knows you're being attacked by waswas. He knows you're trying your best. He knows the difference between genuine transgression and OCD torture.

Trust that.

How OCD Exploits Religious Devotion

Now we get to the mechanism that makes religious OCD so insidious. OCD doesn't attack your faith. It *exploits* your faith. It takes what's beautiful about Islam—care for purity, devotion in worship, consciousness of Allah—and twists these virtues into weapons against you.

Here's how it works:

Islam teaches: Cleanliness is half of faith

OCD twists this into: "Unless you're absolutely certain you're clean—and I mean 100% certain—your faith is invalid. Better wash one more time. Actually, start over completely."

Islam teaches: Pray with focus and sincerity

OCD twists this into: "If you had even one distracted thought during that prayer, it doesn't count. Your focus wasn't perfect. Do it again."

Islam teaches: Allah is aware of your intentions

OCD twists this into: "But what if your intention wasn't pure? What if there was some hidden pride or ego? You need to analyze every thought to make sure your intention was 100% for Allah."

Islam teaches: Avoid major sins like shirk

OCD twists this into: "Every random thought might be shirk. Every doubt might mean you've left Islam. Better constantly check your faith to make sure you still believe."

See the pattern? OCD takes a legitimate Islamic teaching and demands an impossible standard of perfection. It takes a reasonable religious practice and makes it excessive. It takes a source of comfort (Allah's mercy and awareness) and turns it into a source of anxiety.

Dr. Steven Phillipson, who specializes in OCD treatment, explains that OCD targets our most valued domains—relationships, morality, safety, and for religious people, faith (Phillipson, 2018). It's like OCD asks, "What do you care about most?" and then creates doubt and fear around precisely that.

For Muslims, this often means:

Purity becomes contamination obsessions: The Islamic emphasis on ritual cleanliness becomes fear that everything is najis, that you can never be truly pure, that one molecule of impurity invalidates everything.

Devotion becomes scrupulosity: The call to worship becomes a demand for perfect prayer performance, with no wandering thoughts, perfect recitation, and absolute certainty about every movement.

Intention becomes paralysis: The beautiful teaching that actions are judged by intentions becomes constant analysis of whether your intentions are pure enough, whether you're doing things for the right reasons.

Protection from sin becomes harm OCD: The desire to avoid shirk and major sins becomes intrusive fears of having accidentally committed them, magical thinking about punishment, and constant reassurance-seeking.

And here's the cruelest part: **The more you care about Islam, the more material OCD has to work with**.

A person who barely practices Islam might have contamination fears about germs. A deeply devoted Muslim with OCD will have contamination fears specifically about najis, making it harder to separate the disorder from faith.

A person with minimal religious background might have intrusive blasphemous thoughts that bother them a little. A Muslim who loves Allah deeply will be absolutely tormented by such thoughts—precisely because they care so much.

OCD is like a parasite that feeds on what you value. And for Muslims who value their faith above everything else, OCD has an endless buffet of religious content to exploit.

The OCD-Waswas Connection: Where Theology and Psychology Meet

So where do we land? How do Islamic concepts of waswas relate to the psychological understanding of OCD?

Here's the synthesis:

Waswas describes the *source* of intrusive thoughts from a theological perspective—the whispers of shaytan meant to create doubt, anxiety, and distance from Allah.

OCD describes the *pattern* that develops when someone responds to waswas with compulsive behaviors, reassurance-seeking, and avoidance instead of dismissing the thoughts and moving forward.

Everyone experiences waswas occasionally. That's normal human experience. But when someone:

1. Takes the waswas seriously and believes it must be addressed
2. Develops compulsive responses to reduce the anxiety
3. Seeks certainty beyond what Islam requires
4. Allows the thoughts to control their behavior
5. Spends significant time on these patterns

...then waswas has become OCD.

Islamic scholars throughout history recognized the first part—that waswas exists and should be dismissed. Modern psychology has mapped out the second part—exactly how the pattern of OCD develops and how to break it.

The treatment isn't religious vs. psychological. It's both/and.

You need to understand that Islamic theology supports ignoring intrusive thoughts (waswas should be dismissed, not engaged). And you need to understand the psychological mechanisms of OCD (why compulsions make things worse, how avoidance increases fear, why reassurance-seeking perpetuates the cycle).

The 12th-century Muslim scholar telling you to trust your initial certainty and ignore subsequent doubts is giving the same advice as the 21st-century OCD therapist telling you to resist compulsions and tolerate uncertainty.

The Prophet (peace be upon him) telling you to seek refuge and stop engaging with doubts is teaching the same principle as exposure and response prevention therapy.

Islam and psychology are describing the same struggle from different angles. And both offer the same core solution: **Don't engage with the intrusive thoughts. Trust in Allah's mercy. Move forward despite uncertainty**.

What This Means for Your Recovery

Islamic tradition has recognized waswas and excessive religious scrupulosity for over 1,400 years. The guidance has been consistent: These thoughts come from outside you (shaytan), they're not sins, they should be dismissed rather than engaged, and excessive doubt in worship contradicts the ease and mercy that Islam teaches.

Modern psychology has identified the same pattern and given it a name: OCD. And the treatment approach—exposure and response prevention—mirrors what Islamic scholars prescribed centuries ago.

This means several critical things:

1. Treatment is religiously permissible—it's actually religiously supported

When a therapist tells you to resist compulsions and tolerate uncertainty, they're teaching what Islam has taught all along. You're not weakening your faith through treatment; you're removing the waswas that was interfering with proper practice.

2. The excessive demands are from OCD, not from Allah

If your religious practice feels crushing, exhausting, and overwhelming, that's a sign of OCD, not a sign of weak faith. Allah's actual requirements are manageable.

3. Intrusive thoughts don't count as sins and don't affect your faith

This isn't just therapy-speak to make you feel better. It's Islamic theology. The Prophet (peace be upon him) himself confirmed that disturbing thoughts are not sins and may even be a sign of strong faith.

4. You can trust Allah's knowledge of your heart

You don't need 100% certainty that your intentions were pure or your prayers were perfect. Allah knows what's in your heart. He knows the difference between waswas and your actual will.

In the next chapter, we'll examine the specific ways OCD presents in Muslim communities—the exact forms these obsessions and compulsions take when Islam is the framework—so you can recognize the disorder's fingerprints on your own experience.

Chapter 3: Muslim-Specific OCD Presentations

OCD is universal. You'll find it in every culture, every country, every religious tradition. But the specific form it takes—the exact obsessions and compulsions—varies based on what matters in that culture.

In Japan, OCD might center on social errors and offending others, because social harmony is culturally paramount. In the United States, you'll see a lot of contamination OCD focused on germs and disease, because there's cultural emphasis on health and cleanliness.

And in Muslim communities? OCD latches onto Islamic practices, concepts, and values—wudu, prayer, purity laws, the fear of shirk, the importance of intention. These aren't random targets. OCD goes after what you care about most.

So let's map out the specific landscape of OCD in Muslim contexts. We'll look at the actual presentations—the real obsessions and compulsions that Muslim individuals experience—so you can recognize if this is what's happening to you.

Because here's the thing: Until you can clearly identify "This is OCD, not Islam," you'll keep feeding the disorder while thinking you're being a better Muslim.

Religious/Scrupulosity OCD

This is the big one. Religious scrupulosity—excessive fear about religious obligations, moral purity, and spiritual correctness—is the most common form of OCD in Muslim populations.

Research examining OCD across different cultures found that over 50% of Middle Eastern OCD patients reported religious obsessions, compared to about 10-15% in Western countries where religion plays a less central role (Fontenelle et al., 2004). We're not talking about a minor subset here. We're talking about the majority presentation.

Let's break down the specific forms this takes.

Purity and Tahara Obsessions

Islam places significant emphasis on tahara (ritual purity). Muslims learn from childhood about najis (impurities) and how to maintain the state of purity required for prayer and other acts of worship.

For most Muslims, this is straightforward: You perform wudu before prayer, you shower after sexual activity or menstruation, you clean yourself after using the bathroom. It takes a few minutes and you move on.

For someone with OCD, tahara becomes a nightmare.

Common obsessions include:

- "What if there's a drop of urine on my clothes that I can't see?"
- "Did I clean myself thoroughly enough after using the bathroom?"
- "If I touched something that might have been touched by someone who might not have been pure, am I now impure?"
- "What if there's a microscopic particle of najis somewhere on my body?"

The compulsions that follow:

- Showering for 1-2 hours, scrubbing until skin is raw
- Changing clothes multiple times daily due to contamination fears
- Excessive use of water in istinja (cleaning after using bathroom)
- Avoiding certain areas of the home deemed "contaminated"
- Researching Islamic rulings on purity obsessively online

A young man named Tariq described his experience: "I would shower for two hours before Friday prayer. I knew it was excessive. My family would pound on the bathroom door. But I couldn't stop. Every time I thought I was clean, a thought would come—'But what if you missed a spot? What if there's still najis somewhere?' And I'd have to start over."

The Islamic reality: Tahara has clear parameters in fiqh (Islamic jurisprudence). Visible impurities need to be washed. If you can't see impurity, you're not required to assume it's there. The scholarly principle is that certainty isn't removed by doubt—if you were certain you were pure, later doubt doesn't change that.

Wudu Rituals Becoming Compulsions

Wudu (ritual ablution) is performed before the five daily prayers. It's meant to take 1-2 minutes—wash hands, rinse mouth, rinse nose, wash face, wash arms to elbows, wipe over head, wash feet.

Simple, right?

For someone with OCD, wudu becomes an exhausting ordeal.

Common obsessions:

- "Did I wash each part the required number of times?"
- "Did I wash in the exact right order?"
- "Did water reach every single hair and every fold of skin?"
- "Did I have a distracting thought during wudu that invalidates it?"

The compulsions:

- Rewashing each body part multiple times
- Starting wudu over completely at the slightest doubt
- Spending 30-45 minutes on one wudu
- Asking family members to watch and confirm wudu was done correctly
- Setting timers to ensure each step gets enough time
- Researching specific rulings about wudu technique constantly

Layla, a university student, described it this way: "I was doing wudu seven times before each prayer. I'd finish, start walking to my prayer mat, and the thought would come—'You didn't wash your elbows completely.' Back to the bathroom. Then, 'You lost count of how many times you washed your face.' Start over. I was late to class almost every day."

The Islamic reality: Fiqh specifies the requirements of wudu clearly. Wash each required area once (washing three times is recommended but not required). The order matters. Getting water to the area matters—you don't need to scrub or ensure every microscopic space is touched. Normal wudu takes 1-2 minutes.

Prayer Contamination Fears

Some Muslims with OCD develop specific fears about contamination during prayer itself.

Common obsessions:

- "What if there's najis on my clothes and my prayer doesn't count?"
- "What if the prayer mat I'm using was touched by something impure?"
- "What if there's najis in the area where I'm praying?"
- "Did I step in something najis on my way to pray?"

The compulsions:

- Checking clothes extensively before each prayer
- Using only specific "safe" prayer mats and washing them obsessively
- Avoiding praying in certain locations
- Removing and checking shoes/socks multiple times
- Scrutinizing the prayer area for any speck that might be impure

A woman named Sumaya wouldn't pray in her workplace prayer room because other people used it and "they might track in najis." She'd wait until she got home, often missing prayers entirely because she couldn't achieve certainty about the prayer space being pure.

The Islamic reality: Your prayer space needs to be clean—not sterile, just clean. If you can see impurity, remove it. If you can't see impurity, you're not required to investigate or assume it's there. The Prophet (peace be upon him) prayed in various locations, including outdoors where absolute certainty of purity would be impossible.

Doubts About Intention (Niyyah)

Islam teaches that "actions are judged by intentions" (hadith in Sahih Bukhari). This beautiful teaching—that Allah cares more about why you do something than the outward action itself—becomes weaponized by OCD.

Common obsessions:

- "Was my intention truly for Allah, or was there some ego involved?"
- "Did I form the intention correctly before prayer?"
- "What if I'm praying to show off rather than for Allah?"
- "Is my intention pure enough?"

The compulsions:

- Standing for extended periods trying to "achieve" the right intention before prayer
- Mentally reviewing intentions repeatedly
- Starting prayers over because you're not sure the intention was correct
- Seeking reassurance about whether your intentions are acceptable
- Analyzing motivations for every good deed obsessively

Hassan from Chapter 1 exemplified this. Before each prayer, he'd try to form the perfect intention. But doubts would flood in: "Am I really doing this for Allah? Or am I just going through the motions? Is there pride in my heart?" He'd try again. And again. Twenty minutes would pass before he could start the prayer itself.

The Islamic reality: Intention is in the heart. If you intend to pray, you've fulfilled the requirement. You don't need to verbally state the intention in a specific formula. You don't need perfect mental clarity. The fact that you're praying *is* evidence that you intend to pray. OCD creates false standards of intention-purity that Islam doesn't require.

Blasphemous Intrusive Thoughts

This might be the most tormenting form of religious OCD for Muslims. Horrifying, graphic blasphemous thoughts intrude into consciousness—often during the most sacred moments like prayer or Quran recitation.

Common obsessions:

- Explicit curse words directed at Allah during prayer
- Images of disrespecting the Quran or the Prophet (peace be upon him)
- Thoughts questioning Allah's existence or attributes
- Urges to say or do something blasphemous
- "What if I accidentally commit shirk in my thoughts?"

The compulsions:

- Excessive istighfar (seeking forgiveness) after each intrusive thought
- Repeating prayers that were "contaminated" by blasphemous thoughts
- Avoiding Quran recitation or prayer out of fear of having such thoughts
- Seeking reassurance from scholars that the thoughts don't invalidate faith
- Mental rituals to "undo" or neutralize the blasphemous thoughts

Ahmed from Chapter 1 experienced this intensely. During prayer, graphic thoughts about disrespecting Allah would intrude. He was horrified—these were the last thoughts he'd ever want. But the more he tried not to have them, the more persistent they became. He started repeating prayers 10, 15, 20 times, convinced that a prayer with such thoughts "didn't count."

The Islamic reality: As we covered in Chapter 2, the Prophet (peace be upon him) explicitly said that such thoughts are not sins and may even indicate strong faith (because only someone who cares deeply about Allah would be distressed by them). You are not accountable for thoughts that simply cross your mind. The thought itself is not the same as speaking or acting on it.

Perfectionism in Recitation

Some Muslims with OCD become paralyzed by the need for perfect Quran recitation or perfect pronunciation during prayer.

Common obsessions:

- "Did I pronounce that Arabic letter correctly?"
- "What if I made a mistake that changes the meaning?"
- "Was my recitation good enough for Allah to accept?"
- "Did I pause in the right places?"

The compulsions:

- Repeating verses or entire surahs multiple times during prayer
- Recording your recitation to analyze it later for errors
- Spending hours researching the exact pronunciation of letters
- Avoiding leading prayer due to fear of making mistakes
- Restarting prayers from the beginning after perceived errors

Mariam, who had memorized significant portions of the Quran, started taking 45 minutes to complete a single prayer. She'd recite Al-Fatiha, doubt whether she pronounced a letter correctly, and start over. This would repeat 10-15 times before she could move to the next part of prayer.

The Islamic reality: The Quran should be recited with effort to pronounce correctly, but perfection is not required. The Prophet (peace be upon him) accepted the recitation of people with heavy accents, speech impediments, and limited Arabic knowledge. What matters is making an effort and reciting to the best of your ability—not achieving flawless pronunciation beyond your skill level.

Contamination OCD with Islamic Themes

Pure contamination OCD exists in Muslim communities just like anywhere else—fear of germs, chemicals, illness. But in Muslim contexts, contamination fears often intertwine with Islamic concepts of najis.

Najis (Impurity) Obsessions

Islam categorizes certain substances as najis—things like urine, feces, blood (with some scholarly differences on menstrual blood), wine, pork, dead animals, and certain other substances.

For someone with contamination OCD, these categories become a source of terror.

Common obsessions:

- "What if I touched something with pork in it?"
- "What if there's blood somewhere that I can't see?"
- "Did that person who touched me have najis on their hands?"
- "If najis gets on me, how far does it spread?"

The compulsions:

- Washing hands 50+ times daily
- Avoiding restaurants out of fear of cross-contamination with pork

- Refusing to shake hands with non-Muslims
- Throwing away clothes that might have touched something najis
- Creating elaborate cleaning rituals for everyday objects

A man named Ibrahim would spend hours cleaning groceries when he got home from the store. Each item had to be washed because "maybe the person who stocked it had najis on their hands." His wife found him scrubbing canned goods with soap and bleach at 2 AM.

The Islamic reality: Yes, najis exists. No, you don't need to become a forensic investigator to avoid it. The default assumption in Islamic law is that things are pure unless you have clear evidence of impurity. You can't see najis on something? It's pure. Someone's hands look clean? They're pure. You're allowed to function in the world without assuming invisible contamination everywhere.

Bathroom Rituals

Islamic hygiene practices include specific guidelines for using the bathroom (istinja). For most people, these are simple cleanliness practices.

For someone with OCD, bathroom use becomes a multi-hour ordeal.

Common obsessions:

- "Did I clean myself completely after urinating?"
- "Is there any trace of urine still on my body?"
- "Did I use enough water for istinja?"
- "What if there's a droplet I missed?"

The compulsions:

- Spending 1-2 hours in the bathroom for simple urination
- Using excessive amounts of water to ensure cleanliness
- Wiping or washing hundreds of times
- Checking underwear constantly throughout the day
- Avoiding certain activities (like meetings or travel) due to bathroom fears

Fatima from Chapter 1 spent 45 minutes in the shower after using the bathroom. She'd wash, check, wash again, check again. Her water bills were astronomical. She was chronically late to work. Her skin was damaged from excessive washing.

The Islamic reality: Islamic bathroom hygiene requires cleaning the area properly— not perfectly. Fiqh scholars specify that you need to remove najis. Once you've cleaned yourself normally, you're done. You don't need absolute certainty that every microscopic particle is gone.

Menstruation-Related Compulsions

Muslim women know that menstruation affects prayer and fasting obligations. During menstruation, women don't pray or fast. After menstruation ends, they perform ghusl (full-body purification) before resuming prayers.

For women with OCD, this becomes a source of intense anxiety and compulsion.

Common obsessions:

- "Has my period actually ended, or is that just spotting?"
- "What if I pray while still menstruating and it doesn't count?"
- "Did I perform ghusl correctly after my period?"
- "What if there's still some blood internally that makes me impure?"

The compulsions:

- Checking for signs of blood dozens of times daily
- Delaying prayer for days after period appears to end, "just to be sure"
- Performing ghusl multiple times
- Seeking constant reassurance from other women or scholars
- Taking days off work or avoiding activities during menstruation

A young woman named Zainab would check for blood every 15-30 minutes during her period and for several days after. She'd delay resuming prayer for 5-7 days past when her period typically ended, terrified that she might pray while still menstruating. When she did resume, she'd perform ghusl 3-4 times before feeling "safe."

The Islamic reality: There are clear signs that menstruation has ended (cessation of bleeding or white discharge, depending on scholarly opinion). Once you've seen those signs, you perform ghusl once and resume normal practice. You don't need to investigate internally for hidden blood. You trust the signs you can observe.

Harm OCD

Harm OCD involves intrusive thoughts, images, or urges related to causing harm—to oneself, to others, or in religious contexts, to one's spiritual state.

Fear of Committing Shirk Accidentally

Shirk—associating partners with Allah—is described as the one unforgivable sin in Islam (if one dies without repenting from it). For someone with OCD, this teaching becomes a source of terror.

Common obsessions:

- "What if that thought I had was shirk?"
- "Did I just commit shirk without realizing it?"
- "Is asking for help from someone (a doctor, teacher) a form of shirk?"
- "What if I attributed something to other than Allah?"

The compulsions:

- Constantly reviewing thoughts to check for shirk
- Excessive istighfar and shahada (declaration of faith) recitation
- Seeking reassurance from scholars: "Is this shirk?"
- Avoiding certain words or phrases out of fear they might be shirk
- Mental rituals to "cancel out" potential shirk

Omar became terrified of metaphorical language. If someone said, "This medicine saved my life," he'd panic—"Only Allah saves! Is thinking that shirk?" He started speaking in rigid, literal terms to avoid any phrase that could possibly attribute power to something other than Allah.

The Islamic reality: Shirk is deliberately placing something at the level of Allah in worship, devotion, or ultimate reliance. It's not about accidentally using a figure of speech or having an intrusive thought. Islamic scholars throughout history have explained that shirk requires intention and action—not fleeting thoughts or common expressions.

Fear of Cursing Allah or the Prophet

Some Muslims with OCD experience intrusive urges to say or do something disrespectful to sacred things.

Common obsessions:

- Urges to curse while holding the Quran
- Thoughts about disrespecting the Prophet (peace be upon him)
- Fears of accidentally saying something blasphemous
- "What if I have the urge to do something terrible in the mosque?"

The compulsions:

- Avoiding the Quran or Islamic books out of fear
- Not attending mosques due to fear of intrusive urges
- Constant monitoring of thoughts to ensure no disrespect occurs
- Seeking reassurance that urges don't equal sins
- Performing specific prayers or supplications to "prevent" acting on urges

Aisha would get intrusive urges to throw the Quran when she held it. She was horrified. She'd never want to disrespect the Quran—it was the last thing she'd consciously choose. But the urge was there, terrifying her. She stopped touching the Quran entirely, convinced that having such urges meant she was a terrible Muslim.

The Islamic reality: Intrusive urges are not the same as intentions. Everyone's brain generates random "what if" scenarios—"what if I jumped off this balcony," "what if I said something completely inappropriate right now." These are not desires; they're just how brains work. You're not accountable for fleeting urges you don't act on.

Magical Thinking About Punishment

OCD often involves magical thinking—irrational beliefs that your thoughts or behaviors can cause or prevent specific outcomes in ways that defy normal causality.

In religious OCD, this takes the form of believing that thoughts or minor actions will result in divine punishment.

Common obsessions:

- "If I don't pray perfectly, something terrible will happen to my family"
- "This illness is punishment from Allah for a sin I committed"
- "I need to do this ritual to prevent Allah's anger"
- "If I have this thought, it will bring punishment"

The compulsions:

- Performing specific prayers or supplications to prevent disaster
- Avoiding certain numbers or actions deemed "unlucky" in religious terms
- Interpreting every negative event as divine punishment requiring response
- Creating personal rituals to "earn" Allah's protection

Abdul started believing that if he didn't pray each prayer exactly perfectly, his mother would get sick. He had no logical reason to think this—he just "felt" it was true. So he'd repeat prayers until they felt "right," convinced he was protecting his mother through perfect prayer performance.

The Islamic reality: Allah's relationship with you is not based on magic formulas or perfect ritual performance. Negative events are not necessarily punishments—they're part of life in this world. The Prophet (peace be upon him) taught that even the prick of a thorn can be a means of erasing sins and increasing reward, meaning suffering isn't always punishment.

Relationship OCD (ROCD)

Relationship OCD in Muslim contexts often centers on marriage concerns, particularly about whether you're with the "right" person Islamically or whether your relationship is properly halal.

Marriage Doubts

Common obsessions:

- "Is this person really my soulmate that Allah intended for me?"
- "What if I married the wrong person?"
- "Do I really love my spouse, or am I just going through the motions?"
- "What if there's someone better for me out there?"

The compulsions:

- Constantly analyzing feelings for spouse
- Comparing spouse to others to determine if you made the right choice
- Seeking reassurance from family or friends about the marriage
- Researching Islamic rulings on divorce obsessively
- Testing your love by seeing if you have specific thoughts or feelings

Samira had been married for three years to a kind, practicing Muslim man. But OCD told her, "What if he's not THE ONE Allah meant for you? What if you're missing out on your real match?" She'd spend hours analyzing her feelings, comparing her marriage to friends' marriages, wondering if the fact that she sometimes felt annoyed meant she'd made a mistake.

The Islamic reality: Islam doesn't teach that there's one perfect soulmate predetermined for you. Marriage is a choice, an effort, and a commitment. Having doubts or moments of frustration doesn't mean you married the wrong person—it means you're human.

Halal Relationship Concerns

Some Muslims with OCD become obsessed with whether every aspect of their relationship (pre-marriage or within marriage) is perfectly halal.

Common obsessions:

- "Was that touch inappropriate and sinful?"
- "Is this conversation crossing boundaries?"
- "Did I look at my spouse in a way that's somehow wrong?"
- "Is our level of physical intimacy exactly what Islam prescribes?"

The compulsions:

- Constantly seeking Islamic rulings on relationship boundaries
- Avoiding all physical contact even within marriage out of fear
- Confessing every perceived boundary violation to spouse or scholars
- Mentally reviewing interactions to check for any haram element
- Creating rigid rules beyond what Islam requires

Yusuf and Noor were engaged. Yusuf started obsessing: "We shook hands when we got engaged. Was that haram? Should I ask her forgiveness? Should I confess to the imam?" He'd research online for hours, finding conflicting opinions, getting more confused. The engagement period became consumed with religious anxiety rather than preparation for marriage.

The Islamic reality: Yes, Islam has boundaries for relationships. No, you don't need to scrutinize every micro-interaction. Within marriage, physical intimacy is actually *encouraged* as part of a healthy relationship. Islam provides general guidelines, not forensic-level specifications for every moment.

Moral Scrupulosity

This form of OCD involves excessive fear of sinning, hypervigilance about moral behavior, and compulsive confession or forgiveness-seeking.

Constant Fear of Sinning

Common obsessions:

- "Did I just commit a sin without realizing it?"
- "Was that thought sinful?"
- "Is this action permissible, or is it haram?"
- "What if I'm sinning in ways I don't know about?"

The compulsions:

- Researching Islamic rulings constantly
- Seeking reassurance from multiple sources

- Avoiding activities out of fear they might be haram
- Creating personal restrictions beyond Islamic requirements
- Mental reviewing of all actions to check for sins

Tariq would wake up in the middle of the night, suddenly anxious: "Wait, when I said that joke today, was I backbiting? Was I mocking someone?" He'd lie awake for hours, replaying the conversation, trying to determine if he'd sinned. He'd text friends the next day: "When I said that yesterday, did it sound like I was making fun of someone?"

The Islamic reality: Islam provides clear guidance on major sins. For gray areas, the general principle is that if something is not clearly prohibited, it's permissible. You're not expected to achieve a state where you commit zero sins ever—even the Prophet (peace be upon him) sought forgiveness 70-100 times daily (hadith in Sahih Bukhari), not because he was sinning constantly, but because seeking forgiveness is part of maintaining connection with Allah.

Excessive Confession/Seeking Forgiveness

Common obsessions:

- "I need to confess this sin to someone"
- "I must seek forgiveness right now or it doesn't count"
- "What if I haven't sought forgiveness enough times?"
- "Did I repent correctly?"

The compulsions:

- Repeating istighfar hundreds of times for small transgressions
- Confessing perceived sins to family, friends, or imams excessively
- Following specific formulas for repentance ritually
- Feeling compelled to verbalize every tiny mistake
- Mental tallying of sins and forgiveness requests

Amina would say "Astaghfirullah" (I seek Allah's forgiveness) over 200 times daily—not as a general remembrance of Allah, but compulsively after every perceived mistake. Bad thought? Ten astaghfirullah. Annoyed with someone? Twenty astaghfirullah. Didn't smile at a stranger? Five astaghfirullah.

The Islamic reality: Tawbah (repentance) has specific conditions—recognize the sin, feel remorse, stop doing it, intend not to return to it, and if it harmed someone, make amends. That's it. You don't need to say istighfar a specific number of times. You don't need to confess to other humans (except for rights violations that require making amends). Allah accepts sincere repentance the first time.

Recognizing the Pattern

Look across all these presentations. Different specific obsessions, different compulsions—but the same underlying structure:

1. **Intrusive thought or doubt** related to Islamic practice or theology
2. **Intense anxiety** about having done something wrong or being impure
3. **Compulsive behavior** to reduce that anxiety (washing, checking, seeking reassurance, mental rituals)
4. **Temporary relief** followed by return of the obsession
5. **Life interference** as time and energy are consumed by the cycle

Whether it's spending three hours on wudu, avoiding the Quran due to intrusive urges, checking for najis constantly, or seeking reassurance about intentions—it's all OCD.

The content is Islamic. The mechanism is OCD. And recognizing that difference is the first step toward breaking free.

In the next chapter, we'll examine exactly how OCD hijacks Islamic concepts and practices—the specific mechanisms that keep you trapped in the cycle—so you can start seeing where the disorder ends and real Islam begins.

Chapter 4: How OCD Hijacks Your Faith

By now, you understand what OCD is. You recognize what waswas means in Islamic tradition. You've seen the specific forms OCD takes in Muslim communities. But here's the question that probably keeps you up at night:

How do I tell the difference between OCD and genuine religious obligation?

Because that's the trap, isn't it? OCD doesn't announce itself. It doesn't show up wearing a name tag that says "Hi, I'm a mental disorder here to torture you." Instead, it disguises itself as religious devotion. It speaks in the language of Islam. It quotes principles you've been taught since childhood.

It whispers: "Allah deserves perfection in worship, doesn't He?" And you think, "Yes, of course." And OCD has you.

So we need to understand the exact mechanisms—the specific ways OCD takes Islamic concepts and twists them into weapons. Because once you can see how the hijacking works, you can start taking your faith back.

The OCD Cycle Explained

Before we look at Islamic-specific mechanisms, let's establish the basic OCD cycle. This pattern is universal, whether your OCD focuses on religion, contamination, harm, or anything else.

Step 1: Trigger

Something happens—internal or external—that activates anxiety. For religious OCD, common triggers include:

- Beginning wudu or prayer
- Thinking about Islamic obligations
- Hearing about sins or consequences
- Physical sensations that might indicate impurity
- Random intrusive thoughts during worship

Step 2: Intrusive Thought/Obsession

Your brain generates a "what if" question or doubt:

- "What if I didn't wash completely?"
- "What if that thought was shirk?"

- "What if my intention wasn't pure?"
- "What if I'm in a state of najis right now?"

Here's the critical part: **Everyone gets intrusive thoughts**. Research shows that up to 90% of people experience occasional unwanted, disturbing thoughts (Rachman & de Silva, 1978). The content might be different, but the experience is universal.

What separates OCD from normal experience is what happens next.

Step 3: Anxiety Spike

Instead of dismissing the thought ("That's just a random brain blip"), you take it seriously. The thought feels deeply meaningful. You can't let it go.

Anxiety floods your system. Your heart rate increases. You feel urgency—"I need to deal with this NOW."

Dr. Jonathan Abramowitz explains that in OCD, intrusive thoughts become fused with danger signals (Abramowitz, 2018). Your brain treats the thought itself as an emergency requiring immediate action.

Step 4: Compulsion

To reduce the anxiety, you perform a compulsion:

- Redo wudu "to be sure"
- Seek reassurance from a scholar or website
- Mentally review your actions
- Repeat prayers
- Say istighfar multiple times
- Check your body or clothes for najis
- Analyze your intentions

And it works! Kind of. The anxiety decreases. You feel temporary relief.

Step 5: Temporary Relief

For a few minutes, maybe an hour, you feel better. "Okay, I redid wudu, so my prayer will definitely count now."

This relief is what keeps the cycle going. Psychologically, this is called "negative reinforcement"—the compulsion is reinforced because it removes the unpleasant anxiety (Mowrer, 1960).

Your brain learns: "Anxiety appeared → I did the compulsion → anxiety left. Therefore, the compulsion works and I should keep doing it."

Step 6: Return of Doubt

But the relief never lasts. Soon, another thought appears:

- "But wait, did I do that wudu correctly just now?"
- "What if I had a distracting thought during the prayer I just completed?"
- "Actually, did I really clean properly earlier?"

And you're back at Step 2. The cycle repeats, often getting worse over time.

Why the Cycle Intensifies

Each time you perform a compulsion, you're sending your brain a message: "That intrusive thought was a real danger that required action."

You're training your brain that these thoughts are emergencies. So your brain, trying to protect you, generates *more* of them. More warnings. More doubts. More "what ifs."

The compulsions that were supposed to solve the problem are actually *creating* the problem.

Dr. Edna Foa, one of the pioneers of OCD treatment, describes this as a "fear reinforcement loop" (Foa & McLean, 2016). The very behaviors you use to reduce anxiety are maintaining and strengthening the anxiety long-term.

And in religious OCD, this cycle is supercharged because each compulsion feels like religious devotion rather than disorder.

How Certainty-Seeking Feeds OCD

Here's one of the most important concepts to understand about OCD: **The disorder feeds on certainty-seeking**.

OCD asks: "Are you 100% sure?" And if you can't provide absolute certainty, OCD demands action to achieve it.

Did you wash completely during wudu? "Well, I think so... but can I be 100% sure?"

Was your intention purely for Allah? "I believe so... but how can I be *certain* there wasn't some hidden ego?"

Are you definitely free of najis right now? "I don't see any... but what if there's something I can't see?"

The Islamic problem: Islam values sincerity, purity, and correct practice. These are genuine religious concerns. But OCD takes these reasonable values and demands an impossible standard: **absolute certainty**.

And here's the kicker: **Absolute certainty is impossible in most areas of life**.

You can't be 100% certain that you washed every microscopic area during wudu. You can't be 100% certain that your intention had zero ego component. You can't be 100% certain that no invisible najis exists on your body.

Why? Because certainty requires complete information, and complete information is often unavailable. You can't see inside your own mind with perfect clarity. You can't trace every molecule of water. You can't verify the absence of invisible substances.

So when OCD demands certainty, and you try to provide it through compulsions, you're fighting a battle you can't win.

Research on OCD has identified "intolerance of uncertainty" as a key maintaining factor (Steketee et al., 1998). People with OCD struggle more than average with ambiguity. When most people think, "I'm pretty sure I locked the door," that's sufficient. But for someone with OCD, "pretty sure" isn't good enough. They need certainty.

And in religious contexts, certainty-seeking seems reasonable: "Shouldn't I be sure my prayers are valid? Shouldn't I be certain I'm following Islam correctly?"

But here's what Islam actually teaches about certainty.

The Islamic Position on Certainty vs. Doubt

Islamic jurisprudence has a principle: **"Certainty is not removed by doubt."** (اليقين لا يزول بالشك)

What this means: If you were certain of something initially, then later doubt appears, the doubt doesn't override the original certainty.

Example: You performed wudu carefully. You were certain it was done correctly. Later, doubt enters: "But maybe I didn't wash my arms completely." Islamic principle says: Your original certainty stands. The doubt is dismissed.

Another principle: **"The basic principle is the continuance of what was."** (الأصل بقاء ما كان)

Meaning: Things are assumed to continue in their previous state until you have clear evidence of change.

Example: You were in a state of purity. Now you doubt whether something happened that breaks purity. Islamic principle says: Assume you're still in the state of purity unless you have clear evidence of impurity.

These principles exist *specifically* because Islamic scholars recognized that human beings can't achieve perfect certainty in all matters. They built in flexibility—not because they didn't care about correct practice, but because they understood the limitations of human perception.

OCD violates these principles. OCD says: "Doubt is more powerful than certainty. Possibility is more important than probability. What if is more real than what is."

And that's not Islam. That's disorder.

Why Reassurance Doesn't Work

When you're trapped in OCD's cycle, reassurance seems like the obvious solution.

You're worried your prayer didn't count? Ask a knowledgeable friend. You're concerned that action was haram? Look up a fatwa online. You doubt your wudu? Ask your spouse if they saw you do it correctly.

Makes sense, right? You have a question, you get an answer, problem solved.

Except it never works that way with OCD.

You ask a scholar: "If I had a distracting thought during prayer, is it invalid?"

The scholar says: "No, random thoughts during prayer don't invalidate it. The Prophet (peace be upon him) himself said that shaytan comes to disturb you during prayer."

You feel relief. For ten minutes.

Then OCD whispers: "But your thought was *really* distracting. More than just a random thought. Maybe the sheikh didn't understand how bad it was. You should ask someone else."

So you ask another person. They give the same answer. Brief relief. Then: "But what if both scholars are wrong? What if your specific situation is different? Better research more."

Reassurance is a compulsion. It's a behavior you perform to reduce anxiety. And like all compulsions, it provides temporary relief while strengthening the disorder long-term.

Here's why reassurance fails:

1. OCD Moves the Goalposts

No amount of reassurance is ever enough. OCD will always generate a new doubt: "But what about THIS specific situation?" "But what if they didn't understand the question?" "But what about this other detail?"

Research shows that reassurance-seeking in OCD leads to increased frequency of asking, not decreased anxiety over time (Parrish & Radomsky, 2010).

2. Reassurance Teaches You to Doubt Yourself

Every time you seek external reassurance, you're implicitly saying: "I can't trust my own judgment. I need someone else to tell me reality."

This erodes your confidence in your own perceptions and reasoning. You become dependent on others to validate even basic facts: "Did I actually do that? Am I really clean? Is this really okay?"

3. Reassurance Prevents Learning

Real learning happens when you sit with uncertainty and discover that the feared outcome doesn't occur.

If you sit with the doubt ("Maybe my prayer had a mistake") without seeking reassurance, eventually you learn: "The anxiety decreased on its own. Nothing terrible happened. I survived uncertainty."

But when you immediately seek reassurance, you never learn this. You remain convinced that only the reassurance saved you from disaster.

4. Reassurance Can't Provide the Certainty OCD Demands

Even the best Islamic scholar can't give you 100% certainty about your internal mental state or about microscopic particles of potential najis. They can provide general principles and likely scenarios, but they can't verify your specific, impossible-to-verify fears.

So OCD will always find a gap in the reassurance: "Yes, but what about..."

What Islam Says About Excessive Questioning

Interestingly, Islamic tradition recognized the problem of excessive reassurance-seeking and questioning.

The Prophet (peace be upon him) said: "Leave me as I leave you, for the people who were before you were ruined because of their questions and their differences with their prophets." (Sahih Bukhari, Book 92, Hadith 391)

This doesn't mean don't ask any questions. It means don't obsessively question to the point of creating hardship for yourself and paralysis in practice.

The Quran mentions that the Children of Israel, when told to sacrifice a cow, kept asking for more and more specifications—what color, what age, what markings. They turned a simple command into a burden through excessive questioning (Quran 2:67-71).

Islamic scholars throughout history warned against excessive questioning in religion—not to discourage learning, but because they recognized that some people get trapped in endless questioning that creates anxiety rather than knowledge.

The Role of Anxiety vs. Actual Sin

This distinction is *critical* for Muslim OCD sufferers: **Anxiety about sin is not the same as actually sinning**.

Let's break this down clearly.

Anxiety tells you: "You might have done something wrong. You might be impure. You might be sinning right now."

Reality might be: You're completely fine. You performed wudu correctly. You're in a state of purity. You're not sinning.

But anxiety *feels* like truth. The stronger the anxiety, the more convinced you become that the feared outcome is real.

Dr. David Clark, who studies anxiety disorders, calls this "emotional reasoning"—using how you feel as evidence for how things are (Clark & Beck, 2010).

"I feel anxious about my prayer, therefore something must be wrong with my prayer."

"I feel contaminated, therefore I must be in a state of najis."

"I feel guilty, therefore I must have sinned."

But feelings are not facts. Anxiety is not a reliable indicator of spiritual state.

Think about it: Does the most anxious person have the most sins? Does the person with the most religious anxiety have the weakest faith? Obviously not. Often it's the opposite—people who care deeply about their faith experience more religious anxiety because they care so much.

The Companions of the Prophet (peace be upon him) experienced intrusive disturbing thoughts that horrified them. Were these thoughts evidence of their sin? No—the Prophet said they were evidence of faith.

Here's the Islamic reality:

- Actual sin requires intention and action (for most sins)
- Intrusive thoughts are not sins
- Anxiety about having committed a sin is not the same as having committed it
- Doubt about purity doesn't create impurity
- Fear of shirk is not shirk

Your anxiety is the waswas. It's the disorder. It's not a spiritual fact-checker accurately identifying your sins.

OCD's Exploitation of Islamic Values

OCD is insidious because it doesn't attack your faith—it hijacks it. Let's look at specific Islamic values and see how OCD twists them.

Islamic Value: Cleanliness is Part of Faith

The Prophet (peace be upon him) said: "Cleanliness is half of faith" (Sahih Muslim, Book 2, Hadith 432).

Islam emphasizes tahara, hygiene, maintaining purity for worship. This is beautiful. It makes worship a mindful, intentional act.

OCD's Twist: "Cleanliness is half of faith, so you need to be *perfectly* clean. 100% certain. No trace of any impurity anywhere. Can't see najis? Doesn't matter—might still be there. Better wash again. And again. And again. Because half your faith depends on being clean enough."

What started as a value of basic cleanliness becomes a compulsion for sterile perfection that Islam never demanded.

Islamic Value: Sincerity of Intention

Islam teaches that actions are judged by intentions. Sincerity (ikhlas) in worship is critical—doing things for Allah, not for show.

OCD's Twist: "Your intention needs to be *perfectly* pure. Zero ego. Zero distraction. Zero mixed motives. Can't be absolutely certain your intention was pure? Better analyze it for the next hour. Better redo the action until the intention *feels* perfect. Because if there was even 1% ego, the whole action might not count."

What started as a teaching about genuine sincerity becomes paralysis in trying to achieve impossible mental purity.

Islamic Value: Excellence in Worship

The concept of *ihsan*—excellence, doing things beautifully—is praised in Islam. Praying with focus, reciting Quran well, performing actions properly.

OCD's Twist: "Excellence means perfection. No mistakes. Not even tiny ones. Mispronounced one letter in Quran? Doesn't count. Lost focus for two seconds during prayer? Invalid. Better keep redoing it until it's flawless. Because Allah deserves perfection, right?"

What started as aspiration for excellence becomes tyrannical demand for errorless performance.

Islamic Value: Fear of Allah and Accountability

Islam teaches *taqwa*—consciousness of Allah, awareness of accountability, healthy concern about pleasing Allah and avoiding His displeasure.

OCD's Twist: "Fear Allah means be terrified constantly. Assume every action might be haram. Assume every thought might be shirk. Assume you're always potentially in trouble. Better obsessively check everything. Better seek forgiveness 500 times. Because if you're not anxious, you're not really fearing Allah."

What started as God-consciousness becomes pathological anxiety.

Islamic Value: Avoiding Major Sins

Islam is clear about major sins—shirk, murder, theft, lying, adultery, etc. Believers should obviously avoid these.

OCD's Twist: "Every random thought might be a major sin. Every action might secretly be haram. That metaphor you used? Might be shirk. That handshake? Might be forbidden touch. Better research every tiny detail of every action. Better assume the worst about yourself."

What started as avoiding clear prohibitions becomes paralysis over imagined transgressions.

See the pattern? **OCD takes legitimate Islamic values and demands impossible, exhausting, excessive versions of them**.

Islam teaches cleanliness; OCD demands sterility.

Islam teaches sincerity; OCD demands thought-crime-free mental purity.

Islam teaches excellence; OCD demands errorless perfection.

Islam teaches God-consciousness; OCD demands paranoid terror.

The Difference Between Taqwa (God-Consciousness) and OCD

This might be the most important distinction in this entire book. Because "taqwa" and "OCD" can look similar on the surface—both involve attention to religious detail, concern about pleasing Allah, and careful practice.

But they're fundamentally different. Completely opposite, actually.

Taqwa (تقوى):

- Rooted in love and awareness of Allah
- Creates peace, tranquility (sakina)
- Makes worship feel like connection
- Brings you closer to Allah and to others
- Can be adjusted with flexibility when needed
- Follows established Islamic guidelines
- Trusts in Allah's mercy
- Accepts human limitation
- Creates balance in life
- Makes you more compassionate toward yourself and others

OCD:

- Rooted in fear and anxiety
- Creates distress, agitation
- Makes worship feel like torture
- Isolates you from Allah and from others
- Becomes increasingly rigid over time
- Creates rules beyond Islamic requirements
- Doubts Allah's mercy (or your access to it)
- Demands impossible perfection
- Consumes and dominates life
- Makes you harsh and critical toward yourself and others

A person with taqwa might think: "I should pray with focus and sincerity because I love Allah and want to connect with Him."

A person with OCD thinks: "If I don't pray perfectly, something terrible will happen. Allah might not accept it. I might be sinning. I need to redo it until the anxiety stops."

A person with taqwa might think: "I'll perform wudu carefully and properly because this is how I prepare to stand before Allah."

A person with OCD thinks: "I need to wash until I'm absolutely, 100% certain there's no possible impurity anywhere, or my prayer won't count and I'll be sinning."

Taqwa is consciousness *of* Allah. OCD is anxiety *about* religious performance.

The Prophet Muhammad (peace be upon him) said: "The strong believer is better and more beloved to Allah than the weak believer, although both are good" (Sahih Muslim, Book 33, Hadith 6441). Notice—*strong* believer. Not anxious believer. Not paralyzed believer. Strong.

Taqwa makes you stronger. OCD makes you weaker.

How OCD Creates "False Prophets" of Doubt

Here's a metaphor that helps clarify the dynamic:

Imagine you're trying to practice Islam and follow the guidance of the Prophet (peace be upon him) and the scholars of your madhab (school of thought).

The Prophet taught: Wudu is washing each required area once (washing three times is recommended). Takes 1-2 minutes.

The scholars you follow have given clear guidance on what constitutes purity, what breaks wudu, how to perform it.

But then OCD shows up. OCD is like a false prophet whispering contradictory commands:

"The Prophet said wash once? Actually, you need to wash until you have absolute certainty. Seven times might not be enough. Keep washing until it *feels* right."

"The scholars said that level of cleanliness is sufficient? Actually, they don't understand your specific situation. You need to research more. Find more specific rulings. Get more reassurance."

"Islam teaches that Allah is merciful and forgiving? Actually, you need to be terrified constantly. Any mistake might mean your prayer doesn't count. Better be obsessively careful."

OCD sets itself up as an authority *above* the actual teachings of Islam. It claims to know better than the Prophet, better than 1,400 years of Islamic scholarship, better than the clear texts.

And here's the tragedy: **People with religious OCD often follow the false prophet of doubt while thinking they're being extra pious**.

You're not being extra pious by washing for 45 minutes. You're following OCD's commands, not Islam's.

You're not being extra devoted by repeating prayers 20 times. You're following OCD's demands, not the Sunnah.

You're not showing superior taqwa by analyzing every thought for shirk. You're following OCD's paranoia, not Quranic teaching.

The real Prophet (peace be upon him) taught ease, mercy, balance, and manageable practice.

The false prophet of OCD teaches excessive hardship, constant doubt, rigid extremism, and unsustainable demands.

Which one are you following?

This is the question you need to ask yourself honestly.

When you spend three hours on acts of worship that should take fifteen minutes—whose teaching are you following?

When you reject the clear guidance of Islamic scholars because "they don't understand how serious this is"—whose authority are you accepting?

When you're exhausted, anxious, and disconnected from actual spiritual connection with Allah—whose path are you on?

If it's the path of OCD, it's time to recognize it as such.

Because Islam has a clear principle: **The religion is ease, not hardship**. Allah intended to make life manageable for believers, not torture them with impossible standards.

Any "religious" practice that makes you miserable, exhausted, and further from Allah needs to be questioned. Not your faith. Not your commitment. But whether what you're doing is actually Islam or whether it's OCD wearing an Islamic costume.

Breaking Free from the Hijacking

Understanding how OCD hijacks faith is the first step toward reclaiming it.

You now know:

- The basic OCD cycle and how compulsions maintain the disorder
- Why certainty-seeking is a trap OCD uses
- Why reassurance doesn't work and often makes things worse
- That anxiety about sin is different from actually sinning
- How OCD twists Islamic values into excessive demands
- The difference between taqwa and OCD
- How OCD sets itself up as a false authority

With this understanding, you can start seeing your experience clearly: "This demand to wash for 45 minutes? That's OCD, not Islam." "This need to achieve perfect certainty? That's the disorder, not religion." "This anxiety telling me my prayer doesn't count? That's waswas, not spiritual fact."

And once you can see the difference, you can start making different choices.

In the next chapters, we'll explore Islamic perspectives on treatment, evidence-based therapeutic approaches, and specific protocols for reclaiming your worship from OCD's grip.

But right now, the most important thing is this clarity: **OCD is not your faith. It's what's blocking you from practicing your faith properly**.

The path forward isn't less Islam. It's less OCD. And Islam itself—the actual teachings, not the OCD-twisted versions—supports that recovery.

Chapter 5: Is Seeking Treatment Permissible? The Islamic Case for Therapy

You've recognized the OCD. You understand how it's hijacked your worship. You see the difference between what Islam requires and what the disorder demands.

So now what?

Here's where a lot of Muslim OCD sufferers get stuck. Even when they know they need help, a voice in their head says: "Wait. Isn't this a spiritual problem? Shouldn't I just pray more? Isn't seeking therapy somehow... un-Islamic?"

And then there's the cultural weight. In many Muslim communities, mental health treatment carries stigma. People whisper. They suggest you're weak in faith. They say, "If you just trusted Allah more, you wouldn't need therapy."

So let's settle this question right now, with evidence from Islamic sources: **Is seeking treatment for OCD permissible in Islam?**

Short answer: Yes. Not just permissible—encouraged.

Long answer: That's what this chapter is about.

Prophetic Tradition of Seeking Treatment

The Prophet Muhammad (peace be upon him) didn't just allow seeking treatment for illness. He actively commanded it.

One of the clearest hadiths on this topic is narrated in Sunan Abi Dawud:

"Seek treatment, for Allah has not sent down a disease except that He has sent down a cure for it." (Sunan Abi Dawud, Book 29, Hadith 3855)

Notice the verb: *seek*. It's a command, not just a suggestion.

Another narration makes this even more explicit:

"Make use of medical treatment, for Allah has not made a disease without appointing a remedy for it, with the exception of one disease, namely old age." (Sunan al-Tirmidhi, Book 28, Hadith 2038)

The Prophet (peace be upon him) didn't say, "Pray and hope for healing." He said, *use medical treatment*.

But here's the hadith that really seals the case. It's often called the "tie your camel" hadith:

A Bedouin asked the Prophet: "Should I tie my camel and trust in Allah, or leave it untied and trust in Allah?" The Prophet replied: "Tie your camel and trust in Allah." (Sunan al-Tirmidhi, Book 33, Hadith 2517)

This is the perfect metaphor for mental health treatment.

Should you seek therapy and trust in Allah? Or skip therapy and just trust in Allah?

The answer: **Do both**. Take action *and* trust in Allah. Use the means Allah has provided, then rely on Him for the outcome.

The Prophet (peace be upon him) himself sought medical treatment. He used cupping therapy (*hijama*). He prescribed certain foods and herbs for illnesses. He visited sick people and recommended treatments to them.

If seeking treatment was somehow a sign of weak faith, the Prophet wouldn't have done it. He wouldn't have commanded it. He wouldn't have practiced medicine himself.

The early Muslim community followed this example. They developed hospitals, studied medicine, translated medical texts, and created entire fields of medical science. Muslim physicians like Ibn Sina (Avicenna) and Al-Razi (Rhazes) made groundbreaking contributions to medicine specifically because they understood that treating illness was part of Islamic practice, not opposed to it (Haque, 2004).

So when someone says, "Just pray more instead of getting therapy," they're not giving Islamic advice. They're contradicting the Prophet's explicit command to seek treatment.

Scholarly Consensus on Mental Health Treatment

Modern Islamic scholars across all major schools of thought agree: seeking treatment for mental health conditions is not only permissible but recommended.

Sheikh Yusuf al-Qaradawi, one of the most influential contemporary Islamic scholars, has stated that mental illnesses are like physical illnesses and should be treated by professionals (Al-Qaradawi, 1997).

Dr. Yasir Qadhi has spoken publicly about mental health, emphasizing that there's no shame in seeking professional help. He's pointed out that just as you'd see a cardiologist for heart disease, you should see a mental health professional for conditions like OCD or depression.

The Islamic Medical Association of North America (IMANA) has published statements affirming that mental health treatment, including therapy and medication when needed, is consistent with Islamic values and should be pursued (Padela & Curlin, 2013).

The European Council for Fatwa and Research has issued rulings supporting mental health treatment, including psychotherapy, as long as the treatment doesn't contradict core Islamic principles.

Here's what's interesting: **There's actually no scholarly disagreement on this**. You won't find any credible Islamic scholar saying, "Mental health treatment is haram" or "Therapy is forbidden." The consensus is clear.

The disagreement you might encounter isn't at the scholarly level. It's at the cultural level—uninformed opinions, stigma, misunderstanding. But Islamic scholarship? Unanimous support for seeking treatment.

Addressing Common Concerns

Even with clear Islamic evidence, people still have doubts. Let's tackle the big ones.

"Isn't this a test from Allah I should endure?"

Yes, difficulties are tests from Allah. The Quran says: "And We will surely test you with something of fear and hunger and a loss of wealth and lives and fruits, but give good tidings to the patient" (Quran 2:155).

But here's the question: **How does Allah want you to respond to tests?**

If you break your leg (a test), does Allah want you to refuse medical treatment and just endure the pain? No. You seek treatment *while* being patient with the process.

If you develop cancer (a test), does Allah want you to skip chemotherapy and just pray? No. You get treatment *while* trusting in Allah's plan.

The test isn't "Can you suffer without seeking help?" The test is: "Will you trust Allah, seek the means He's provided, be patient with the process, and maintain good character through difficulty?"

OCD is a test, yes. But **the test includes whether you'll seek appropriate treatment**, not whether you'll white-knuckle through suffering alone.

Think about it this way. The Prophet (peace be upon him) faced tremendous tests—persecution, warfare, the loss of loved ones. Did he just passively endure? No. He took action. He strategized. He sought help from companions. He used available resources. All while trusting in Allah's plan.

The concept of *sabr* (patience) in Islam doesn't mean passive resignation. It means active perseverance while taking appropriate action.

A scholar named Khaled Abou El Fadl explained this beautifully: Patience in Islam means bearing hardship with dignity while working to improve your situation, not simply accepting suffering as your permanent fate (Abou El Fadl, 2001).

So yes, OCD might be a test. And seeking treatment is part of passing that test.

"Will treatment weaken my faith?"

This fear makes sense on the surface. If therapy teaches you to dismiss religious doubts, won't that make you less conscientious about faith?

Actually, the opposite happens. Research shows that when religious OCD is treated effectively, people often report *stronger* faith afterward (Abu Raiya, Pargament, & Mahoney, 2011).

Why? Because OCD was blocking real spiritual connection. It turned worship into torture. It made Islam feel like an impossible burden. Treatment removes those barriers.

After treatment, people often say things like:

- "I can finally pray without anxiety and actually feel connected to Allah"
- "I enjoy reading Quran again instead of fearing it"
- "I can focus on being a better person instead of obsessing over ritual perfection"
- "My faith feels like it's mine again, not controlled by disorder"

Here's an example. Rashid had severe wudu OCD. He'd spend 45 minutes on ablution, miss prayers because he couldn't finish in time, and feel constant anxiety about purity. His faith felt like prison.

After treatment, he performed wudu in two minutes, prayed on time, and felt peaceful during worship. Did treatment weaken his faith? No. It freed his faith from OCD's grip.

The Islamic scholar Hamza Yusuf has talked about this—how excessive religious anxiety actually *damages* faith by making Islam feel oppressive rather than liberating (Yusuf, 2009). Treatment restores the ease and mercy that Islam is supposed to embody.

"Should I just make more dua?"

Make dua. Absolutely. But also take action.

Islam teaches both components. The Quran repeatedly combines spiritual practice with practical action:

"O you who have believed, seek help through patience and prayer." (Quran 2:153)

Notice: seek help through *both* patience and prayer. Not just prayer alone.

The Prophet (peace be upon him) would make dua *and* take practical steps. When preparing for battle, he didn't just pray for victory—he strategized, trained soldiers, gathered intelligence. When facing illness, he didn't just make dua—he sought treatment.

Dua is asking Allah for help. Treatment is *using* the help Allah has provided.

Think about it. If you're starving, you make dua for sustenance. But you also eat when food is available. You don't refuse food and say, "I'm just making dua for Allah to sustain me." That's not tawakkul (trust)—that's foolishness.

Same with OCD. Make dua for healing. Absolutely. But also use the treatment Allah has made available through modern psychology.

A contemporary scholar, Sheikh Omar Suleiman, puts it this way: Dua is the spiritual component of seeking Allah's help; taking action is the practical component. Islam requires both (Suleiman, 2018).

And here's something beautiful: Making dua *while* getting treatment is incredibly powerful. You're acknowledging that ultimate healing comes from Allah, while also using the means He's created. That's the perfect balance of spiritual and practical.

The Concept of Tawakkul (Trust in Allah) Alongside Action

Tawakkul is one of the most misunderstood concepts in Islam. People think it means passive reliance—"I'll just trust Allah and not do anything."

That's not what tawakkul means.

Ibn al-Qayyim, the great Islamic scholar, explained tawakkul as having two components: (1) using the means Allah has provided, and (2) trusting Allah for the outcome (Ibn al-Qayyim, 2000).

Notice both components are required.

The "tie your camel" hadith perfectly illustrates this. You tie the camel (take action), *then* trust in Allah. You don't skip tying the camel and claim that's trust. That's not trust—that's negligence.

A farmer who has tawakkul doesn't say, "I trust Allah to grow crops, so I won't plant seeds or water the field." He plants, waters, and tends the crops (action), while trusting Allah to provide rain, sunshine, and harvest (outcome).

Same with OCD treatment. You seek therapy, practice the techniques, take medication if needed (action), while trusting that Allah is the ultimate source of healing (outcome).

Dr. Ingrid Mattson, a prominent Islamic scholar, explains that tawakkul means "trusting Allah's wisdom while taking responsible action in the world" (Mattson, 2013). The two go together.

Actually, refusing treatment while claiming tawakkul could be considered a misuse of the concept. It's like the story of the man in a flood:

A flood is coming. Someone offers him a ride to safety. He refuses: "I trust Allah to save me." Water rises. A boat comes. He refuses: "I trust Allah." Water rises more. A helicopter arrives. He refuses: "I trust Allah." He drowns. In the afterlife, he asks Allah, "Why didn't you save me?" Allah says, "I sent you a car, a boat, and a helicopter. What more did you want?"

The modern version for OCD: Allah has provided therapy, medication, trained professionals, research, treatment protocols. Refusing all of this while claiming trust in Allah isn't tawakkul—it's refusing the help Allah sent.

Real tawakkul for someone with OCD looks like this:

1. Recognize you have a disorder that needs treatment (awareness)
2. Seek qualified mental health care (action)

3. Follow through with treatment recommendations (responsibility)
4. Make dua and trust that Allah controls the outcome (spiritual component)
5. Be patient with the process (sabr)

That's the Islamic approach. Action plus trust.

Mental Health as Physical Health

Here's a question that cuts through a lot of confusion: **Would you refuse treatment for diabetes?**

If you had diabetes, would you say, "I'll just pray more and skip the insulin"? Would you say, "Seeking treatment shows weak faith"? Would you say, "This is a test I should endure without medical intervention"?

Of course not. You'd see an endocrinologist. You'd manage your blood sugar. You'd take medication if needed. And nobody would question your faith for doing so.

So why is mental health different?

Biologically, it's not. OCD involves the brain—an organ, just like the pancreas or heart. When the brain's circuitry malfunctions (as it does in OCD), that's a medical condition requiring treatment, just like when the pancreas can't produce insulin (Pauls, Abramovitch, Rauch, & Geller, 2014).

Research using brain imaging shows that OCD involves specific abnormalities in brain circuits, particularly involving the orbitofrontal cortex, anterior cingulate cortex, and striatum (Saxena, Brody, Schwartz, & Baxter, 1998). This isn't theoretical—we can literally see the differences on brain scans.

And treatment works by changing brain function. Cognitive-behavioral therapy for OCD has been shown to normalize activity in these brain circuits (Schwartz, 1997). The brain is a physical organ that responds to treatment, just like other organs.

Islamic theology has never separated "mental" from "physical" in the way Western culture sometimes does. The classical Islamic scholars recognized that psychological states had physical bases. They treated mental disturbances as medical conditions requiring intervention.

Al-Razi, the 9th-century Persian physician, wrote extensively about psychological disorders and their treatment. He didn't say, "These people just need more faith." He developed therapeutic approaches based on what we'd now call cognitive and behavioral techniques (Haque, 2004).

Ibn Sina wrote about anxiety, obsessions, and compulsive behaviors in his medical texts. He classified them as illnesses requiring treatment, not spiritual failures (Haque, 2004).

So the idea that mental health somehow doesn't deserve medical treatment? That's not Islamic. That's stigma dressed up in religious language.

The brain is part of the body Allah created. When it malfunctions, you treat it. Simple as that.

Fatawa from Contemporary Scholars on OCD Treatment

Let's look at what actual Islamic legal opinions (fatawa) say about OCD treatment.

Sheikh Assim Al-Hakeem, a Saudi scholar known for answering questions online, has repeatedly stated that OCD is a medical condition and people should seek professional help. He's specifically advised people to see mental health professionals rather than just seeking Islamic advice for what is fundamentally a psychiatric disorder.

Dr. Hatem al-Haj, a professor of Islamic jurisprudence, issued a detailed fatwa explaining that OCD-driven excessive doubt in worship should be treated by (1) following the basic requirements of fiqh without elaboration, and (2) seeking professional mental health treatment (Al-Haj, 2019).

Sheikh Dr. Yasir Qadhi has discussed OCD in multiple lectures and podcast episodes, explicitly stating that it's a neurobiological disorder that requires professional treatment. He's encouraged people to seek therapy and medication when needed, while maintaining Islamic spiritual practices.

Mufti Abdur-Rahman ibn Yusuf Mangera has written about waswas and OCD, clarifying that when religious doubts become pathological (consuming hours daily, causing severe distress), the person needs mental health treatment, not just more Islamic education.

The Assembly of Muslim Jurists of America (AMJA) has issued fatawa supporting mental health treatment for various conditions, including OCD. They've clarified that seeking therapy and taking psychiatric medication when prescribed by qualified professionals is permissible and often necessary.

Here's a specific fatwa from AMJA regarding mental health treatment:

"There is no Islamic prohibition against seeking mental health treatment, including therapy and medication. Mental illness is like physical illness and should be treated by qualified professionals. Seeking such treatment does not contradict tawakkul (trust in Allah)."

Sheikh Abdullah bin Bayyah, one of the most respected contemporary scholars, has emphasized the importance of addressing mental health conditions through professional treatment, noting that Islamic law operates on the principle of preventing harm and seeking benefit (Bin Bayyah, 2015).

What's striking is the consistency. Across different schools of thought, different regions, different scholars—the answer is the same: **OCD is a medical condition; seek professional treatment**.

Some scholars have even gone further, saying that if OCD is significantly impairing your ability to function, seeking treatment becomes *obligatory* (*wajib*), not just permissible (*ja'iz*).

Why? Because Islam requires you to preserve your health and well-being. The Quran says: "And do not kill yourselves" (Quran 4:29), which scholars interpret broadly as an obligation to protect your physical and mental health.

If you had a serious infection that could be cured with antibiotics but you refused treatment, you'd be harming yourself—which is prohibited. Same logic applies to mental health conditions.

What Treatment Actually Looks Like

So you've decided to seek treatment. What happens next?

Professional Assessment

First, you'd see a mental health professional—psychologist, psychiatrist, or licensed therapist who specializes in OCD. They'll conduct an assessment to confirm the diagnosis and understand your specific symptoms.

For religious OCD, it's helpful if the therapist has cultural competence about Islam, though it's not absolutely required. Many therapists who don't know much about Islamic practice can still effectively treat the OCD mechanism while you provide the religious context.

Evidence-Based Therapy

The gold standard treatment for OCD is Exposure and Response Prevention (ERP), a specific type of cognitive-behavioral therapy. We'll discuss this in detail in Chapter 7.

Basically, ERP involves gradually exposing yourself to situations that trigger OCD anxiety while preventing the compulsive responses. For example, performing wudu once without repeating, even while feeling anxious about whether it was perfect.

Other effective approaches include cognitive therapy (challenging OCD thoughts) and acceptance-based therapies (learning to coexist with intrusive thoughts without reacting to them).

Treatment typically involves weekly therapy sessions over several months. You'll practice techniques between sessions and gradually build up your ability to resist compulsions.

Medication (Sometimes)

For moderate to severe OCD, medication is often recommended alongside therapy. The most common are SSRIs (Selective Serotonin Reuptake Inhibitors), which help regulate brain chemistry (Soomro, Altman, Rajagopal, & Oakley-Browne, 2008).

Some people worry: "Is taking psychiatric medication permissible in Islam?"

Yes. Islamic scholars have ruled that psychiatric medication is permissible and often recommended when prescribed by qualified physicians. There's a detailed scholarly discussion about this in Chapter 19, but the short answer: medication for mental health is no different from medication for any other medical condition.

Integration with Faith

Good treatment doesn't ask you to abandon Islam. It asks you to separate Islam from OCD.

You'll still pray, but you'll pray according to Islamic guidelines rather than OCD's demands. You'll still maintain purity, but according to fiqh requirements rather than obsessive standards. You'll still practice your faith—just without the disorder hijacking it.

Many people find that treatment actually *strengthens* their faith because they can finally practice Islam the way it's meant to be practiced—with ease, sincerity, and genuine connection to Allah.

What About Spiritual Alternatives?

"Okay, but what about ruqyah? What about just going to the mosque more? What about Islamic counseling?"

Here's the nuanced answer: **Spiritual practices have their place, but they're not a substitute for professional mental health treatment for OCD.**

Ruqyah (Islamic spiritual healing) can be appropriate for spiritual concerns. If someone believes they're experiencing the influence of jinn or the evil eye, ruqyah might be sought alongside medical treatment.

But OCD is not a jinn problem. It's a neurobiological disorder. Treating it primarily with ruqyah instead of evidence-based therapy is like treating diabetes primarily with spiritual healing instead of insulin. You might pray for healing (which is good), but you still need the medical treatment.

Islamic counseling can be helpful for navigating religious questions, finding community support, and integrating faith into your recovery. But Islamic counselors, unless they're also trained mental health professionals, typically aren't equipped to provide the specialized OCD treatment you need.

The best approach: See a qualified OCD therapist for the disorder itself, while maintaining spiritual practices and seeking Islamic guidance for religious questions that arise during treatment.

Some Muslims have found therapists who are also knowledgeable about Islam, which can be ideal. Organizations like the Khalil Center, a Muslim mental health organization, provide therapy services with Islamic cultural competence (Keshavarzi & Haque, 2013).

But even if you can't find a Muslim therapist, a skilled OCD specialist can help you effectively, and you can consult Islamic scholars separately for religious questions.

Take Aways

Is seeking treatment permissible in Islam?

Yes. Absolutely. Unequivocally.

The Prophet (peace be upon him) commanded it. Islamic scholars across history have supported it. Contemporary fatawa affirm it. The entire Islamic medical tradition is built on it.

OCD is not a spiritual problem that you solve through more prayer alone. It's a medical condition that requires professional treatment. Getting that treatment isn't a sign of weak faith—it's a sign of wisdom, responsibility, and proper tawakkul.

You tie your camel *and* trust in Allah.

You seek treatment *and* make dua.

You use the means Allah provided *and* rely on Him for the outcome.

That's the Islamic way. That's what the Prophet taught. That's what the scholars affirm.

If you've been hesitating to seek help because of religious doubts, put those doubts aside. They're not from Islam—they might actually be from the OCD itself, which wants to keep you trapped in the cycle.

You have Islamic permission—actually, Islamic encouragement—to get the help you need.

Now let's talk about what that help looks like and how it works within an Islamic framework.

Chapter 6: Distinguishing Religious Obligation from OCD Compulsion

Here's the problem that keeps Muslim OCD sufferers trapped: OCD makes itself look exactly like good Islamic practice.

Spending two hours on wudu? OCD says that's thoroughness in worship. Repeating prayers 15 times? OCD says that's striving for excellence. Researching Islamic rulings for six hours online? OCD says that's seeking knowledge.

And because Islam *does* value thoroughness, excellence, and knowledge, you can't tell where proper practice ends and disorder begins.

You need clear criteria. Bright lines. Specific guidelines that help you distinguish between what Islam actually requires and what OCD is demanding in Islam's name.

That's what this chapter provides. We're going to look at the actual Islamic legal principles (*fiqh*) that define religious obligations, so you can see clearly when you've crossed from requirement into compulsion.

Because here's the truth: **Islamic law is way more flexible and merciful than OCD will ever let you believe**.

Fiqh Principles for Minimum Requirements

Islamic jurisprudence (fiqh) operates on clear principles. Scholars throughout history established these principles specifically to prevent the kind of excessive religiosity that OCD creates.

Here are the core principles you need to know:

Principle 1: Certainty is Not Removed by Doubt

Arabic: اليقين لا يزول بالشك (al-yaqeen la yazool bi'l-shakk)

This is perhaps the most important fiqh principle for someone with OCD.

What it means: If you were certain of something initially, and then doubt appears later, the doubt doesn't override the original certainty.

Example: You performed wudu carefully. You were certain it was done correctly at the time. Five minutes later, doubt appears: "Wait, did I wash my left arm completely?"

Islamic ruling: Your original certainty stands. You're still in a state of wudu. The doubt is dismissed.

OCD wants you to repeat wudu "just to be sure." But Islamic law says: No. The certainty you had when you completed wudu is what counts. Later doubt is irrelevant (Al-Suyuti, 1983).

Principle 2: The Basic Principle is Continuance of What Was

Arabic: الأصل بقاء ما كان (al-asl baqa' ma kan)

What it means: Things continue in their previous state unless there's clear evidence of change.

Example: You were in a state of purity. You now doubt that you might have broken your wudu—maybe you passed gas, maybe you didn't.

Islamic ruling: Assume you're still in a state of purity. Why? Because that was the last state you were certain of. Without clear evidence that it changed, it continues (Al-Nawawi, 1996).

OCD wants you to assume impurity and redo wudu. Islamic law says: No. Assume continuance of the previous certain state.

Principle 3: Hardship Brings Ease

Arabic: المشقة تجلب التيسير (al-mash'aqqa tajlib al-taysir)

This is one of the five major universal principles (*qawa'id kulliyyah*) in Islamic jurisprudence.

What it means: When something becomes genuinely difficult, Islamic law provides accommodations and relaxations.

The Quran establishes this: "Allah intends for you ease and does not intend for you hardship" (Quran 2:185).

Example: If performing wudu in the normal way causes genuine hardship (extreme cold, no water access, skin condition), alternatives are permitted—you can wipe over socks, perform tayammum (dry ablution), etc.

But OCD creates *manufactured* hardship—spending 45 minutes on wudu not because it's physically necessary, but because of anxiety.

Islamic law says: The wudu itself shouldn't be hard. If you're making it hard, you're exceeding requirements (Al-Qarafi, 2004).

Principle 4: Harm Must Be Removed

Arabic: الضرر يزال (ad-darar yuzal)

What it means: Actions or practices that cause harm should be stopped, even if they seem religious.

The Prophet (peace be upon him) said: "There should be neither harming nor reciprocating harm" (Sunan Ibn Majah, Book 13, Hadith 2340).

Example: If your "religious practice" is causing you to miss work consistently, damaging relationships, creating severe distress, or harming your physical health (like skin damage from excessive washing), that practice needs to stop—even if you think it's religious.

Islamic law prioritizes preventing harm. If your worship is harming you, something is wrong with *how* you're worshiping, not with Islam itself (Ibn Nujaym, 1999).

Principle 5: Actions are Judged by Intentions

Arabic: الأمور بمقاصدها (al-umoor bi-maqasidiha)

From the hadith: "Actions are by intentions" (Sahih Bukhari, Book 1, Hadith 1).

What it means: Allah judges the intention behind your actions, not just the outward form.

Example: You intended to pray properly. You performed the prayer with sincere intention to worship Allah. Did you have some random distracting thoughts during it? That doesn't invalidate the prayer—your intention to pray is what counts.

OCD wants to invalidate prayers based on intrusive thoughts, wavering attention, or uncertainty about whether your intention was "pure enough." Islamic law says: If you intended to pray, you prayed (Al-Nawawi, 1996).

The Concept of "Al-Mash'aqqa Tajlib al-Taysir" (Hardship Brings Ease)

This principle deserves special attention because it directly contradicts everything OCD tells you.

OCD says: "The harder and more painful worship is, the more Allah will accept it. Push yourself. Make it difficult. Suffering means sincerity."

Islamic law says: **The opposite**. When worship becomes genuinely difficult, Islam provides ease.

The classical scholar Al-Qarafi explained that this principle means: When religious obligations create genuine hardship, accommodations are made to ease the difficulty (Al-Qarafi, 2004).

Examples from fiqh:

- Can't stand for prayer? Sit.
- Can't sit? Lie down.
- Can't find water for wudu? Use tayammum (dry ablution).
- Traveling? Shorten and combine prayers.
- Sick during Ramadan? Don't fast; make it up later.
- Genuinely can't afford Hajj? Not obligated to go.

Every area of Islamic law contains these accommodations. Why? Because Allah says: "Allah does not burden a soul beyond that it can bear" (Quran 2:286).

Now, here's the critical question: **Does OCD create genuine hardship?**

Yes. Absolutely. OCD is intensely difficult—psychologically, emotionally, and physically.

So Islamic law should provide ease for someone struggling with OCD. And it does. The ease is: **Follow the minimum requirements, not the OCD-driven maximums**.

Ibn Taymiyyah addressed people experiencing excessive waswas. His advice was consistent: Perform the religious obligation once, properly, according to its minimum requirements, and then stop. Ignore subsequent doubts. That's the "ease" provision for people experiencing pathological religious doubt (Ibn Taymiyyah, 1995).

Rulings on Excessive Wudu

Let's get specific. What do Islamic scholars say about wudu, one of the most common OCD battlegrounds?

The Requirements

According to all four major schools of Islamic jurisprudence, wudu requires:

1. Intention (niyyah) in the heart
2. Washing the entire face once
3. Washing both arms up to and including the elbows once
4. Wiping over the head (or part of it, depending on school)
5. Washing both feet up to and including the ankles once

That's it. Once. One time for each required area.

Washing three times is recommended (*sunnah*) but not required. The Prophet (peace be upon him) would sometimes wash once, sometimes twice, sometimes three times (Sahih Bukhari, Book 4, Hadith 159).

The entire process should take 1-2 minutes when done properly.

What About Doubts During Wudu?

If you're in the middle of wudu and you doubt whether you washed a particular area, the ruling depends on timing:

- If you're still in the act of wudu: Wash the area you doubted.
- If you've finished and moved on: Ignore the doubt. Your wudu is valid (Al-Nawawi, 1996).

What About Doubts After Wudu?

If you've completed wudu and later doubt whether you did it correctly, the ruling is clear across all schools: **Ignore the doubt**. Your wudu is valid. The doubt doesn't invalidate it.

Ibn Taymiyyah specifically addressed people who keep repeating wudu due to doubt. He said: This is from shaytan's whisperings. Perform wudu once, properly, then ignore any subsequent doubts—no matter how strong they feel (Ibn Taymiyyah, 1995).

What If You Can't Tell If You Washed Thoroughly Enough?

If water touched the required area, you washed it. You don't need to ensure water reached every microscopic bit of skin or every individual hair.

The legal standard is: reasonable washing of the required area. Not forensic, microscopic, absolute certainty of total coverage.

Time Limits

Some scholars advise people with excessive waswas to set a time limit: 5 minutes maximum for wudu. When the time is up, you're done—even if doubts remain. This approach has scholarly precedent and is particularly recommended for those with OCD (Al-Haj, 2019).

Rulings on Excessive Prayer Repetition

Prayer (salah) is another common OCD target. Let's look at what Islamic law actually requires versus what OCD demands.

The Requirements

A valid prayer requires:

1. Being in a state of purity
2. Facing the qiblah (direction of Mecca)
3. Proper intention
4. Reciting the opening takbir ("Allahu Akbar")
5. Standing (if able)
6. Reciting Al-Fatiha
7. Performing the movements (bowing, prostration, etc.) in proper order
8. The final tashahhud (testimony of faith) and tasleem (saying "As-salamu alaykum")

If you did these things, your prayer is valid. Period.

What About Mistakes During Prayer?

If you make a clear, definite mistake during prayer (like skipping a required part), you can do the prostrations of forgetfulness (sujood as-sahw) at the end.

But if you're just uncertain—"Did I recite Al-Fatiha correctly? Did I bow for the right amount of time?"—the ruling is: Continue the prayer. Don't stop. Don't restart (Al-Nawawi, 1996).

What About Intrusive Thoughts During Prayer?

The Prophet (peace be upon him) explicitly addressed this:

"Shaytan comes to one of you in his prayer and confuses him so he does not know how much he has prayed. If any one of you experiences that, let him perform two prostrations of forgetfulness while sitting." (Sahih Muslim, Book 4, Hadith 1208)

Notice: The remedy for confusion during prayer is two prostrations at the end. Not repeating the entire prayer. Not starting over 15 times.

What If You Had Blasphemous Intrusive Thoughts?

We covered this in Chapter 2, but it bears repeating: Intrusive thoughts don't invalidate prayer. If you had unwanted, disturbing thoughts during prayer, the prayer is still valid. Your intention to pray is what matters, not random mental content.

Ibn Taymiyyah clarified: Waswas during prayer is from shaytan and doesn't affect the validity of the prayer as long as you intended to pray and completed the required components (Ibn Taymiyyah, 1995).

The One-Time Rule

Many scholars recommend this for people with OCD: **Pray each prayer once and move on, regardless of doubts**.

Even if you feel uncertain about whether you did it "right," even if intrusive thoughts occurred, even if your concentration wasn't perfect—the prayer counts. Don't repeat it.

Sheikh Dr. Hatem al-Haj specifically advises this for OCD sufferers: Establish the intention to pray each prayer only once, and then consider it done when you finish, regardless of any doubts that arise (Al-Haj, 2019).

When Uncertainty is Acceptable in Worship

OCD tells you that uncertainty in worship is unacceptable. You must be 100% sure.

Islamic law says: **Uncertainty is often not just acceptable, but expected**.

Here are areas where Islamic scholars explicitly acknowledge that certainty isn't required:

Qiblah Direction

If you're in an unfamiliar location and you're not sure which direction is toward Mecca, you make your best estimate and pray. Even if you later discover you were facing the wrong direction, your prayer was valid—you did your best with the information available (Al-Kasani, 1986).

Amount of Water in Wudu

You don't need to measure exactly how much water you used or ensure every microscopic area was touched. Reasonable washing is sufficient.

Pronunciation in Recitation

Unless you're a Quran teacher or imam leading prayer, small mispronunciations that don't change the meaning are overlooked. You recite to the best of your ability. Perfect pronunciation isn't required for valid prayer (Al-Nawawi, 1996).

Time of Prayer

If you're uncertain whether the prayer time has entered or left, you can follow a reasonable estimate. Many mosques call the adhan slightly early or late for logistical reasons—this is accepted as part of normal practice.

State of Purity

As we discussed, if you're uncertain whether you broke wudu, you assume you're still in a state of purity. Certainty isn't required—reasonable belief is sufficient.

Intention Purity

You can't perfectly analyze whether your intention is 100% pure with zero ego. Islamic law doesn't require that. If you intended to worship Allah, that's sufficient—even if human imperfection means mixed motivations exist (Al-Ghazali, 1989).

In all these cases, **Islam accepts human limitation**. You do your reasonable best, and that's what counts.

OCD demands superhuman certainty. Islam requires human reasonableness.

The Danger of Bid'ah (Innovation) Through OCD

Here's something most people don't consider: **OCD-driven religious practices can actually become religious innovation (bid'ah)**.

Bid'ah means introducing practices into Islam that weren't part of the original religion. The Prophet (peace be upon him) warned against this: "Whoever introduces something into this matter of ours that is not part of it will have it rejected" (Sahih Muslim, Book 18, Hadith 4266).

How does OCD create bid'ah?

By adding requirements that Islam never established.

Examples:

- Washing each body part in wudu seven times every time (the Prophet sometimes washed once)
- Reciting specific phrases exactly 100 times to "ensure" Allah's acceptance (no such requirement exists)
- Creating personal rules about what breaks wudu that go beyond Islamic scholarship
- Refusing to pray unless you've achieved a specific mental state that Islam doesn't require
- Developing elaborate rituals before worship that have no basis in Sunnah

When you create requirements beyond what Allah and His Messenger established, you're essentially saying: "The religion as revealed isn't sufficient. I need to add to it."

That's bid'ah.

Ibn Taymiyyah specifically warned about this in the context of excessive religious scrupulosity. He noted that people who add extra requirements to worship—thinking they're being extra pious—are actually contradicting the Prophet's teaching that the religion is complete and sufficient as revealed (Ibn Taymiyyah, 1995).

The Prophet (peace be upon him) gave us a complete religion. Adding to it—even with good intentions—is problematic. And when those additions come from OCD rather than from revelation or scholarship, they're definitely not from Islam.

So here's an uncomfortable question: **Are you practicing Islam, or are you practicing OCD-modified Islam?**

If your religious practices include requirements that no scholar recognizes, that the Prophet never taught, that create hardship beyond what Islam intends—you might be inadvertently innovating.

The solution isn't less Islam. It's *actual* Islam, stripped of the OCD additions.

Consulting Qualified Scholars vs. OCD-Driven Research

Google has made religious OCD worse.

Think about it. Thirty years ago, if you had a question about whether your wudu was valid, you'd ask your local imam. He'd give you an answer. Done.

Now? You can spend six hours reading conflicting fatawa from dozens of websites, finding minority opinions that support your worst fears, and emerging more confused than when you started.

This is OCD-driven research, and it makes everything worse.

What Qualified Scholar Consultation Looks Like

Real Islamic consultation involves:

1. Identifying a knowledgeable scholar or imam you trust
2. Asking your question clearly and concisely
3. Listening to the answer
4. Following that answer
5. Not asking the same question again

Notice step 5: **Not asking the same question again**.

If you ask a qualified scholar about whether your prayer was valid, and they say yes, the conversation is over. You don't ask three more scholars to "make sure." You don't research online to see if maybe this scholar was wrong.

The classical Islamic tradition of *taqlid* (following scholarly authority) exists partly to prevent the kind of paralysis that OCD creates. You choose a qualified scholar or school of thought, you learn their rulings, you follow them. That provides stability and clarity (Hallaq, 2009).

What OCD-Driven Research Looks Like

OCD research involves:

1. Having a doubt or fear
2. Searching online for rulings
3. Finding both permissive and restrictive opinions
4. Latching onto the most restrictive, fear-based opinion
5. Seeking more opinions because you're not "sure" yet
6. Finding conflicting views
7. More anxiety
8. More research
9. Never reaching resolution

The key difference: Real scholarship seeks knowledge to guide action. OCD research seeks certainty to relieve anxiety. And because certainty is impossible, the research never ends.

How to Stop OCD-Driven Research

If you have a genuine Islamic question that's preventing you from practicing your faith:

Step 1: Ask one qualified, trusted scholar

Step 2: Accept their answer

Step 3: Follow it

Step 4: Do not research further

If the doubt returns later ("But what if that scholar was wrong?"), that's OCD. Don't engage with it. You got your answer. Move on.

Some people with OCD benefit from a blanket rule: **No independent Islamic research during recovery**. If a question arises, they can ask their designated scholar. But no browsing fatwa websites, no Googling "is this halal," no reading forums about Islamic rulings.

This might feel restrictive. But it breaks the reassurance-seeking cycle that feeds OCD.

Setting Boundaries with Islamic Practices During Treatment

This is where things get practical and sometimes uncomfortable.

When you're in treatment for religious OCD, you need to set boundaries around religious practices. This doesn't mean abandoning Islam. It means practicing Islam in a structured way that breaks the OCD cycle.

Time Limits

Example boundaries:

- Wudu: 5 minutes maximum
- Each prayer: 10-15 minutes maximum
- Bathroom/istinja: 10 minutes maximum
- Pre-bedtime dua: 5 minutes maximum

These aren't Islamic limits—they're treatment boundaries designed to prevent compulsive behavior.

Initially, these limits might feel impossibly restrictive. "How can I do wudu properly in 5 minutes?" (Most people do it in 2 minutes, so 5 minutes is actually generous.)

But the point isn't speed. The point is preventing the compulsive extensions that keep you trapped.

One-Time Rules

Example boundaries:

- Pray each prayer once; never repeat
- Perform wudu once; never redo it based on doubt
- If you make istighfar once for something, don't repeat it
- Ask an Islamic question once; don't ask again for reassurance

These rules prevent the compulsive repetition that characterizes OCD.

Research Restrictions

Example boundaries:

- No browsing Islamic Q&A websites
- No Googling Islamic rulings during anxious moments
- Limit Islamic study to scheduled times (not when anxious)
- No asking family members for reassurance about religious validity

Prayer Modifications (Temporary)

In some severe cases, therapists recommend temporarily modifying how you pray to break compulsive patterns. For example:

- Pray only the mandatory (*fard*) parts, skipping the recommended (*sunnah*) portions temporarily
- Recite shorter surahs in prayer to reduce opportunities for OCD to create doubts
- Set a timer and end prayer when it goes off, even if doubts remain

Is this ideal Islamic practice? No. But it's therapeutic practice that allows you to *return* to proper Islamic practice once the OCD is under control.

Think of it like physical therapy. If you injured your leg, the physical therapist might restrict your movement temporarily—not as the permanent state, but as part of healing so you can eventually move normally again.

Same with religious OCD treatment. You might restrict certain practices temporarily so you can eventually practice Islam freely and without compulsion.

Getting Scholarly Permission for Treatment Boundaries

Some people feel more comfortable setting these boundaries if they have explicit Islamic permission.

You can consult with a qualified Islamic scholar, explain that you have diagnosed OCD and are in treatment, and ask about temporary modifications to worship during recovery.

Many scholars, when they understand the medical reality of OCD, will give permission for treatment-related boundaries, understanding that the goal is to eventually restore normal Islamic practice.

Dr. Hatem al-Haj, for example, has specifically addressed this, noting that people with OCD should follow their therapist's treatment plan, even if it involves temporary modifications to how they practice, because the alternative—remaining trapped in OCD—is worse (Al-Haj, 2019).

When to Follow Fiqh vs. When to Follow Your Therapist

Here's a question that creates confusion: If Islamic law says one thing and your therapist says another, who do you follow?

Example scenario: Islamic law says it's recommended to pray the sunnah prayers before and after the fard prayers. Your therapist says, "For now, just pray the fard and skip the sunnah to reduce compulsive opportunities."

Who's right?

Short answer: Follow your therapist for treatment, while understanding it's temporary.

Islamic scholars have a principle: Preventing harm takes priority over gaining benefit (دفع المفاسد مقدم على جلب المصالح).

The "benefit" of praying sunnah prayers is real but not obligatory. The "harm" of OCD preventing you from functioning, destroying your relationship with faith, and consuming your life is severe.

So temporarily reducing practice to prevent severe harm is Islamically justifiable—especially when the goal is to eventually restore full practice.

Think of it this way:

Fiqh tells you what normal Islamic practice looks like. This is your goal. This is where you're headed.

Therapy tells you how to get there when OCD is blocking the path. This is your method. This is the route.

They're not contradictory—they're addressing different questions.

Fiqh says: "Wudu should be done like this."

Therapy says: "Because OCD is interfering, here's how to relearn doing wudu without compulsion."

Both are correct. One describes the destination; the other describes the journey.

What This Means for Your Recovery

You need clarity about what Islam actually requires so you can see when OCD is demanding extra.

Islamic law is built on principles of ease, mercy, and human limitation. It accounts for doubt. It accepts reasonable uncertainty. It provides accommodations for difficulty.

OCD creates rules that contradict these principles—demanding perfect certainty, rejecting reasonable estimates, refusing accommodations, and making worship harder than Allah intended.

When you know the fiqh principles—certainty isn't removed by doubt, hardship brings ease, actions are judged by intentions—you can recognize OCD's lies.

When you know the actual requirements for wudu and prayer, you can see that spending three hours on worship that should take fifteen minutes isn't piety—it's disorder.

When you understand that Islamic scholars throughout history have addressed excessive religious scrupulosity and consistently advised: Do the minimum requirements and move on—you have permission to resist OCD's demands.

Islamic law is your ally in recovery, not your obstacle. The religion provides exactly the structure and flexibility you need to break free from OCD.

You just need to learn what Islam actually teaches—not what OCD claims in Islam's name.

Chapter 7: Exposure and Response Prevention (ERP)

You understand the problem. You've recognized the OCD. You've got Islamic permission to seek treatment. You know what Islam actually requires versus what the disorder demands.

Now comes the hard part: **Actually changing the behavior**.

Because here's the thing—you can understand OCD intellectually and still be trapped in it behaviorally. Knowledge doesn't automatically change the compulsion to wash your hands for the fifteenth time or to restart prayer for the tenth time.

You need a method. A specific approach that breaks the cycle.

That method is Exposure and Response Prevention (ERP).

ERP is the most researched, most effective treatment for OCD. Studies show that 60-80% of people who complete ERP treatment experience significant symptom reduction (Öst, Havnen, Hansen, & Kvale, 2015). It works across cultures, across different OCD subtypes, and yes—it works for religious OCD.

But let's be honest: ERP sounds terrifying when you first hear about it. Face your fears? On purpose? Without doing the compulsion that makes the anxiety go away?

Yeah. That's exactly what it is.

And it works.

What is ERP and Why It Works

ERP has two components: **Exposure** and **Response Prevention**.

Exposure means deliberately putting yourself in situations that trigger OCD anxiety. If you're afraid of najis contamination, you'd deliberately touch things you consider impure. If you fear your prayers don't count, you'd pray once and stop, even with uncertainty.

Response Prevention means blocking the compulsion you'd normally do to reduce anxiety. No excessive washing. No repeating prayers. No seeking reassurance. No mental rituals.

Put them together: You trigger the anxiety on purpose and then don't do anything to make it go away. You just... sit with it.

This sounds insane if you've never heard of it before. Why would you deliberately cause yourself anxiety and then refuse to relieve it?

Because **that's how you break the OCD cycle**.

OCD works like this:

1. Trigger → 2. Anxiety → 3. Compulsion → 4. Temporary relief → 5. Reinforcement of the cycle

ERP changes it to:

1. Trigger → 2. Anxiety → 3. **No compulsion** → 4. **Anxiety decreases on its own** → 5. Learning that compulsions aren't necessary

Dr. Edna Foa, one of the developers of ERP, explains it like this: OCD is maintained by avoidance and compulsions. When you stop avoiding triggers and stop performing compulsions, your brain learns that the feared outcome doesn't actually happen, and the anxiety naturally decreases over time (Foa & McLean, 2016).

The technical term is **extinction learning**. You're extinguishing the association between the trigger and the fear response by repeatedly experiencing the trigger without the feared outcome occurring.

The Neuroscience of OCD and Extinction Learning

Here's what's happening in your brain during OCD.

Research using functional MRI shows that people with OCD have overactivity in certain brain circuits—particularly involving the orbitofrontal cortex (OFC), anterior cingulate cortex (ACC), and striatum (Pauls et al., 2014).

The OFC is involved in detecting errors and potential problems. In OCD, it's hyperactive—constantly signaling "Something's wrong! Something's dangerous!"

The ACC generates the feeling of anxiety and distress. In OCD, it overreacts to the OFC's signals.

The striatum is involved in forming habits and repetitive behaviors. In OCD, it creates the compulsive behaviors in response to the anxiety.

Together, these circuits create a loop: Detect potential problem → Feel anxiety → Perform compulsion → Temporary relief → Circuit is reinforced.

Every time you do a compulsion, you're strengthening this circuit. Your brain learns: "Compulsion = safety."

ERP works by changing what your brain learns.

When you do exposure without response prevention, your brain initially panics. The OFC screams "Danger!" The ACC floods you with anxiety. But then... **nothing bad happens**. And the anxiety starts to decrease on its own.

Your brain learns new information: "Actually, not doing the compulsion is safe. The feared outcome didn't occur."

Research shows that successful ERP treatment actually *changes brain activity patterns* in people with OCD. The overactivity in the OFC and ACC decreases. The brain circuits normalize (Nakao et al., 2005).

This isn't just "mind over matter" or "trying harder." It's literally retraining your brain's circuitry through new learning experiences.

Islamic Compatibility: ERP as Trusting Allah's Plan

Some Muslims worry: "Isn't ERP just psychology? What does this have to do with Islam?"

Here's the beautiful part: **ERP aligns perfectly with Islamic teachings about waswas**.

Think about what Islamic scholars have said for centuries:

- Ibn Taymiyyah: When waswas creates doubt about whether you did something correctly, **ignore the doubt and move on**. Don't repeat the action.
- Al-Ghazali: When excessive doubt attacks you in worship, **dismiss it without engaging** and continue your practice.
- The Prophet (peace be upon him): When shaytan whispers disturbing thoughts, **seek refuge in Allah and stop thinking about it**.

What is this if not response prevention?

You're having the intrusive thought (exposure to the trigger), and you're instructed to not engage with it, not seek reassurance, not perform rituals to "undo" it (response prevention).

Islamic tradition has been teaching a form of ERP for 1,400 years. Modern psychology just mapped out the mechanism and systematized the approach.

The concept of *tawakkul* (trust in Allah) is actually at the heart of ERP. When you resist compulsions and sit with uncertainty, you're practicing profound trust. You're saying:

"I don't know for certain if my wudu was perfect. But I trust that Allah knows my intention and accepts my effort. I'm not going to keep repeating it."

"I don't know if that intrusive thought means something terrible. But I trust that Allah knows the difference between waswas and my actual will. I'm not going to perform rituals to 'fix' it."

That's tawakkul. That's surrendering the outcome to Allah while doing your reasonable best with the means available.

ERP isn't asking you to abandon faith. It's asking you to trust Allah enough to stop trying to achieve superhuman certainty through compulsions.

Creating Your Fear Hierarchy

ERP works by gradually facing fears, starting with easier situations and working up to harder ones.

You don't start by tackling your biggest fear. You build up to it.

This is called a **fear hierarchy**—a ranked list of situations that trigger OCD anxiety, ordered from least to most distressing.

Here's how to create one:

Step 1: List Your OCD Triggers and Compulsions

Write down all the situations that trigger OCD anxiety and the compulsions you perform in response.

Example for someone with purity OCD:

Trigger: Using public bathroom Compulsion: Showering for 1 hour when I get home

Trigger: Touching shoes Compulsion: Washing hands 20 times

Trigger: Doubting whether I washed my arm completely in wudu Compulsion: Redoing entire wudu 3-5 times

Step 2: Rate Each Item's Anxiety Level

Use a 0-100 scale, where:

- 0 = No anxiety at all
- 25 = Mild anxiety
- 50 = Moderate anxiety
- 75 = Severe anxiety
- 100 = Extreme, unbearable anxiety

Be honest about the numbers. This is about what actually causes anxiety for you, not what "should" cause anxiety.

Step 3: Order Items from Lowest to Highest

Arrange your list from lowest anxiety rating to highest.

Example hierarchy for religious OCD:

Situation	Anxiety Rating
Perform wudu in 7 minutes instead of 15	30
Pray without checking if my shoes touched najis	40
Touch a doorknob without washing hands after	45
Perform wudu in 5 minutes	55
Pray with one minor distraction and not repeat	60
Touch the bottom of my shoe and not wash for 1 hour	65
Perform wudu only once even with doubt	70
Pray without repeating even with intrusive thought	80
Let an intrusive blasphemous thought pass without saying astaghfirullah	90

Step 4: Fill In Gaps

If you have large jumps between items (like from 40 to 70), create intermediate steps.

Example: If "Pray without repeating" is 80 and "Pray with one minor distraction" is 60, add "Pray without repeating when anxiety is mild" at maybe 70.

Step 5: Identify Response Prevention Goals

For each exposure, clearly identify what compulsion you're *not* doing.

Example:

Exposure: Perform wudu in 5 minutes Response Prevention: Don't redo wudu based on doubt. Don't check each body part multiple times. Don't seek reassurance from family members.

This clarity is important. You need to know exactly what behavior you're preventing.

Planning Exposures

Once you have your hierarchy, you start working through it—beginning with lower-anxiety items.

Here's how to plan each exposure:

Choose Your Starting Point

Pick an item rated between 30-50 on your hierarchy. You want something challenging but not overwhelming.

If even your lowest-rated item is 70+, you might need to create easier versions first. Example: If "Perform wudu once" is 70, maybe start with "Perform wudu twice instead of five times" at a lower rating.

Plan the Specific Exposure

Be concrete. "Practice not repeating wudu" is too vague.

Better: "Tomorrow before Dhuhr prayer, I will perform wudu in 5 minutes. I will use a timer. When the timer goes off, I'm done—even if I feel uncertain about whether I washed completely."

Identify the Response Prevention

What compulsions will you resist?

Example: "I will not redo wudu based on doubt. I will not ask my spouse if they think my wudu was correct. I will not mentally review whether I washed each part the required number of times."

Predict the Anxiety

Before doing the exposure, predict how anxious you expect to feel (0-100 scale).

During the exposure, check your actual anxiety every few minutes.

After the exposure, notice how your anxiety changed over time.

This helps you learn that anxiety peaks and then naturally decreases—even without compulsions.

Repeat the Exposure

You don't just do each exposure once. You repeat it multiple times—daily if possible—until your anxiety rating for that item drops significantly (by 50% or more).

Example: If "Perform wudu in 5 minutes" initially causes 55 anxiety, you repeat it daily until it only causes 20-30 anxiety. Then you move to the next item on your hierarchy.

Stay in the Exposure Long Enough

This is critical. You need to stay in the anxiety-provoking situation long enough for your anxiety to decrease *while you're still in it*.

If you do the exposure, panic, and escape immediately, you don't learn anything except "This is unbearable."

But if you do the exposure and stay with it—letting the anxiety peak, plateau, and start to come down—you learn: "I can handle this. The anxiety doesn't last forever."

Most experts recommend staying in the exposure until your anxiety decreases by at least 50%. If it starts at 70, stay until it's down to 35 or less.

This might take 15 minutes. It might take an hour. The timing varies, but the principle is the same: **Stick with it until you learn that the anxiety naturally decreases**.

Response Prevention Strategies

Response prevention—not doing the compulsion—is often harder than the exposure itself.

Your brain is screaming, "Do the compulsion! Wash again! Repeat the prayer! Seek reassurance! Fix this!" And you have to say no.

Here are strategies that help:

Strategy 1: Delay and Distract

You might not be ready to completely eliminate a compulsion immediately. That's okay. Start by delaying it.

Example: If you normally wash your hands immediately after touching something you consider contaminated, try waiting 5 minutes first. Then 10 minutes. Then 30 minutes.

During the delay, distract yourself with another activity. Call a friend. Watch a video. Cook something. The goal is to interrupt the automatic anxiety-to-compulsion pathway.

Often, after delaying, you'll find the urge to do the compulsion has decreased. You might be able to resist it entirely.

Strategy 2: Do It Differently

If you're not ready to stop a compulsion cold, modify it.

Example: If you normally repeat a prayer 10 times, try repeating it only 5 times. Then 3 times. Then once. Then zero.

This gradual reduction can be easier than jumping straight to complete response prevention.

Strategy 3: Set Clear Rules

Give yourself clear, specific rules about when compulsions are and aren't allowed.

Example: "I am allowed to perform wudu once before each prayer. I am not allowed to redo wudu based on doubt. If I broke wudu with certainty (like actually using the bathroom), I can redo it. But not based on doubt."

Write these rules down. When OCD pushes you to break the rule, you can point to it: "No. I have a rule about this."

Strategy 4: Recruit Support

Tell someone you trust about your ERP goals. Ask them to support your response prevention.

Example: "I'm working on not seeking reassurance. If I ask you whether my wudu was valid, please remind me that I'm in treatment and I need to tolerate the uncertainty. Don't answer the question."

This external support can help when your own willpower is struggling.

Strategy 5: Accept the Discomfort

This is the core skill. The anxiety will come. You can't prevent that. But you can change how you respond to it.

Instead of fighting the anxiety or trying to make it go away through compulsions, you practice accepting it:

"Okay, there's anxiety. It's uncomfortable. But it's not dangerous. I can feel anxiety and still not do the compulsion. The anxiety won't last forever."

Some people find it helpful to talk to the anxiety:

"Thanks for trying to protect me, anxiety. I know you think I'm in danger. But I'm actually safe. I'm going to sit with you for a while."

This isn't magical thinking. It's a way of defusing from the anxiety—recognizing it's a feeling, not a fact.

Working with Uncertainty in a Faith Context

The hardest part of ERP for religious OCD is tolerating spiritual uncertainty.

You're not just accepting uncertainty about germs or whether you locked the door. You're accepting uncertainty about your prayers, your purity, your standing with Allah.

That feels different. More serious. More consequential.

And that's exactly why it's the most important work.

Here's the reframe that helps many Muslim OCD sufferers:

Certainty-seeking is trying to control what only Allah controls. Accepting uncertainty is surrendering to Allah's wisdom.

Think about it. When you demand 100% certainty that your prayer was valid, you're essentially saying: "I need to verify this myself. I can't trust Allah to judge my intention fairly. I can't rely on His mercy unless I'm absolutely certain I performed perfectly."

That's not trust. That's trying to guarantee your outcome through your own verification.

Real tawakkul says: "I did my best. I prayed sincerely. I followed the basic requirements. Now I trust Allah to judge my intention and accept my effort, even if it wasn't perfect."

The Quran says: "Allah does not burden a soul beyond that it can bear" (Quran 2:286). You *can't* achieve absolute certainty in many areas of worship. If Allah required that, He'd be burdening you beyond what you can bear.

So accepting uncertainty isn't abandoning faith. It's trusting Allah enough to let Him be the judge of your efforts without you needing absolute verification.

Case Examples: Muslim Individuals in ERP

Let's see what this looks like in practice.

Case Example 1: Zahra's Wudu Exposure

Zahra spent 30-45 minutes on wudu before each prayer. She'd wash each body part 7-10 times, check constantly, and restart if any doubt appeared.

Her ERP hierarchy started with: "Perform wudu in 15 minutes" (rated 40 anxiety).

First exposure:

- She set a timer for 15 minutes
- Began wudu normally
- When the timer went off, she stopped—even though she'd only washed her arms 3 times instead of her usual 7
- Anxiety spiked to 75
- She wanted desperately to redo it
- Instead, she sat with the anxiety, made dua: "Allah, I'm trusting You to accept this effort"
- After 20 minutes, anxiety dropped to 45
- She prayed with that wudu
- Anxiety during prayer: 60, but she completed it
- After prayer, anxiety dropped to 30

She repeated this exposure daily for a week. By day 7, the 15-minute wudu only caused 25 anxiety.

Next step: 10-minute wudu. Then 7-minute. Then 5-minute.

After three months of daily ERP practice, Zahra could perform wudu in 3-4 minutes with minimal anxiety. She prayed on time. She had her life back.

Case Example 2: Bilal's Prayer Repetition

Bilal would repeat prayers 5-15 times due to intrusive blasphemous thoughts during prayer.

His ERP started with: "Pray with one intrusive thought and don't repeat" (rated 65 anxiety).

First exposure:

- He began Maghrib prayer
- Intrusive blasphemous thought appeared during first rakah
- Massive anxiety spike to 85
- Strong urge to restart prayer
- He reminded himself: "This is waswas. The Prophet (PBUH) said these thoughts aren't sins. I'm going to finish this prayer."
- Continued prayer despite ongoing intrusive thoughts
- Anxiety remained high (75) throughout prayer
- Finished prayer, wanted desperately to repeat it
- Sat with the urge for 30 minutes
- Anxiety gradually decreased to 50

He repeated this exposure daily. Some prayers were harder than others. But each time he practiced finishing prayer once and sitting with the uncertainty.

After six weeks, intrusive thoughts still occurred, but they didn't trigger the same panic. He could notice them and continue praying. Anxiety dropped from 85 to 30-40.

He learned: "The thoughts appear, but they're not me. They don't invalidate my prayer. Allah knows the difference."

Case Example 3: Aisha's Contamination Fears

Aisha feared najis contamination constantly. She wouldn't touch certain objects, avoided certain areas of her home, and changed clothes multiple times daily.

Her ERP included: "Touch the bathroom door handle and don't wash hands for 1 hour" (rated 55 anxiety).

First exposure:

- She deliberately touched the bathroom door handle
- Immediately wanted to wash hands
- Set a timer for 1 hour
- Anxiety: 70
- Sat on the couch, hands deliberately unwashed
- Watched TV to distract
- Every few minutes, urge to wash
- She reminded herself: "I'm trusting Allah. If there's actual najis, minimal amounts don't invalidate prayer according to most scholars. I'm being reasonable."
- After 45 minutes, anxiety dropped to 40
- At 1 hour, she washed hands normally (not excessively)

She repeated this exposure multiple times per week, gradually increasing difficulty—touching shoes, touching public doorknobs, etc.

After two months, her contamination anxiety had decreased significantly. She could function normally without constant washing.

What All Three Cases Show

Notice the pattern:

1. **Gradual progression**: They didn't start with their worst fear. They built up to it.
2. **Repeated practice**: One exposure wasn't enough. They did the same exposure multiple times until anxiety decreased.
3. **Sitting with discomfort**: They didn't escape when anxiety peaked. They stayed in the situation until anxiety started to drop.
4. **Islamic framework**: They incorporated Islamic concepts—trusting Allah, referencing scholarly rulings, making dua—while doing the psychological work.
5. **Measurable progress**: Over weeks and months, what initially caused 70-85 anxiety dropped to 30-40 or less.

This is how ERP works. It's not magic. It's not overnight. It's systematic, gradual retraining of your brain's fear response.

And it works.

The Path Forward

ERP is the most effective treatment we have for OCD. Research consistently shows response rates of 60-80% for people who complete the treatment (Öst et al., 2015).

But "completing the treatment" is the key phrase. ERP requires commitment. You have to do the exposures. You have to resist the compulsions. You have to sit with discomfort.

For Muslim individuals with religious OCD, this means deliberately triggering spiritual anxiety and sitting with uncertainty about religious validity. That's hard. Really hard.

But it's the path to freedom.

The alternative is staying trapped in OCD's cycle—performing compulsions that provide temporary relief but keep you imprisoned long-term.

ERP offers an exit. A way out. A method that actually works.

And it aligns beautifully with Islamic teachings: Trust Allah, resist shaytan's whisperings, accept reasonable uncertainty, and move forward with your worship.

In the next chapter, we'll look at cognitive approaches—how to challenge the specific thoughts that fuel religious OCD and develop new ways of thinking that support recovery.

Chapter 8: Cognitive Approaches: Restructuring OCD Thoughts

ERP targets the behavior—you do exposures and resist compulsions, and your brain gradually learns that the feared outcomes don't occur.

But there's another piece: **the thoughts themselves**.

OCD isn't just compulsive behavior. It's also a pattern of thinking—specific cognitive distortions that keep the disorder running.

When you think "If I don't repeat this prayer perfectly, Allah won't accept it," that thought drives the compulsion. When you think "I might have najis on my hands and one molecule will invalidate my entire prayer," that thought fuels the washing.

So changing the behavior (ERP) works even better when combined with changing the thoughts (cognitive therapy).

That's what this chapter covers: How to identify the distorted thinking patterns in religious OCD and replace them with more accurate, Islamic-aligned thoughts.

Because here's the truth: **Most OCD thoughts aren't just anxiety-based. They're factually incorrect**.

They contradict Islamic theology. They violate logic. They ignore evidence. And once you can see that clearly, the thoughts lose their power.

Cognitive Behavioral Therapy (CBT) for OCD

Cognitive Behavioral Therapy (CBT) is based on a simple premise: **Thoughts, feelings, and behaviors are interconnected**. Change one, and you can change the others.

Standard CBT teaches you to:

1. Identify automatic negative thoughts
2. Examine the evidence for and against those thoughts
3. Develop alternative, more balanced thoughts
4. Test out the new thoughts through behavioral experiments

For OCD specifically, cognitive therapy focuses on challenging the *appraisals* you make about intrusive thoughts (Wilhelm & Steketee, 2006).

An appraisal is the meaning you attach to something. Everyone gets random intrusive thoughts. But in OCD, you appraise those thoughts as highly significant and dangerous:

- "This thought means I'm a bad Muslim"
- "Having this thought is the same as doing the action"
- "I'm responsible for preventing terrible outcomes by doing rituals"
- "I must have perfect certainty or I'm being negligent"

These appraisals are cognitive distortions—thinking errors. And they're learnable to recognize and challenge.

Identifying Cognitive Distortions

Let's map out the specific thinking errors that show up in religious OCD.

Distortion 1: Thought-Action Fusion

Definition: Believing that thinking about something is morally equivalent to doing it, or that thinking about something makes it more likely to happen.

Example: "I had a blasphemous thought about Allah during prayer. That's the same as actually blaspheming. I'm committing shirk in my mind."

Why it's false: Islamic theology explicitly distinguishes thoughts from actions. The Prophet (PBUH) said you're not accountable for what crosses your mind unless you act on it or speak it.

Alternative thought: "This is an intrusive thought, not an action. Islam holds me accountable for intentions and deeds, not fleeting mental content. Allah knows I don't want this thought."

Distortion 2: Intolerance of Uncertainty

Definition: Believing that uncertainty is unacceptable and you must achieve complete certainty before acting.

Example: "I can't pray until I'm 100% certain my wudu was perfect. What if there's najis somewhere on my body that I didn't notice? I need to keep checking."

Why it's false: Islamic law operates on reasonable certainty, not absolute certainty. The fiqh principle is: certainty isn't removed by doubt. Normal human uncertainty is expected and accepted.

Alternative thought: "I performed wudu normally. I have reasonable certainty that it's valid. Later doubts don't override that. I can proceed to prayer."

Distortion 3: Inflated Responsibility

Definition: Believing you have the power and duty to prevent all possible negative outcomes through your actions.

Example: "If I don't pray perfectly, something terrible might happen to my family. I need to repeat this prayer until it's perfect to protect them."

Why it's false: You don't control outcomes through ritual perfection. Allah controls what happens. Your responsibility is to do your reasonable best; outcomes are in Allah's hands.

Alternative thought: "My family's well-being is in Allah's hands, not dependent on my prayer being perfect. I'll pray sincerely, and trust Allah with the results."

Distortion 4: Overestimation of Threat

Definition: Believing that potential dangers are much more likely and severe than they actually are.

Example: "If there's even a tiny bit of najis on my clothes, my prayer is completely invalid and I'll be sinning."

Why it's false: Islamic law has specific thresholds for what amount of impurity actually invalidates prayer. Small, unavoidable amounts are overlooked. The religion is merciful, not punitive.

Alternative thought: "Islamic scholars say minor, unavoidable impurities don't invalidate prayer. I'm catastrophizing. If I have obvious najis, I'll clean it. Otherwise, I'm fine."

Distortion 5: Perfectionism

Definition: Believing that anything less than perfect performance is failure and unacceptable.

Example: "If I don't recite Al-Fatiha with absolutely perfect pronunciation and zero wandering thoughts, my prayer doesn't count."

Why it's false: Islam requires sincere effort and reasonable ability, not flawless performance. The Prophet (PBUH) accepted the worship of people with limited ability, speech impediments, and varying skill levels.

Alternative thought: "Allah judges my sincerity and effort, not whether I'm objectively perfect. I recite to the best of my ability, and that's what counts."

Distortion 6: Should Statements

Definition: Rigid rules about how you "must" or "should" behave that go beyond actual requirements.

Example: "I should be able to pray without any distracting thoughts whatsoever. If my mind wanders even once, I failed."

Why it's false: The Prophet (PBUH) himself taught that shaytan will cause distractions during prayer—it's a normal human experience, not a failure.

Alternative thought: "Everyone's mind wanders during prayer sometimes. The goal is to gently return focus when I notice distraction, not to achieve perfect concentration throughout."

Distortion 7: Black-and-White Thinking

Definition: Seeing things in all-or-nothing terms without recognizing middle ground.

Example: "Either my intention was 100% purely for Allah with zero ego, or the whole action is worthless and hypocritical."

Why it's false: Human intentions are complex. Pure sincerity is the goal, but human limitation means mixed motivations often exist. Islam judges based on the primary intention, not perfection.

Alternative thought: "I intended this action primarily for Allah. Even if some human imperfection exists in my motivation, Allah knows my heart and judges my overall intention."

Thought Records from Islamic Perspective

A thought record is a CBT tool for challenging distorted thoughts. You write down:

1. The situation
2. The automatic thought
3. The emotion and its intensity

4. Evidence for the thought
5. Evidence against the thought
6. Alternative, balanced thought
7. The emotion after reframing

Let's see this in action with Islamic examples.

Example 1: Wudu Doubts

Component	Content
Situation	Finished wudu, starting to walk to prayer, doubt appears about whether I washed my elbows completely
Automatic thought	"I might not have washed completely. My wudu might be invalid. If I pray with invalid wudu, the prayer won't count."
Emotion	Anxiety (85/100)
Evidence for thought	I can't perfectly recall every moment of wudu. Maybe I rushed the elbows.
Evidence against thought	I performed wudu carefully and was certain it was complete when I finished. The fiqh principle is certainty isn't removed by doubt. Islamic law doesn't require perfect memory of each moment. Reasonable effort is sufficient.
Alternative thought	"I performed wudu properly and was certain at the time. This is later doubt, which Islamic scholars say to ignore. My wudu is valid. I'm going to trust Allah and proceed to prayer."
New emotion	Anxiety (40/100)

Example 2: Blasphemous Intrusive Thought

Component	Content
Situation	During prayer, horrible blasphemous thought intrudes
Automatic thought	"I just committed shirk in my mind. Allah won't accept this prayer. I might have left Islam."
Emotion	Terror (95/100), Shame (90/100)
Evidence for thought	The thought was really blasphemous. I had it during prayer, a sacred time.
Evidence against thought	The Prophet (PBUH) explicitly said intrusive thoughts aren't sins. The Companions experienced disturbing thoughts and the Prophet said it was evidence of faith, not lack of faith. The thought was unwanted—the fact that I'm horrified proves I didn't want it. Islamic

Component	Content
	theology says thoughts aren't sins unless you act on them or speak them.
Alternative thought	"This is waswas—shaytan's whisper designed to disturb me. It's not my thought; it's an intrusion. Allah knows the difference. Having this thought doesn't mean anything about my faith. I'll continue my prayer and ignore the thought."
New emotion	Anxiety (50/100), Shame (30/100)

Example 3: Contamination Fear

Component	Content
Situation	Touched doorknob at grocery store, now worried my hand has najis that will spread
Automatic thought	"What if someone who had najis on their hands touched this doorknob? Now I have it. If I touch my clothes, they're contaminated. I can't pray in contaminated clothes."
Emotion	Disgust (80/100), Anxiety (75/100)
Evidence for thought	It's technically possible someone with najis touched the doorknob. I can't prove they didn't.
Evidence against thought	The default assumption in Islamic law is things are pure unless I have clear evidence of impurity. I can't see any najis. Islamic scholars say you can't function in life if you assume invisible contamination everywhere. The Prophet (PBUH) and his companions touched public objects without obsessing about potential invisible najis. Possibility doesn't equal probability.
Alternative thought	"I have no evidence of actual najis. Islamic law says I should assume purity in the absence of clear evidence of impurity. I'm going to wash my hands normally later and trust that's sufficient. I don't need to investigate invisible possibilities."
New emotion	Anxiety (35/100), Disgust (30/100)

Notice the pattern: The emotion decreases when you challenge the thought and develop an alternative based on evidence, logic, and Islamic theology.

Challenging OCD "Fatwas"

OCD loves to issue religious rulings. It sets itself up as an authority on Islam and delivers verdicts:

"Your prayer doesn't count because..." "You committed shirk when you..." "Allah won't accept this because..."

These are what I call "OCD fatwas"—pronouncements that sound religious but are actually disorder-driven distortions.

You need to challenge them the way you'd challenge any questionable fatwa: by examining the evidence.

OCD Fatwa: "If you had any distracting thought during prayer, the whole prayer is invalid."

Challenge it:

- Is this supported by Quran? No. The Quran never says this.
- Is this supported by hadith? No. In fact, the Prophet (PBUH) acknowledged that distractions happen and taught the sujood as-sahw (prostrations of forgetfulness) as a remedy—not invalidation of the whole prayer.
- Do Islamic scholars teach this? No. All four madhabs recognize that passing distractions don't invalidate prayer.
- Does this align with the principle that "Allah does not burden a soul beyond that it can bear"? No. Expecting zero mental distractions is beyond human capability.

Verdict: This is an OCD fatwa, not an Islamic ruling. Rejected.

OCD Fatwa: "If you can't achieve 100% certainty about your intention, the action doesn't count."

Challenge it:

- Is this supported by Islamic sources? No. Islamic law requires sincerity of intention, not absolute certainty that your intention was perfect.
- Is this practically achievable? No. Human beings can't have perfect clarity about internal mental states.
- Do scholars require this? No. They recognize that intention is in the heart, and if you intended to do something for Allah, that's sufficient even if doubts later arise.

Verdict: OCD fatwa. Dismissed.

OCD Fatwa: "Any possible najis, no matter how small or uncertain, invalidates your state of purity."

Challenge it:

- What do actual fiqh rulings say? They say the default is purity unless you have clear evidence of impurity. They specify thresholds for what amounts of najis actually matter.
- Is this consistent with how the Prophet (PBUH) practiced? No. He lived in a world without modern plumbing, walked on dusty roads, and didn't obsess about invisible contamination possibilities.
- Is this sustainable? No. Following this principle would make normal life impossible.

Verdict: OCD fatwa. Overruled.

Islamic Cognitive Reframes

Let's look at specific Islamic teachings that counter OCD thoughts.

Reframe 1: "Allah is Merciful, Not a Tyrant"

OCD presents Allah as a harsh judge waiting to reject your worship for any tiny imperfection.

Islamic reality: Allah is *Ar-Rahman* (The Most Merciful), *Ar-Raheem* (The Especially Merciful), *Al-Ghafoor* (The Forgiving), *Al-Afuww* (The Pardoner).

The Quran says: "Say, 'O My servants who have transgressed against themselves, do not despair of the mercy of Allah. Indeed, Allah forgives all sins. Indeed, it is He who is the Forgiving, the Merciful.'" (Quran 39:53)

If Allah forgives *actual sins*, do you really think He rejects prayers because you had an intrusive thought? Or because you weren't 100% certain your wudu was microscopically perfect?

When OCD says, "Allah won't accept this," respond: "Allah is merciful and knows my sincere effort. He doesn't expect perfection; He expects sincerity."

Reframe 2: "The Prophet (PBUH) Taught Ease, Not Hardship"

OCD makes Islam feel like torture—exhausting, demanding, impossible.

Islamic reality: The Prophet (PBUH) said, "Make things easy and do not make them difficult" (Sahih Bukhari, Book 3, Hadith 125).

He also said: "This religion is easy. No one becomes harsh and strict in the religion without it overwhelming him. So do what is right, and come as close as you can, and receive the good news" (Sahih Bukhari, Book 2, Hadith 38).

When the Companions were too harsh on themselves in worship, the Prophet corrected them and told them to be moderate.

When OCD says, "You need to do more, be perfect, never stop until you're certain," respond: "The Prophet (PBUH) taught ease. If my practice is overwhelming me, I'm exceeding what Islam requires."

Reframe 3: "My Intention is Pure; the Waswas is Not From Me"

OCD tries to make you own intrusive thoughts as if they reflect your character or faith.

Islamic reality: The concept of waswas in Islamic theology explicitly recognizes that disturbing thoughts come from outside you—from shaytan, not from your own heart.

The Prophet (PBUH) confirmed that experiencing horrible thoughts is not sinful and may even indicate strong faith—because only someone who cares deeply would be disturbed by them.

When OCD says, "This thought means you're a bad Muslim," respond: "This is waswas. It's not my thought. The fact that I'm horrified by it proves my faith, not the opposite."

Reframe 4: "Allah Knows the Difference Between Waswas and My Will"

OCD creates fear that Allah can't distinguish between intrusive thoughts and actual intentions.

Islamic reality: The Quran says, "And We have already created man and know what his soul whispers to him, and We are closer to him than [his] jugular vein" (Quran 50:16).

Allah knows what's in your heart. He knows the difference between a thought that intruded without permission and a choice you made. He knows your true intentions from OCD-generated doubts about those intentions.

When OCD says, "But what if Allah thinks you meant that thought?" respond: "Allah is Al-Aleem (The All-Knowing). He knows exactly what I intended and what was waswas. I trust His knowledge."

Reframe 5: "Certainty Isn't Required; Reasonable Effort Is"

OCD demands absolute certainty. Islam requires reasonable effort.

Islamic reality: The fiqh principle "certainty is not removed by doubt" exists precisely because Islamic scholars recognized humans can't achieve perfect certainty in many situations.

The legal maxim is: Do your best with what you know, and that's sufficient.

When OCD says, "You need to be absolutely certain," respond: "Islamic law doesn't require absolute certainty. I did my reasonable best. That's what Allah asks for."

Inference-Based Cognitive Behavioral Therapy (I-CBT)

There's a specific type of cognitive therapy designed for OCD called Inference-Based CBT (I-CBT), developed by researchers at the Université de Montréal (Aardema & O'Connor, 2012).

I-CBT focuses on something called the "obsessional doubt"—the story your OCD tells about why something might be dangerous or wrong.

The key insight: **OCD generates doubts that are based on imagination, not on actual perception or evidence**.

Distinguishing Imagined Possibility from Reality

Here's how OCD works in I-CBT terms:

You performed wudu. Your senses tell you: "I washed my arms. They're clean."

But OCD generates an alternative story: "What if when you washed your left arm, the water didn't reach all the way to the elbow? What if there's a tiny dry patch? What if that invalidates your wudu?"

This story is **inference-based**—it's not based on what you actually observed. It's based on imagined possibilities that OCD presents as likely.

I-CBT teaches you to distinguish:

What you actually perceived (sensory reality):

- I washed my arms under running water
- I saw and felt water on my skin

- I was paying attention while I did it

What OCD infers (imagined doubt):

- "Maybe water didn't reach everywhere"
- "Maybe there's a spot you missed"
- "Maybe it's not valid"

The OCD inference is asking you to distrust your direct experience and instead believe a story about *possible* problems that you have no evidence actually exist.

I-CBT response: **Trust what you actually perceived. Reject the imagined doubt.**

The Obsessional Story vs. What Actually Happened

Let's see this with examples.

Example 1: Wudu Validity

What actually happened (direct perception):

- I performed wudu
- I washed each required body part
- I was careful and attentive
- I felt water on my skin
- I saw that I was washing properly
- I completed wudu

The obsessional story (OCD inference):

- "But what if when you washed your elbows, the water didn't quite reach the required point? What if there's a microscopic dry area? What if you were distracted for a second and didn't wash thoroughly enough? What if..."

I-CBT response: "These are imagined possibilities that OCD is generating. I have no actual evidence that any of this is true. I trust what I directly perceived: I washed properly. I'm rejecting the OCD story."

Example 2: Prayer Validity

What actually happened:

- I intended to pray
- I performed the prayer

- I recited what I needed to recite
- I did the movements in order
- I completed the prayer

The obsessional story:

- "But what if your intention wasn't pure? What if there was some hidden ego? What if when you said 'Allahu Akbar' you weren't fully focused? What if that blasphemous thought that appeared means the prayer doesn't count?"

I-CBT response: "I'm distinguishing what actually happened from OCD's story. I actually did pray with sincere intention. The intrusive thought is not evidence of anything—it's just waswas. I'm trusting my direct experience that I prayed sincerely."

Example 3: Contamination

What actually happened:

- I touched a doorknob
- I don't see any najis on my hand
- I don't smell anything
- I don't feel anything wet or unusual on my hand

The obsessional story:

- "But what if someone who had najis on their hands touched this doorknob earlier? What if there's invisible najis that transferred to your hand? What if it spreads to everything you touch? What if..."

I-CBT response: "I have no actual evidence of najis. I'm trusting my senses—what I see, smell, and feel—rather than an imagined story about possible invisible contamination."

Trusting Your Senses (A Form of Tawakkul)

I-CBT teaches you to trust your direct perceptions over OCD-generated inferences.

From an Islamic perspective, this is actually a form of *tawakkul* (trust in Allah).

Allah gave you senses—sight, touch, smell—to navigate the world. Trusting those senses is trusting the faculties Allah provided.

OCD asks you to distrust your senses and instead believe elaborate "what if" stories. That's not piety. That's actually distrusting Allah's design.

The Prophet (PBUH) taught: "Seek refuge in Allah and stop" when doubts arise. He didn't say, "Investigate every possible imagined scenario until you achieve certainty." He said trust Allah and move forward based on what you actually know.

So when OCD generates doubt based on imagined possibilities, the Islamic response aligns perfectly with I-CBT: Trust what you actually perceived, reject the imagined doubt, and move forward with tawakkul.

Putting It All Together

Cognitive approaches work alongside ERP. You're doing exposures (behavioral change) while also challenging the thoughts (cognitive change).

Example: You're doing an exposure where you perform wudu once and don't repeat it.

During the exposure, OCD generates thoughts: "This wudu might not be valid. You should repeat it to be safe."

You use cognitive tools:

- Identify the distortion: "This is intolerance of uncertainty and overestimation of threat."
- Challenge with evidence: "I performed wudu properly. The fiqh principle says certainty isn't removed by later doubt."
- Use an Islamic reframe: "Allah is merciful and knows I did my best. I trust His acceptance."
- Apply I-CBT: "I'm trusting what I actually perceived—that I washed properly—rather than OCD's imagined story about possible problems."

The thoughts lose their power. You can sit with the exposure more effectively. Your anxiety decreases faster.

That's the power of combining behavioral and cognitive approaches.

You're not just resisting compulsions (ERP). You're also changing the thinking patterns that fuel the compulsions (CBT). Together, they create lasting change.

In the next chapter, we'll look at acceptance-based approaches—how to coexist with intrusive thoughts without fighting them, and how this aligns with Islamic concepts of patience and surrender.

Chapter 9: Acceptance and Commitment Therapy (ACT): Living with Uncertainty

ERP teaches you to face your fears and resist compulsions. Cognitive therapy teaches you to challenge OCD thoughts and replace them with more accurate ones.

But here's another approach, one that might sound strange at first: **Stop fighting the thoughts altogether**.

Not because the thoughts are true. Not because you should believe them. But because fighting intrusive thoughts is what gives them power.

This is Acceptance and Commitment Therapy (ACT, pronounced as one word: "act"). And it offers a radically different relationship with OCD.

Instead of trying to control, challenge, or eliminate intrusive thoughts, ACT teaches you to let them exist while you move toward what matters to you. Instead of getting tangled up in whether a thought is true or false, you notice it's just a thought and refocus on your values.

Think of it like this: Cognitive therapy says, "Let's examine whether this thought is accurate and replace it with a better one." ACT says, "This thought showed up. Okay. I'm going to acknowledge it's here and then do what's important anyway."

Both work. And interestingly, both align beautifully with Islamic teachings—just from different angles.

ACT Principles and Islamic Compatibility

ACT has six core processes. Let's look at each one and see how it connects with Islamic concepts.

1. Acceptance

In ACT, acceptance means allowing thoughts, feelings, and sensations to be present without trying to control or eliminate them (Hayes, Strosahl, & Wilson, 2011).

You can't control what thoughts pop into your head. But you can control whether you engage with them, struggle against them, or let them pass like clouds in the sky.

Islamic connection: The concept of *sabr* (patience) includes accepting what you cannot change while working to change what you can. You can't stop waswas from occurring—that's shaytan's doing. But you can accept that it appears and then choose not to engage with it.

The Prophet (peace be upon him) taught this when he said to seek refuge in Allah and stop thinking about disturbing thoughts. That's acceptance—acknowledge the thought appeared, seek Allah's protection, and move on. Don't wrestle with it.

2. Cognitive Defusion

Defusion means separating yourself from your thoughts—recognizing that thoughts are just mental events, not facts or commands (Hayes et al., 2011).

Instead of "I'm having the thought that my prayer doesn't count" becoming "My prayer doesn't count," you create space: "I notice I'm having the thought that my prayer doesn't count. That's what my brain is producing right now."

Islamic connection: The concept of waswas explicitly teaches this. The whispers aren't you. They're external intrusions from shaytan. When you recognize "This is waswas, not my own thinking," you're practicing defusion—separating yourself from the thought.

3. Being Present

ACT emphasizes staying connected to the present moment rather than getting lost in worries about the past or future (Hayes et al., 2011).

Islamic connection: Mindfulness in ACT is remarkably similar to the concept of *muraqabah* (consciousness of Allah's presence) in Islamic spirituality. Being present to Allah in the current moment, rather than ruminating about past sins or future worries, is classical Islamic teaching.

The practice of *dhikr* (remembrance of Allah) grounds you in the present moment—you're aware of Allah right now, in this breath, in this moment.

4. Self as Context

This means recognizing that you are not your thoughts, feelings, or experiences—you're the awareness that observes them (Hayes et al., 2011).

Islamic connection: Islam teaches that your true self (*ruh*, soul) is distinct from the fleeting contents of your mind. A blasphemous intrusive thought isn't you—it's a mental event you're experiencing. Your essential self, created by Allah and accountable to Him, is separate from the waswas.

5. Values

ACT asks: What matters to you? What kind of life do you want to live? What kind of person do you want to be?

Then it guides you to let those values direct your behavior, rather than letting anxiety and avoidance control you (Hayes et al., 2011).

Islamic connection: This is profoundly Islamic. What kind of Muslim do you want to be? What does Allah want from you? Living according to Islamic values (justice, mercy, sincerity, kindness, devotion) rather than according to OCD's demands is exactly what Islam teaches.

6. Committed Action

This means taking action aligned with your values, even when it's uncomfortable—even when anxiety is present (Hayes et al., 2011).

Islamic connection: This is *jihad al-nafs* (struggle against the self)—doing what's right even when it's difficult. It's praying on time even when OCD creates anxiety. It's being kind to people even when you're obsessing about purity. It's living your faith despite internal struggle.

Psychological Flexibility and Surrender to Allah

The core concept in ACT is **psychological flexibility**—the ability to stay present, accept your internal experiences, and take action aligned with your values despite discomfort (Kashdan & Rottenberg, 2010).

OCD creates psychological rigidity. It says: "You can't move forward until the anxiety is gone. You can't act until you're certain. You can't pray until you've achieved the perfect mental state."

ACT (and Islam) says: You can do what matters while feeling uncertain, anxious, or uncomfortable.

Here's where this gets really Islamic: *Tawakkul* (trust in Allah) doesn't mean waiting until you feel confident and anxiety-free before acting. It means taking action *while* accepting uncertainty about the outcome, trusting Allah with the results.

Psychological flexibility is the psychological version of tawakkul. You accept the presence of difficult internal experiences (anxiety, doubt, intrusive thoughts) while moving forward with what Allah requires from you.

The Quran describes believers as those who "establish prayer" (Quran 2:3) and "give zakah" (Quran 2:43)—it doesn't say "establish prayer once you've eliminated all religious anxiety" or "give charity after you've achieved perfect certainty about your intentions."

You establish prayer now. With the anxiety. With the intrusive thoughts. With the uncertainty. That's tawakkul. That's psychological flexibility.

Defusion from Intrusive Thoughts

Let's get practical. How do you actually practice defusion—creating distance from thoughts without fighting them?

Technique 1: Name It

When an intrusive thought appears, simply label it.

Instead of: "My wudu might not be valid!" (fused with the thought)

Try: "I'm having the thought that my wudu might not be valid." (defused)

Or even simpler: "There's an OCD thought."

This tiny linguistic shift creates psychological distance. You're observing the thought rather than being consumed by it.

Technique 2: Thank Your Mind

This sounds weird, but it works. When OCD generates a doubt, you can say (internally or out loud): "Thanks for that thought, mind. I know you're trying to protect me. But I'm going to keep going anyway."

This acknowledges the thought appeared without taking it seriously as a command.

Example: Intrusive blasphemous thought during prayer.

Response: "Okay, that thought showed up. Thanks, brain. I know this is waswas. I'm going to continue my prayer."

Technique 3: Sing It

This is a classic ACT technique. Take the OCD thought and sing it to the tune of "Happy Birthday" or any silly song.

"My wudu isn't valid, my wudu isn't valid, my wudu isn't vaa-lid, my wudu isn't valid."

Why does this work? It's nearly impossible to take a thought seriously when you're singing it to a ridiculous tune. You're defusing from it—it's still there, but it loses its threatening quality.

Technique 4: Watch It Pass

Imagine thoughts are like cars driving by on a highway. You're standing on the sidewalk watching. The OCD thought is just another car—you notice it, you let it pass, you don't jump in front of it or chase it down.

Intrusive thought appears: "What if that was shirk?"

Response: "There goes an OCD thought. I see it. It's passing by. I'm staying here on the sidewalk."

Technique 5: Name the Waswas

Some people find it helpful to personify the waswas—to treat it like a separate entity trying to distract you.

"Oh, there's shaytan trying to make me doubt my prayer again. Nice try. I'm not engaging."

This aligns with Islamic teaching that waswas comes from outside you, and it creates psychological distance—it's not your doubt; it's an external whisper you're choosing to dismiss.

Values Clarification: What Kind of Muslim Do You Want to Be?

ACT asks you to get clear about your values—what really matters to you, what kind of person you want to be, what kind of life you want to live.

For Muslims with religious OCD, this question becomes: **What kind of Muslim do you want to be?**

Not "What kind of Muslim does OCD demand you be?" But what does *Islam* actually call you toward? What kind of life does *Allah* want for you?

Let's do this exercise.

Step 1: Identify Your Islamic Values

What matters to you in your practice of Islam? What kind of Muslim do you aspire to be?

Examples people commonly identify:

- Someone who prays regularly and on time
- Someone who treats family with kindness and patience
- Someone who serves the community
- Someone who studies and understands Islam
- Someone who remembers Allah throughout the day
- Someone who gives charity generously
- Someone whose faith brings peace, not anxiety
- Someone who reflects Allah's mercy to others

Step 2: Describe Your "OCD Muslim" vs. Your "Values-Based Muslim"

Now contrast: What kind of Muslim does OCD want you to be?

OCD Muslim:

- Spends hours on wudu and prayer rituals
- Constantly anxious and uncertain
- Isolated from community (too anxious to attend mosque)
- Exhausted from compulsions
- Unable to help others (too consumed with personal rituals)
- Harsh and critical toward self
- Disconnected from spiritual joy
- Focused on ritual perfection rather than sincerity

Values-Based Muslim:

- Prays five times daily, on time, with sincerity
- Feels peace and connection in worship
- Engaged in community
- Energy to serve family and others
- Balanced practice across all pillars of Islam
- Compassionate toward self and others
- Experiences spiritual joy and closeness to Allah
- Focused on sincerity and character development

Step 3: Notice the Discrepancy

OCD is moving you *away* from the Muslim you want to be. It's preventing you from living according to your values.

You value being engaged in community, but OCD keeps you home doing excessive rituals.

You value kindness to family, but OCD makes you irritable and unavailable.

You value remembering Allah with joy, but OCD turns worship into torture.

Step 4: Let Values Guide Action

Once you see the discrepancy, you can make a choice: "Which direction am I moving in? Toward my values or toward OCD's demands?"

Example scenario: You just finished wudu. Doubt appears—"Did you wash thoroughly enough?"

OCD wants you to redo wudu (moving away from values: wastes time, increases anxiety, prevents timely prayer).

Values want you to pray on time with sincerity (moving toward values: fulfilling obligation, trusting Allah, experiencing worship).

In that moment, you can ask: "Which wolf am I feeding? The OCD or my values?"

And then choose the values-based action, even if it feels uncomfortable.

Committed Action Despite Discomfort

This is where ACT gets hard—and where it overlaps completely with *jihad al-nafs* (struggle against the lower self).

ACT says: **You don't wait until you feel good to do what matters. You do what matters, and feelings follow**.

OCD says: "You can't pray until the anxiety is gone. You can't skip the compulsion until you feel comfortable doing so. Wait until you're ready."

That's a trap. You'll never feel "ready." Anxiety won't magically disappear before you take action.

Instead, you act *with* the anxiety present. You commit to values-based action despite discomfort.

Example 1: Praying with Intrusive Thoughts

You start prayer. Intrusive blasphemous thought appears. Massive anxiety.

OCD says: "Stop. Restart. You can't pray with that thought in your mind."

Values say: "I value fulfilling my prayers properly. Properly means once, with sincere intention. The thought is waswas—it doesn't invalidate the prayer."

Committed action: You acknowledge the thought ("There's the intrusive thought"), accept the discomfort, and continue praying. You don't stop. You don't restart. You do what Islam requires despite the internal struggle.

Example 2: Leaving Wudu Imperfect

You perform wudu in 5 minutes. Doubt and anxiety appear: "You didn't wash completely!"

OCD says: "Redo it until you're sure. You can't move forward with this uncertainty."

Values say: "I value praying on time and trusting Allah's mercy. I performed reasonable wudu. That's sufficient."

Committed action: You walk to prayer with the anxiety. You acknowledge it ("Yep, there's the OCD doubt"), accept it's uncomfortable, and proceed to prayer anyway.

The action comes first. The comfort comes later (if at all).

Example 3: Resisting Reassurance-Seeking

You have a question about whether something was halal. You want to Google it immediately.

OCD says: "You need to know right now. Research until you're certain."

Values say: "I value living with tawakkul and not feeding OCD through compulsive research. If this is a genuine question, I'll ask my imam this week. If it's OCD reassurance-seeking, I need to sit with the uncertainty."

Committed action: You close the laptop. You don't Google. You sit with the discomfort of not knowing. You tolerate the anxiety because it's aligned with your values (not feeding OCD).

Mindfulness Practices Compatible with Dhikr

ACT includes mindfulness—paying attention to the present moment without judgment (Kabat-Zinn, 2003).

For Muslims, dhikr (remembrance of Allah) is a form of mindfulness that's been practiced for 1,400 years.

The difference: ACT mindfulness is often secular (just awareness of breath, body, surroundings). Islamic dhikr is awareness *of Allah's presence*.

But the mechanism is similar—both ground you in the present moment and create distance from anxious thoughts.

Mindful Dhikr Practice

Try this:

1. Sit comfortably
2. Choose a dhikr phrase: "SubhanAllah" (Glory be to Allah), "Alhamdulillah" (Praise be to Allah), "Allahu Akbar" (Allah is Greater), or "La ilaha illa Allah" (There is no god but Allah)
3. Repeat it slowly, staying present to each word
4. When your mind wanders to OCD thoughts, gently notice ("There's a thought") and return to the dhikr
5. Don't fight the intrusive thoughts—just keep returning to the dhikr

This is mindfulness. And it's profoundly Islamic.

You're training your mind to stay present (with Allah) rather than getting lost in OCD rumination about past doubts or future worries.

Walking Meditation with Dhikr

Another practice: Walk slowly while repeating dhikr, paying attention to each step, each breath, each word.

When OCD thoughts intrude (and they will), you notice them, let them be, and return attention to the dhikr and the walking.

You're practicing being present to Allah's remembrance while allowing thoughts to come and go without engagement.

Daily Life Mindfulness

You can bring this awareness into daily activities.

Performing wudu mindfully: Pay attention to the sensation of water, the act of washing, the intention to prepare for prayer. When OCD doubts appear ("Did I wash enough?"), notice the thought and return to the present-moment experience of wudu.

Eating mindfully: Pay attention to taste, texture, the blessing of food. When OCD creates fears ("What if this has najis?"), notice the thought and return to the experience of eating with gratitude.

The pattern is always the same: Be present. Notice when thoughts pull you away. Gently return.

The Concept of Sabr (Patience) in ACT Context

Sabr is one of the most important concepts in Islam. It's usually translated as patience, but it means more than just waiting passively.

Sabr means:

- Persevering through difficulty
- Restraining yourself from harmful actions
- Accepting what you cannot control while working to change what you can
- Maintaining good character despite hardship

Sound familiar? That's exactly what ACT teaches—psychological flexibility, committed action despite discomfort, acceptance of difficult internal experiences.

ACT is essentially a psychological framework for practicing sabr.

The Quran says: "O you who have believed, seek help through patience and prayer. Indeed, Allah is with the patient." (Quran 2:153)

What does patience with OCD look like?

It's not: "I'll just suffer forever with these compulsions and not try to change."

It's: "I'll accept that anxiety and intrusive thoughts appear (can't control that), while I work to change my behavioral response to them (can control that). I'll persevere through the discomfort of resisting compulsions, trusting that Allah is with me in this struggle."

That's sabr. And it's ACT.

Example: Sabr in ERP

You're doing an exposure—performing wudu once and not repeating despite doubt.

The anxiety is intense. You want to redo wudu so badly.

Sabr doesn't mean: "This doesn't bother me." (That's not patience; that's denial.)

Sabr means: "This is really hard. I feel intense anxiety. But I'm going to bear this discomfort for the sake of Allah and my recovery. I'm going to restrain myself from the compulsion even though every part of me wants to do it. I trust that Allah is with me in this moment of difficulty."

That's sabr in action.

Acceptance Is Not Resignation

Here's something important: ACT's concept of acceptance doesn't mean giving up or resigning yourself to suffering.

You're not accepting OCD as a permanent state you'll never overcome.

You're accepting the present-moment reality of difficult internal experiences (anxiety, doubt, intrusive thoughts) while working to change your behavioral responses to them.

It's like accepting that it's raining outside. You don't stand there getting soaked saying, "I accept this rain and will do nothing." You accept the rain exists, and then you open an umbrella or go inside.

With OCD: You accept the intrusive thought appeared. You accept anxiety is present. And then you choose how to respond—you don't engage with the thought, you don't do the compulsion, you move toward values-based action.

Islam teaches this balance: Accept Allah's decree (*qadr*) while taking action (*ikhtiyar*). Some things are beyond your control—accept them. Other things you can influence—work on those.

You can't control whether OCD generates intrusive thoughts. Accept that they appear.

You can control whether you engage with them and perform compulsions. Work on changing that.

ACT and ERP Together

ACT and ERP work beautifully together.

ERP says: Face your fears, resist compulsions.

ACT says: While doing that, practice accepting discomfort, defusing from thoughts, and moving toward your values.

Example exposure: Touch a doorknob and don't wash hands for 30 minutes.

ERP component: You're exposing yourself to contamination fear and preventing the washing compulsion.

ACT component: While doing this, you practice:

- Accepting the anxiety that appears
- Defusing from thoughts ("There goes the OCD thought about najis")
- Staying present (feeling the anxiety in your body without fighting it)
- Connecting to values ("I'm doing this to reclaim my life and practice Islam without OCD controlling me")
- Committed action (sitting with discomfort because it matters)

Together, they create powerful change.

You're not just white-knuckling through exposures. You're developing a completely different relationship with anxiety and intrusive thoughts.

The Willingness to Struggle

ACT talks about willingness—being willing to experience difficult thoughts and feelings in service of your values (Hayes et al., 2011).

Islamic tradition talks about jihad al-nafs—the struggle against the lower self, against desires and impulses that pull you away from what's right.

Same concept.

Recovery from OCD requires willingness to struggle. To feel anxiety. To tolerate uncertainty. To sit with intrusive thoughts without fixing them.

It's not easy. Nobody's claiming it is.

But here's the question: **What are you willing to struggle for?**

Are you willing to struggle to feed OCD? To spend hours on rituals, to exhaust yourself with compulsions, to let the disorder control your life? Because that's also struggle—it's just struggle that leads nowhere good.

Or are you willing to struggle *for* recovery? To feel anxiety in service of reclaiming your worship? To tolerate intrusive thoughts in service of living according to your values?

Both involve struggle. But only one leads to freedom.

The Prophet (peace be upon him) said the greatest jihad is against the self (narrated in various hadith collections). This is that jihad.

When you sit with OCD anxiety and don't do the compulsion, you're waging jihad al-nafs.

When you let intrusive thoughts pass without engaging, you're waging jihad al-nafs.

When you pray once and move on despite doubt, you're waging jihad al-nafs.

This struggle is Islamic. It's what Allah asks from you—not perfection, but sincere striving.

What This Means for Your Recovery

ACT offers a different path than fighting OCD head-on. Instead of battling thoughts, you learn to coexist with them while living according to your values.

You practice acceptance—letting anxiety and intrusive thoughts be present without trying to control them.

You practice defusion—creating distance from thoughts so they're just mental events, not facts.

You stay present—connected to the moment, to Allah, rather than lost in rumination.

You clarify your values—what kind of Muslim you want to be—and let that guide you.

You take committed action—doing what matters despite discomfort.

And all of this aligns beautifully with Islamic teachings: sabr, tawakkul, jihad al-nafs, dhikr, recognizing waswas as external rather than self.

Combined with ERP and cognitive approaches, ACT gives you a complete toolkit for recovery—one that's psychologically sound and Islamically compatible.

In the next chapter, we'll look at how to use Islamic spiritual practices themselves as part of recovery—without letting them become compulsions.

Chapter 10: Islamic Spiritual Practices as Support (Not Compulsions)

Here's a tricky situation: Islamic spiritual practices—dhikr, dua, Quran recitation, seeking Islamic knowledge—are all good things. They're encouraged in Islam. They bring you closer to Allah.

But when you have OCD, these same practices can become compulsions.

You're supposed to make dua. But if you're repeating dua 500 times because OCD says you haven't said it "right," that's a compulsion.

You're supposed to seek Islamic knowledge. But if you're researching fiqh rulings for six hours a day to relieve anxiety about whether your wudu was valid, that's a compulsion.

You're supposed to remember Allah. But if dhikr becomes a ritual you perform in specific patterns to prevent feared outcomes, that's a compulsion.

So how do you maintain spiritual practices during recovery without feeding OCD?

That's what we need to figure out.

Healthy Use of Dhikr and Dua

Dhikr (remembrance of Allah) and dua (supplication) are core Islamic practices. The Quran encourages them repeatedly:

"And the men who remember Allah often and the women who do so - for them Allah has prepared forgiveness and a great reward." (Quran 33:35)

"And your Lord says, 'Call upon Me; I will respond to you.'" (Quran 40:60)

These are beautiful practices that create connection with Allah, provide comfort, and ground you in faith.

Healthy dhikr and dua look like:

- Spontaneous remembrance throughout the day
- Heartfelt supplication when you feel moved to pray
- Established practices (morning/evening adhkar) done once, with presence
- Gratitude and praise that flows naturally

- Seeking Allah's help for genuine concerns
- Connection and peace as the primary goal

OCD-driven dhikr and dua look like:

- Rigid counting—"I must say SubhanAllah exactly 100 times or it doesn't count"
- Repetition driven by anxiety—"I need to keep making dua until the anxiety goes away"
- Compulsive patterns—"I have to say this specific dua in this exact order or something bad will happen"
- Reassurance-seeking—"If I say astaghfirullah enough times, maybe the intrusive thought will be undone"
- Using spiritual practices as rituals to prevent feared outcomes
- Increased anxiety as the primary outcome

How to Distinguish

Ask yourself:

1. **Why am I doing this?**
   - Healthy: To remember Allah, seek His help, express gratitude
   - OCD: To reduce anxiety, achieve certainty, prevent feared outcomes
2. **What's the outcome?**
   - Healthy: Peace, connection, spiritual nourishment
   - OCD: Temporary relief followed by return of anxiety, exhaustion, feeling trapped
3. **Is there flexibility?**
   - Healthy: If I'm interrupted or can't complete it, I'm okay
   - OCD: If I don't do it exactly right or complete it fully, I panic
4. **What happens if I skip it?**
   - Healthy: I miss the blessing, but I'm not in crisis
   - OCD: Overwhelming anxiety, catastrophic thinking, compulsion to make up for it

Guidelines for Healthy Dhikr and Dua During Recovery

1. **Set time limits**: If you do morning adhkar, set a reasonable time (10-15 minutes) and stop when the time is up, even if OCD says you didn't do it "right."
2. **Do it once**: Don't repeat dhikr or dua because doubt appeared. Say it once with sincerity, and move on.
3. **Focus on meaning over counting**: Pay attention to what you're saying rather than obsessing about numbers.

4. **Allow interruptions**: If you're interrupted mid-dhikr, that's okay. You don't have to start over from the beginning.
5. **Avoid using it as reassurance**: If you find yourself making dua or istighfar compulsively after intrusive thoughts, that's a compulsion. The intrusive thought doesn't require dua—it's waswas that should be dismissed.

Ruqyah: When Is It Appropriate?

Ruqyah is Islamic spiritual healing—reciting Quran and specific duas for protection and healing. It's a legitimate Islamic practice mentioned in hadith.

The Prophet (peace be upon him) allowed and practiced ruqyah, particularly reciting Al-Mu'awwidhatayn (the last two surahs of the Quran, Surah Al-Falaq and An-Nas) for protection (Sahih Bukhari, Book 76, Hadith 60).

When ruqyah is appropriate:

- As a general spiritual practice for protection
- When you believe you may be experiencing spiritual harm (jinn, evil eye)
- Alongside medical treatment for physical or mental illness
- Performed by yourself or by a knowledgeable, trustworthy person

When ruqyah becomes problematic:

- When it's used *instead of* professional mental health treatment for OCD
- When it's performed compulsively (listening to ruqyah audio for hours daily)
- When it becomes reassurance-seeking ("If I do ruqyah enough, the OCD will magically disappear")
- When you avoid proper treatment thinking "this is just a jinn problem, not OCD"

The balanced approach:

OCD is a neurobiological disorder. It's not caused by jinn. It's not caused by insufficient ruqyah.

That said, you can absolutely seek spiritual protection and healing through ruqyah while also getting proper psychological treatment for OCD.

Think of it this way: If you had diabetes, you'd take insulin (medical treatment). You could also make dua for healing (spiritual practice). You wouldn't skip the insulin and only do dua.

Same with OCD. Get therapy (medical treatment). Make dua and seek ruqyah if you wish (spiritual practice). Don't skip therapy and only do ruqyah.

And be aware: If you find yourself doing ruqyah compulsively—listening to it for hours, repeating it constantly, feeling like you must do it to prevent disaster—that's OCD co-opting a spiritual practice.

The Role of Quran Recitation

Reciting Quran is one of the most blessed acts in Islam. The Prophet (peace be upon him) said: "Whoever recites a letter from the Book of Allah, he will be credited with a good deed, and a good deed gets a ten-fold reward" (Sunan al-Tirmidhi, Book 45, Hadith 2835).

Healthy Quran recitation:

- Reciting with focus and reflection on meaning
- Daily recitation as part of regular practice
- Reciting for the sake of Allah and the blessing of His words
- Accepting your current level of ability and working to improve gradually
- Feeling connected to Allah through His words

OCD-driven Quran recitation:

- Repeating verses over and over because you doubt you pronounced something correctly
- Avoiding Quran because intrusive thoughts appear during recitation
- Obsessing over tajweed (pronunciation rules) to the point of paralysis
- Feeling extreme anxiety about making mistakes
- Using Quran recitation compulsively as a ritual to prevent feared outcomes

Guidelines for Healthy Quran Practice

1. **Accept your ability level**: You don't need perfect tajweed unless you're a teacher or imam. Recite to the best of your ability, and that's sufficient.
2. **Don't repeat compulsively**: If you think you mispronounced something, make a mental note to learn it better later, but don't repeat the verse 20 times right now.
3. **One-time rule**: Recite your daily portion once, with attention and sincerity. Don't redo it because of doubts.
4. **Manage intrusive thoughts**: If intrusive thoughts appear during Quran recitation, apply what you've learned—recognize it's waswas, don't engage, continue reciting.

5. **Time limits**: If you find yourself taking hours to read a single page because of OCD doubts, set a time limit. Read for your designated time, then stop.

Distinguishing Spiritual Practice from Reassurance-Seeking

This is one of the trickiest distinctions for Muslim OCD sufferers.

How do you tell if you're seeking knowledge and guidance (healthy) or seeking reassurance to relieve anxiety (compulsion)?

Reassurance-seeking looks like:

- Asking the same question multiple times to different people
- Researching the same Islamic ruling repeatedly
- Feeling temporary relief after getting an answer, then needing to ask again
- Asking for opinions on questions you already know the answer to
- The primary goal is anxiety reduction, not knowledge

Genuine knowledge-seeking looks like:

- Asking a question you truly don't know the answer to
- Accepting the answer and applying it
- Not asking the same question again
- The primary goal is learning and proper practice

Example 1: Reassurance-Seeking

You've asked three different imams whether your wudu is valid if you had a moment of doubt. All three said yes. But you ask a fourth because the anxiety returned. That's reassurance-seeking.

Example 2: Genuine Knowledge

You genuinely don't know the ruling on whether wiping over socks is valid in your madhab (school of thought). You ask a knowledgeable scholar once, get an answer, and follow it. That's genuine knowledge-seeking.

The rule: One question, one answer, move forward. If you find yourself asking the same question repeatedly, that's OCD, not Islam.

Creating a Balanced Spiritual Routine

A healthy spiritual routine supports recovery. An OCD-hijacked routine feeds the disorder.

Here's how to build a routine that helps:

Step 1: Identify Core Practices

What spiritual practices are actually obligatory or highly recommended in Islam?

Obligatory:

- Five daily prayers
- Fasting in Ramadan
- Zakah (if you meet the criteria)
- Hajj (if able)

Highly recommended:

- Daily Quran recitation
- Morning and evening adhkar
- Dua for daily needs
- Seeking Islamic knowledge

Step 2: Establish Time Boundaries

For each practice, set reasonable time limits:

- Each fard prayer: 10-15 minutes maximum
- Morning adhkar: 10 minutes maximum
- Evening adhkar: 10 minutes maximum
- Daily Quran reading: 15-30 minutes (or whatever you can sustain)
- Voluntary prayers: Whatever you choose, but stick to the limit

Step 3: Apply the One-Time Rule

Each practice is done once, properly, then you move on. No repeating based on doubt.

Step 4: Include Non-Religious Activities

A balanced life includes more than just religious rituals. Islam encourages:

- Spending time with family
- Serving community
- Earning a livelihood
- Taking care of health
- Recreation and rest

If your entire day is consumed with religious rituals (driven by OCD), you're actually neglecting other Islamic obligations like caring for family.

Step 5: Monitor for Compulsive Drift

Check in weekly: "Have any of my spiritual practices started becoming compulsive? Am I spending more time? Am I feeling more anxiety? Am I repeating things?"

If yes, pull back. Apply the boundaries again.

Example Balanced Daily Routine

6:00 AM - Wake up, Fajr prayer (10 min) 6:15 AM - Morning adhkar (10 min) 6:30 AM - Quran recitation (15-20 min) 7:00 AM - Breakfast, get ready for day (Throughout day: 4 remaining prayers, ~10 min each) 10:00 PM - Evening adhkar (10 min) 10:15 PM - Personal dua (5 min) 10:30 PM - Bedtime

Total religious practice: ~90 minutes daily. That's healthy, sustainable, and leaves time for work, family, rest, and other life responsibilities.

Compare that to an OCD-driven routine where someone spends 4-6 hours daily on rituals, misses work, neglects family, and feels exhausted. That's not Islam—that's disorder.

When to Seek Islamic Spiritual Counseling vs. Psychological Treatment

Some Muslims wonder: "Should I see an imam or a therapist?"

Here's the answer: **For OCD, you need a therapist. For Islamic guidance, you see an imam. Sometimes you need both.**

See a mental health professional (therapist, psychologist, psychiatrist) for:

- OCD diagnosis and assessment
- Evidence-based OCD treatment (ERP, CBT, ACT)
- Medication management if needed
- Learning skills to manage anxiety and resist compulsions
- Processing the psychological aspects of the disorder

See an Islamic counselor or knowledgeable imam for:

- Islamic guidance on religious questions
- Spiritual support and encouragement
- Understanding Islamic rulings that OCD has confused

- Integration of faith and mental health recovery
- Community connection

See both when:

- You need psychological treatment for the disorder AND Islamic guidance for faith questions
- You want a therapist who understands Islamic practice
- You want an imam who understands mental health

Don't rely on an imam alone for OCD treatment unless they also have professional mental health training. Most imams are trained in Islamic sciences, not clinical psychology. They can provide spiritual guidance, but they can't provide ERP or other evidence-based OCD treatment.

Don't rely on a therapist alone for Islamic questions if they don't have knowledge of Islam. They can treat the OCD mechanism, but you might need Islamic guidance on what Islam actually requires versus what OCD demands.

Ideal scenario: A therapist who specializes in OCD (with or without Islamic knowledge) for treatment, plus a knowledgeable, understanding imam for spiritual support. The two can complement each other.

Integration: Faith as Motivation, Not Compulsion

The goal is for your faith to *motivate* recovery, not become another source of compulsion.

Faith as motivation looks like:

"I want to recover from OCD so I can worship Allah with sincerity and joy rather than anxiety and exhaustion."

"I believe Allah wants ease for me, not hardship, so I'm pursuing treatment."

"My faith teaches me to seek treatment for illness, so I'm honoring that by getting help."

"I want to be able to serve my community and family, which OCD prevents, so recovery is part of fulfilling my Islamic obligations."

Faith as compulsion looks like:

"If I don't get treatment perfectly right, Allah won't accept it."

"I need to do treatment in a specific Islamic way or it won't work."

"I must pray a certain way about recovery or it will fail."

"If I don't recover, it means my faith is weak."

See the difference?

In the first, faith points you toward health and provides meaning for the struggle. In the second, OCD has hijacked faith itself and turned recovery into another arena for anxiety.

How to Keep Faith as Motivation

1. **Connect treatment to Islamic values**: "I'm doing this because Allah commands seeking treatment. Because Islam teaches ease, not hardship. Because I want to worship properly."
2. **Use faith for encouragement**: "Allah is with those who are patient. I trust He's with me in this difficult process."
3. **Make dua for healing**: "Ya Allah, help me overcome this disorder. Give me strength to resist compulsions. Guide me to healing."
4. **Apply Islamic concepts**: Sabr in the struggle. Tawakkul in the outcome. Jihad al-nafs against the disorder.
5. **But don't compulsify recovery**: Don't create rigid rules about how you "must" practice treatment. Don't obsess about doing it the "Islamic way." Just do the treatment and trust Allah with the results.

The Beautiful Balance

Islamic spiritual practices can be powerful sources of comfort, guidance, and connection with Allah during recovery.

Dhikr can ground you when anxiety spikes. Dua can remind you that Allah is with you in the struggle. Quran can provide perspective when OCD feels overwhelming. Community can support you when isolation threatens.

But these same practices can become compulsions if you're not careful.

The key is awareness. Constant checking: "Am I doing this to connect with Allah, or to relieve anxiety? Am I doing this once with sincerity, or compulsively repeating? Is this creating peace or increasing anxiety?"

When spiritual practice brings peace, connection, and moves you toward values—continue.

When it creates more anxiety, becomes time-consuming, and looks like a compulsion—apply the boundaries. Time limits. One-time rules. Therapy principles.

You can be a practicing, spiritual Muslim while recovering from OCD. You just need to ensure that your practice serves Islam, not the disorder.

Chapter 11: Assessment and Preparation

You've learned about OCD, understood Islamic perspectives, and explored treatment approaches. Now it's time to get practical. Before jumping into recovery work, you need to understand exactly what you're dealing with.

Think of this like preparing for a journey. You wouldn't set out on a road trip without knowing your starting point, your destination, and what resources you need along the way. Same with OCD recovery. You need to assess where you are, identify what you're working with, and build the support system that'll get you there.

This chapter walks you through the assessment and preparation process. You'll identify your specific OCD patterns, map out your triggers and compulsions, build your support team, and set realistic goals.

Because recovery works best when you're organized, prepared, and have the right people in your corner.

Self-Assessment Tools (Y-BOCS Adaptation)

The Yale-Brown Obsessive Compulsive Scale (Y-BOCS) is the gold standard assessment tool for OCD. Mental health professionals use it to measure symptom severity and track progress over time (Goodman et al., 1989).

You can't officially diagnose yourself with OCD—that requires a professional. But you can use Y-BOCS principles to understand your symptoms better.

Time Spent on Obsessions and Compulsions

Rate yourself honestly:

Obsessions (intrusive thoughts, doubts, urges):

- 0 = None
- 1 = Less than 1 hour per day
- 2 = 1-3 hours per day
- 3 = 3-8 hours per day
- 4 = More than 8 hours per day

Compulsions (repetitive behaviors, mental rituals):

- 0 = None
- 1 = Less than 1 hour per day

- 2 = 1-3 hours per day
- 3 = 3-8 hours per day
- 4 = More than 8 hours per day

If you're scoring 2 or higher on either, OCD is taking significant time from your life.

Interference with Life

How much does OCD interfere with your daily functioning?

- 0 = No interference
- 1 = Mild interference, but I can mostly function normally
- 2 = Moderate interference, definite impact on life but still manageable
- 3 = Severe interference, substantially impairs functioning
- 4 = Extreme interference, incapacitating

Example: If you're missing work regularly, avoiding mosque, or unable to fulfill family responsibilities because of OCD, you're probably at level 3 or 4.

Distress Level

How distressing are the obsessions and compulsions?

- 0 = No distress
- 1 = Mildly disturbing
- 2 = Moderately distressing, uncomfortable but manageable
- 3 = Severely distressing, very disturbing
- 4 = Extremely distressing, near-constant disabling anxiety

Resistance and Control

How much effort do you make to resist obsessions and compulsions?

Resistance:

- 0 = Always resist
- 1 = Usually resist
- 2 = Sometimes resist
- 3 = Rarely resist
- 4 = Never resist

Control:

- 0 = Complete control

- 1 = Much control, usually can stop
- 2 = Moderate control, sometimes can stop
- 3 = Little control, rarely can stop
- 4 = No control

Low scores on resistance and control mean OCD has a strong grip. That's not a failure on your part—it's an indication of severity.

Interpreting Your Scores

Add up your ratings across all categories. General severity ranges:

- 0-7: Subclinical (minimal symptoms)
- 8-15: Mild OCD
- 16-23: Moderate OCD
- 24-31: Severe OCD
- 32-40: Extreme OCD

This isn't a formal diagnosis, but it gives you a baseline. When you start treatment, you can reassess every few weeks to track improvement.

Identifying Your OCD Subtypes

OCD doesn't look the same for everyone. You need to identify your specific subtypes so you can target treatment effectively.

Common OCD subtypes in Muslim populations:

Religious/Scrupulosity OCD

- Excessive doubt about wudu validity
- Fear of committing shirk
- Intrusive blasphemous thoughts
- Obsessive prayer repetition
- Excessive concern about intentions

Do any of these dominate your experience? That's your primary subtype.

Contamination OCD

- Fear of najis contamination
- Excessive washing
- Avoidance of "impure" objects or places
- Anxiety about bathroom use

Harm OCD

- Fear of accidentally harming others
- Intrusive violent or sexual thoughts
- Fear of causing spiritual harm
- Magical thinking about preventing disasters

Relationship OCD (ROCD)

- Obsessive doubt about marriage
- Constant testing of feelings for spouse
- Fear of not being "truly" in love

Perfectionism/Just Right OCD

- Need for symmetry or exactness in worship
- Repeating actions until they feel "right"
- Arranging items in specific ways

Identify Your Top Three Subtypes

Write them down:

1. Primary subtype: _____
2. Secondary subtype: _____
3. Tertiary subtype: _____

Most people have one dominant subtype and a few minor ones. Knowing this helps you prioritize which exposures to work on first.

Mapping Your Triggers and Compulsions

Now get specific. What exactly triggers your OCD, and what exactly do you do in response?

Create a Trigger List

Triggers are situations, objects, thoughts, or sensations that activate OCD anxiety.

Examples:

External triggers:

- Preparing for prayer

- Using the bathroom
- Touching certain objects
- Being in mosque
- Seeing others pray differently than you

Internal triggers:

- Random intrusive thought
- Physical sensation (feeling "dirty")
- Uncertainty or doubt
- Memory of past action

Write down every trigger you can identify. Be specific. Not just "prayer"—but "when I'm about to start Al-Fatiha" or "when I'm uncertain if I said the opening takbir correctly."

Map Your Compulsions

For each trigger, identify the compulsion(s) you perform.

Example mapping:

Trigger: Finished wudu, walking to prayer mat ↓ Obsession: "Did I wash my elbows completely?" ↓ Compulsions:

1. Mental review of wudu process
2. Trying to remember exact sensations
3. Going back to redo wudu "to be safe"
4. Washing extra times

Trigger: Intrusive blasphemous thought during prayer ↓ Obsession: "That thought might invalidate my prayer or make me a bad Muslim" ↓ Compulsions:

1. Saying astaghfirullah 50 times
2. Repeating the entire prayer
3. Seeking reassurance online about whether such thoughts are sins
4. Mentally reviewing whether I "really" meant the thought

Create these maps for your top 5-10 triggers. This gives you a clear picture of your OCD patterns.

Rate Anxiety Levels

For each trigger-compulsion pair, rate the anxiety (0-100 scale) you feel when the trigger appears and you *don't* do the compulsion.

This becomes your exposure hierarchy (which you'll use in treatment).

Building Your Support Team

Recovery is hard to do alone. You need people in your corner who understand what you're dealing with and can support your efforts.

Your support team typically includes three types of people:

Mental Health Professionals

This is your treatment core. You need someone trained in OCD treatment—ideally someone who specializes in it.

Who to look for:

Psychologist or Licensed Therapist: Trained in Cognitive-Behavioral Therapy (CBT) and Exposure and Response Prevention (ERP). Look for credentials like:

- PhD or PsyD in Clinical Psychology
- Licensed Clinical Social Worker (LCSW)
- Licensed Professional Counselor (LPC)
- Certification in OCD treatment (some therapists get specialized training through organizations like the International OCD Foundation)

Psychiatrist: Medical doctor who can prescribe medication if needed. Many people with moderate to severe OCD benefit from combining therapy with medication (Foa, Liebowitz, et al., 2005).

How to find them:

1. International OCD Foundation therapist directory (lists OCD specialists)
2. Psychology Today therapist finder (filter by specialty: OCD)
3. Ask your primary care doctor for referrals
4. Contact Muslim mental health organizations (like the Khalil Center if available in your area)

What to ask:

When interviewing potential therapists:

- "Do you specialize in OCD treatment?"
- "Do you use Exposure and Response Prevention?"
- "How many OCD clients have you treated?"
- "Are you familiar with religious OCD/scrupulosity?"

If they say they "treat anxiety in general," that's not specific enough. OCD requires specialized treatment.

Cultural competence:

Ideally, find someone who understands Islam. But if that's not available, a skilled OCD therapist who's willing to learn about Islamic practices can work.

You can educate them about wudu, prayer, purity requirements—they treat the OCD mechanism while you provide the religious context.

Understanding Family Members

Your family can either help or hinder recovery. When they understand OCD, they become allies. When they don't, they might unintentionally feed the disorder.

What family members need to understand:

1. **OCD is a medical disorder, not a choice**: You're not being "difficult" or "overly religious." Your brain's circuitry is malfunctioning.
2. **Reassurance feeds OCD**: When you ask, "Do you think my wudu was valid?" and they answer, they're providing temporary relief but strengthening the disorder long-term.
3. **Accommodation enables the disorder**: If family changes their behavior to reduce your anxiety (like not touching certain objects, doing extra cleaning for you), it prevents you from learning to handle anxiety.
4. **Recovery requires discomfort**: You'll be anxious during treatment. That's normal. They need to support you through it, not try to eliminate the discomfort.

How to educate them:

- Share this book with them (or relevant chapters)
- Bring them to a therapy session where your therapist explains OCD
- Direct them to resources from International OCD Foundation about supporting loved ones with OCD
- Explain specifically what helps and what doesn't

What to ask from them:

"When I ask for reassurance about whether my prayer was valid, please remind me that I'm in treatment and need to tolerate the uncertainty. Don't answer the question."

"When I'm doing an exposure and I'm anxious, I need you to encourage me to stick with it, not tell me to stop because you're worried about my discomfort."

"I might ask you to help with accountability—like if I say I'm only performing wudu once, you can support that boundary if I start to waver."

Supportive Imam or Islamic Counselor

This person provides spiritual support and clarity about Islamic requirements versus OCD demands.

What to look for:

- Knowledge of Islamic jurisprudence (fiqh)
- Understanding of mental health (ideally has some training or awareness of OCD)
- Compassionate, not judgmental
- Willing to give clear, direct answers (not long, elaborate explanations that feed OCD research)

What you need from them:

1. **Clear rulings on minimum requirements**: "What's actually required for valid wudu according to my madhab?"
2. **One-time answers**: "I'm going to ask you about prayer validity once. Please give me your answer, and I'm committing to not asking again."
3. **Boundaries around reassurance**: "If I come back asking the same question repeatedly, please remind me that we've already addressed this and it's my OCD, not Islam."
4. **Support for treatment**: "I'm in therapy for OCD. Sometimes my therapist will recommend practices that seem to conflict with Islamic ideals (like deliberately not repeating a prayer even if I feel uncertain). Can you support this as part of medical treatment?"

Who NOT to consult:

- Online forums (you'll find endless conflicting opinions)
- Multiple scholars simultaneously (leads to confusion and reassurance-seeking)
- Anyone who doesn't understand that OCD is a medical condition

Choose one knowledgeable person, ask your questions clearly, accept their answers, and move forward.

Setting Realistic Recovery Goals

OCD recovery is possible, but it's not instant. You need realistic expectations about what recovery looks like and how long it takes.

What Recovery Means

Recovery from OCD doesn't necessarily mean zero symptoms ever again. It means:

- Significant reduction in symptom severity (often 50-80% improvement)
- Ability to function normally in daily life
- Obsessions might still appear occasionally, but you don't engage with them
- Compulsions are either eliminated or drastically reduced
- Quality of life is restored

Think of it like diabetes. Someone with diabetes can manage the condition, live a full life, and keep symptoms under control—but they still have the condition and need to maintain healthy practices. Same with OCD for many people.

Realistic Timeframes

Standard ERP treatment is typically:

- 12-20 weekly therapy sessions
- Daily homework/exposure practice
- 3-6 months for significant improvement
- Ongoing maintenance to prevent relapse

Some people improve faster. Some take longer. Factors affecting timeline:

- Severity of OCD
- How long you've had it (longer duration typically means longer treatment)
- Consistency with exposure practice
- Presence of other conditions (depression, other anxiety disorders)
- Quality of therapist and treatment approach

Short-Term Goals (Weeks 1-4)

- Complete assessment and identify subtypes
- Learn about OCD and treatment
- Build fear hierarchy

- Start with lowest-level exposures
- Begin resisting one compulsion

Example: "In the next month, I'll perform wudu in under 10 minutes at least 5 times per week."

Medium-Term Goals (Months 2-3)

- Work through middle range of fear hierarchy
- Resist multiple compulsions
- Implement response prevention strategies
- Notice reduction in anxiety for lower-level exposures

Example: "By month 3, I'll pray each prayer only once without repeating, even when intrusive thoughts appear."

Long-Term Goals (Months 4-6 and beyond)

- Tackle highest-anxiety exposures
- Maintain gains
- Handle setbacks without returning to compulsions
- Resume normal life activities

Example: "By month 6, I'll spend no more than 90 minutes daily on all religious practices combined (5 prayers, wudu, Quran, etc.), and I'll be attending mosque regularly."

Write Your Goals

Make them specific, measurable, achievable, relevant, and time-bound (SMART goals):

Not this: "Get better at OCD"

This: "Reduce wudu time from current 45 minutes to 5 minutes or less within 12 weeks"

Not this: "Stop being anxious"

This: "Pray each prayer only once without repetition, tolerating the anxiety that appears, within 8 weeks"

Creating Safety Plans

OCD creates distress, but it rarely creates actual danger. That said, some people with OCD experience severe depression, suicidal thoughts, or extreme distress that needs immediate intervention.

You need a plan for those moments.

Recognize Warning Signs

Signs that you need immediate support:

- Thoughts of harming yourself
- Feeling hopeless about recovery
- Unable to function (can't work, can't care for yourself)
- OCD symptoms suddenly spike to unmanageable levels
- Panic attacks that don't resolve

Crisis Contacts

Write down:

1. **Therapist's emergency contact**: Most therapists provide after-hours crisis numbers
2. **Psychiatrist contact** (if you have one)
3. **Crisis hotline**:
   - National Suicide Prevention Lifeline: 988 (in US)
   - Crisis Text Line: Text HOME to 741741
4. **Trusted family member or friend** who knows about your OCD and can provide support
5. **Local emergency services**: 911 (or your country's equivalent)

Self-Soothing Strategies

For moments of high distress that aren't quite crisis-level:

- Call a supportive friend or family member
- Use grounding techniques (5 senses exercise: name 5 things you see, 4 things you hear, 3 things you can touch, 2 things you smell, 1 thing you taste)
- Take a walk outside
- Practice deep breathing
- Make wudu and pray (if this is genuinely comforting and not a compulsion)
- Engage in physical activity
- Listen to Quran recitation

When to Adjust Treatment

Sometimes OCD treatment needs to be modified:

- If exposures are too intense and causing extreme distress, scale back to easier ones
- If you're having suicidal thoughts, pause exposure work and focus on crisis intervention with your therapist
- If you're not making any progress after 6-8 weeks of consistent practice, discuss with your therapist whether the approach needs adjustment

Red Flags That Treatment Isn't Working

- Your therapist is just talking to you about OCD without doing actual exposures
- You've been in treatment for months but haven't been asked to resist any compulsions
- The therapist gives you reassurance ("Don't worry, your prayers are fine") instead of teaching response prevention
- Symptoms are getting worse despite consistent treatment

If you see these flags, it might be time to find a different therapist who actually specializes in OCD.

Practical Assessment Exercise

Before moving into specific treatment protocols, complete this exercise:

My OCD Assessment

1. **Time commitment**: I spend approximately ____ hours per day on OCD-related thoughts and behaviors.
2. **My primary subtypes** (list top 3):
    - _____
    - _____
    - _____
3. **My top 5 triggers**:
    - _____
    - _____
    - _____
    - _____
    - _____
4. **My most time-consuming compulsions**:
    - _____
    - _____
    - _____

5. **My support team members**:
    - Therapist: _____
    - Family supporter: _____
    - Islamic advisor: _____
6. **My 3-month recovery goal**:

___

7. **One thing I'll commit to this week**:

___

Completing this exercise gives you a roadmap. You know where you are, where you're going, and what you need to get there.

Moving Forward

Assessment and preparation set the foundation for recovery. You've identified your specific OCD patterns, built your support network, and established realistic goals.

Now comes the hard work—actual exposure and response prevention targeting specific OCD presentations.

In the next chapters, we'll tackle specific protocols for wudu and prayer OCD, contamination fears, intrusive thoughts, and moral scrupulosity.

Each protocol provides step-by-step guidance for applying ERP to these particular struggles. You'll learn exactly what exposures to do, how to resist specific compulsions, and how to work through the anxiety that appears.

Recovery is possible. You're prepared. Now let's do the work.

Chapter 12: Wudu and Prayer: Reclaiming Your Worship

Wudu and prayer are supposed to be acts of worship that bring you closer to Allah. They should take a few minutes, provide spiritual connection, and ground you in your faith throughout the day.

For someone with OCD, they become torture. Wudu stretches from two minutes to an hour. Prayer gets repeated 10, 15, 20 times because of intrusive thoughts or doubt about pronunciation. What should be peace becomes prison.

So we need to reclaim these acts of worship from OCD's grip. This chapter provides specific protocols—exact steps for how to perform wudu and prayer in a way that breaks OCD patterns while fulfilling Islamic requirements.

This is where theory meets practice. Where you actually start changing behavior.

Wudu Protocol

Fiqh Minimum Requirements

First, you need to know what Islam actually requires for valid wudu. Not what OCD demands—what fiqh (Islamic jurisprudence) establishes.

All four major madhabs (schools of thought) agree on the basic requirements (Al-Kasani, 1986):

Obligatory actions:

1. Intention (in the heart)
2. Washing the face once
3. Washing both arms up to and including the elbows once
4. Wiping over the head (or part of it, depending on madhab)
5. Washing both feet up to and including the ankles once
6. Performing these in order

That's it. Washing once is sufficient. Washing three times is *mustahabb* (recommended), not *wajib* (obligatory).

The entire process should take 1-2 minutes. Maybe 3 minutes if you're being particularly thorough or have long hair.

If you're spending 15, 30, 45 minutes on wudu, you're not being extra pious. You're exceeding Islamic requirements and feeding OCD.

Time standard: A normal, careful wudu takes approximately **2 minutes**.

ERP Hierarchy for Ablution

You're not going to jump immediately from 45-minute wudu to 2-minute wudu. That's too big a leap. You'll work up to it gradually.

Create your wudu exposure hierarchy. Here's an example (adjust based on your current baseline):

Current baseline: 45 minutes for wudu

Level 1 (Anxiety: 30/100): Wudu in 30 minutes Level 2 (Anxiety: 40/100): Wudu in 20 minutes Level 3 (Anxiety: 55/100): Wudu in 15 minutes Level 4 (Anxiety: 60/100): Wudu in 10 minutes Level 5 (Anxiety: 70/100): Wudu in 7 minutes Level 6 (Anxiety: 75/100): Wudu in 5 minutes Level 7 (Anxiety: 80/100): Wudu in 3 minutes (approaching normal) Level 8 (Anxiety: 85/100): Wudu only once before each prayer, never repeating based on doubt Level 9 (Anxiety: 90/100): Performing wudu in 2-3 minutes with interruptions/distractions present

How to progress:

Start with Level 1. Practice daily. When your anxiety for that level drops by 50% (in this example, from 30 to 15), move to the next level.

Don't rush. Some people spend 3-4 days on each level. Some spend a week. That's fine. The point is consistent practice until the anxiety decreases.

Time-Limited Wudu Practice

Here's the actual exposure exercise:

Step 1: Set Your Timer

Choose your current level's time limit. Let's say you're working on "wudu in 15 minutes."

Set a timer for 15 minutes. This is non-negotiable. When the timer goes off, you're done—even if doubt appears, even if you're not "sure" you washed completely.

Step 2: Begin Wudu

Make your intention (niyyah). Begin washing as you normally would.

Step 3: Notice OCD Urges

As you wash, OCD will generate urges:

- "Wash that area one more time"
- "You need to check if you got all the way to the elbow"
- "Start over to be safe"

Notice these urges. Label them: "That's an OCD urge."

Step 4: Resist Compulsions

Don't give in. Continue washing normally according to the requirements. Don't:

- Rewash areas excessively
- Check repeatedly
- Start over based on doubt
- Seek reassurance from family members

Step 5: When Timer Goes Off, Stop

Even if you're mid-arm wash. Even if doubt appears. Even if anxiety is high. Stop.

This is the hardest part. OCD will scream: "You didn't finish! Go back!"

Don't. You're done.

Step 6: Sit with the Anxiety

Don't immediately rush into another compulsion. Sit for 5-10 minutes with the discomfort.

Notice the anxiety. Where do you feel it in your body? What thoughts are appearing? Rate it 0-100.

Step 7: Proceed to Prayer

Pray with that wudu. Don't redo it. Don't check your limbs. Trust that what you did was sufficient.

The anxiety will be present during prayer. That's expected. You're learning to pray *with* anxiety, not waiting for anxiety to disappear before you pray.

Step 8: Record Your Experience

After prayer, write down:

- Time limit you used
- Peak anxiety level (0-100)
- Compulsions you resisted
- How anxiety changed over time
- One success from the practice

This tracking helps you see progress and reinforces the learning.

Managing Doubt During Wudu

Doubt will appear. "Did I wash my right arm to the elbow?" "Was there water on every part of my face?" "Should I do this again to be safe?"

Here's how to handle it:

Strategy 1: Expectation Setting

Before you begin wudu, tell yourself: "Doubt will probably appear. When it does, I'm going to notice it and keep going. I'm not repeating anything based on doubt."

This pre-commitment makes it easier to follow through when the moment arrives.

Strategy 2: The "Good Enough" Standard

OCD wants perfection. Islam requires "good enough."

When you wash your face, if water touched your face, you washed your face. You don't need microscopic certainty that every single pore received water.

When doubt appears, remind yourself: "I washed normally. That's sufficient. Islamic law doesn't require perfect certainty."

Strategy 3: Trust Your Initial Certainty

The fiqh principle: Certainty is not removed by doubt.

When you finished washing your arms, you were certain (or reasonably certain) you'd done it. Later doubt—five seconds later, five minutes later—doesn't change that initial certainty.

Trust what you knew at the time, not what OCD suggests later.

Strategy 4: Verbal Reminder

Some people find it helpful to say out loud (or internally): "Washed my face—done. Washed my right arm—done. Washed my left arm—done."

This creates clear markers. When doubt appears, you can reference: "I said I was done with that step. Moving forward."

Strategy 5: The One-Time Rule

This is the ultimate response prevention strategy for wudu: **You perform wudu once. You don't repeat it based on doubt. Period.**

Doesn't matter how strong the doubt feels. Doesn't matter how uncertain you are. You did it once; you're moving forward.

This is hard. Really hard. But it's also the most effective way to break the compulsion cycle.

Prayer Protocol

Accepting Uncertainty in Recitation

You're reciting Al-Fatiha. You pronounce a letter. Doubt appears: "Did I say that correctly? What if I changed the meaning?"

First, reality check: Unless you're an imam leading prayer or a Quran teacher, small pronunciation errors that don't change meaning are overlooked in Islamic law (Al-Nawawi, 1996).

Second, the protocol: **Recite once. Move on. Don't repeat.**

Even if you're uncertain. Even if you think you might have mispronounced something. Once and done.

The One-Time Rule for Prayers

This is your core commitment: **Each prayer is performed once. You don't repeat it.**

Doesn't matter what happens during the prayer:

- Intrusive thought appeared? Finish the prayer. Don't repeat.
- Lost count of rakats? Make your best estimate, do sujood as-sahw (prostrations of forgetfulness), finish. Don't repeat.
- Felt uncertain about pronunciation? Continue. Don't repeat.
- Mind wandered? Bring focus back. Continue. Don't repeat.

The **only** time you restart a prayer is if you definitively broke it according to Islamic law (like actually laughing out loud, clearly forgetting a required pillar, etc.).

Doubt doesn't count. Intrusive thoughts don't count. Uncertainty doesn't count.

Implementation Steps

1. **Pre-prayer commitment**: Before starting prayer, say to yourself: "I'm praying this prayer once. When I finish, I'm done. I won't repeat it no matter what OCD says."
2. **During prayer**: When intrusive thoughts, doubts, or urges to restart appear, acknowledge them ("There's an OCD thought") and continue praying.
3. **After prayer**: When the urge to repeat appears, sit with it for 5 minutes. Rate your anxiety. Resist the urge to repeat. Move on with your day.
4. **Daily practice**: Do this for all five prayers. Some will be harder than others. That's fine. The point is consistent practice.

Managing Intrusive Thoughts During Salah

Intrusive thoughts during prayer are one of the most distressing OCD symptoms for Muslims. Horrifying blasphemous thoughts, sexual images, violent urges—appearing during the most sacred act.

First, the Islamic foundation: The Prophet (peace be upon him) explicitly said that shaytan comes to disturb you during prayer (Sahih Muslim, Book 4, Hadith 1208). This is normal. It happens to everyone. And it doesn't invalidate your prayer.

The Protocol

Before Prayer: Set your expectation. "Intrusive thoughts might appear. They're waswas. They don't invalidate my prayer. I'm going to acknowledge them and continue."

When Thought Appears:

1. **Notice it**: "There's an intrusive thought."
2. **Don't engage**: Don't try to push it away. Don't mentally argue with it. Don't analyze it.

3. **Don't perform mental rituals**: Don't say astaghfirullah repeatedly. Don't mentally "correct" the thought. Don't seek reassurance from yourself about whether you "really" meant it.
4. **Return to prayer**: Bring your attention back to the words you're reciting, the movements you're performing.

After Prayer:

Don't repeat the prayer because intrusive thoughts appeared. This is critical. The prayer is valid. You're done.

If you repeat, you're teaching your brain: "Intrusive thoughts require action." That strengthens the OCD.

If you don't repeat, you're teaching your brain: "Intrusive thoughts are just mental noise. They don't require action." That weakens the OCD.

What About Really Disturbing Thoughts?

"But my thoughts are really, really blasphemous. Graphic. Terrible. Surely those are different?"

No. The more disturbing the thought, the more it proves you don't want it. Only someone who truly values their faith would be horrified by such thoughts.

The thought content doesn't matter. The process is the same: Notice, don't engage, continue prayer, don't repeat.

Perfection vs. Sincerity

OCD wants perfect prayers. Islam wants sincere prayers.

Perfect prayer (in OCD's definition):

- Zero wandering thoughts
- Flawless pronunciation
- Exact movements at exact times
- Complete certainty about every element

Sincere prayer (in Islam's definition):

- Genuine intention to worship Allah
- Reasonable effort to perform correctly
- Bringing focus back when mind wanders

- Sincerity of heart, even if execution isn't flawless

The Prophet (peace be upon him) accepted the prayers of people with limited ability, heavy accents, speech impediments, and varying levels of knowledge.

What mattered was the heart, the intention, the effort.

The Shift

Instead of asking, "Was this prayer perfect?" ask, "Did I pray sincerely?"

Instead of analyzing every detail, trust that your sincere effort is what Allah accepts.

This isn't about lowering standards. It's about recognizing that **Allah judges the heart, not the microscopic details**.

Prostration and Movement

Not Rechecking Positions

During prayer, you bow (ruku), you prostrate (sujood), you sit.

OCD wants you to check: "Was I low enough in ruku? Did my forehead fully touch the ground in sujood? Was I positioned correctly?"

The protocol: **You don't check**. You perform the movement once, reasonably, and move on.

If you go down for sujood, your forehead touches the ground, and you come up—you did sujood. You don't need to verify that every square centimeter of your forehead made contact.

Accepting "Good Enough" in Movements

Islamic requirements for ruku: Bend until your back is approximately horizontal.

Islamic requirements for sujood: Seven body parts touch the ground (forehead, nose, both hands, both knees, both feet or toes).

That's it. You don't need to measure angles. You don't need to ensure perfect positioning.

If you bent and your back was roughly horizontal, you fulfilled ruku.

If you went down and the required parts touched the ground, you fulfilled sujood.

Good enough is good enough.

Resisting Mental Review

After prayer, OCD wants you to mentally replay every moment: "Did I say 'subhana rabbiyal azeem' three times in ruku? Did I actually say the tashahhud correctly? Maybe I forgot something."

This is mental compulsion. It's as much a compulsion as physically repeating the prayer.

The response prevention: When the urge to mentally review appears, notice it ("There's the urge to review") and redirect your attention to something else.

Call a friend. Read something. Make wudu for the next prayer. Anything except mentally reviewing.

The thoughts will be uncomfortable. "But I need to know if I did it right!"

No, you don't. You prayed. It's done. Allah accepted it based on your sincere intention. Moving on.

Practical Example: Bilal's Prayer Recovery

Bilal used to repeat prayers 5-15 times because of intrusive blasphemous thoughts. Here's what his recovery looked like:

Week 1-2: Building commitment

Bilal committed to the one-time rule for Fajr prayer only (starting with one prayer, not all five).

Day 1: Intrusive thought during first rakah. Massive urge to restart. He noticed the thought, continued praying. After prayer, anxiety was 85/100. He sat with it for 10 minutes. Didn't repeat prayer.

Day 3: Intrusive thought again. Anxiety: 80/100. Resisted repeating.

Day 7: Still getting intrusive thoughts, but anxiety after prayer dropped to 65/100.

Week 3-4: Expanding practice

Added Dhuhr prayer to one-time rule. Some prayers were easier than others. Fajr anxiety now down to 50/100.

Week 5-8: All five prayers

Applied one-time rule to all prayers. Some days were hard. Some days had multiple intrusive thoughts in one prayer. But he stuck with it—never repeated.

By week 8: Intrusive thoughts still occurred occasionally, but anxiety was 30-40/100. He could handle them without panic.

Month 3-6: Maintenance

Intrusive thoughts became less frequent. When they appeared, Bilal knew what to do: notice, continue, don't repeat.

Prayer felt like worship again, not torture.

Your Wudu and Prayer Protocol

Based on what you've learned, create your specific plan:

Wudu Plan:

- Current time: _____ minutes
- Target time (3 months): _____ minutes
- This week's goal: Perform wudu in _____ minutes
- Response prevention commitment: I will not [specific compulsion you're resisting]

Prayer Plan:

- One-time rule: Starting with [which prayer(s)]
- Response prevention: I will not repeat prayers, even if [specific trigger]
- When intrusive thoughts appear during prayer, I will [your coping strategy]

Accountability:

- I'm telling [family member/friend] about this plan
- I'll track my practice using [tracking method]
- I'll reassess progress in [timeframe]

Write this down. Put it somewhere visible. This is your commitment.

What to Expect

The first few times you do this, anxiety will be high. Really high. That's expected.

You'll want desperately to redo wudu, to repeat prayer. The urge will feel overwhelming.

But here's what happens when you resist:

Short-term: Anxiety stays high for 10-20 minutes, then gradually decreases.

Medium-term: After a week of practice, the same exposure causes less anxiety. What was 80/100 becomes 60/100.

Long-term: After consistent practice, you can perform wudu normally and pray once without significant distress.

The anxiety doesn't disappear overnight. But it does decrease. And eventually, wudu and prayer feel normal again.

You're reclaiming your worship. One exposure at a time.

Chapter 13: Purity and Contamination Concerns

Contamination OCD in Islamic contexts is especially tricky because Islam does have legitimate purity requirements. There really is such a thing as najis. There really are rules about cleanliness for prayer.

So OCD takes these legitimate concepts and blows them up into an all-consuming fear of invisible impurity everywhere.

The challenge: How do you maintain proper Islamic hygiene without feeding contamination obsessions?

This chapter gives you the framework—what najis actually means in fiqh, what Islamic law requires versus what OCD demands, and specific ERP protocols for contamination fears.

Understanding Najis from Fiqh Perspective

First, let's get clear on what najis actually is according to Islamic law, not according to OCD.

What Constitutes Najis

The four madhabs have slight differences, but generally agree on major categories (Al-Kasani, 1986):

Definite najis (all schools agree):

- Urine (human and animal)
- Feces (human and animal)
- Blood (with some differences about menstrual blood)
- Dead animals (except fish and locusts)
- Pork
- Alcohol (wine/intoxicants)

Important fiqh principles about najis:

1. **The default is purity**: Unless you have clear evidence that something is najis, it's assumed to be pure (Al-Nawawi, 1996).
2. **Visible vs. invisible**: Generally, if you can't see najis, you're not required to investigate or assume it exists.

3. **Amount matters**: Small, unavoidable amounts of certain impurities are overlooked. The exact thresholds vary by madhab, but all recognize that microscopic or minimal amounts don't invalidate prayer.
4. **Intention and knowledge**: If you prayed not knowing there was najis on you, and later discovered it, your prayer was still valid in most circumstances.

What OCD Does

OCD takes these categories and creates paranoid catastrophizing:

- "That doorknob might have been touched by someone who had najis on their hands"
- "There might be invisible urine droplets in the bathroom that spread everywhere"
- "If one molecule of najis touches my clothes, my entire outfit is contaminated"
- "I need to investigate every surface for potential najis"

This isn't Islamic practice. This is disorder.

ERP for Contamination Fears

Your contamination hierarchy maps specific triggers from least to most anxiety-provoking.

Example Hierarchy:

Level 1 (30/100): Touch a doorknob at home, don't wash hands immediately Level 2 (40/100): Touch bathroom door handle, wait 30 minutes before washing Level 3 (50/100): Wear clothes for a full day even if they brushed against something I consider "contaminated" Level 4 (60/100): Use public bathroom, normal istinja (cleansing), don't shower afterward Level 5 (70/100): Touch the bottom of my shoe, don't wash hands for 1 hour Level 6 (75/100): Pray in clothes I wore outside all day without changing Level 7 (85/100): Touch something I "know" has najis (like a public bathroom floor), minimal hand washing, continue my day Level 8 (90/100): Deliberate contact with feared substance (within Islamic bounds), normal washing only

The Exposure Process

Pick your starting level. Let's use Level 2: Touch bathroom door handle, wait 30 minutes before washing.

Step 1: Set Up

Set a timer for 30 minutes. Touch the bathroom door handle deliberately.

Step 2: Resist Immediate Washing

Your hands feel "contaminated." The urge to wash is overwhelming.

Don't. Sit with your hands unwashed.

Step 3: Notice the Anxiety

Where do you feel it? What thoughts appear? "I need to wash. There might be najis. I can't touch anything else."

Rate the anxiety: 0-100.

Step 4: Engage in Normal Activity

Touch your phone. Touch your face. Sit on the couch. Act as if your hands are clean.

This is the critical part. You're not just abstaining from washing—you're actively doing things that spread the "contamination" (in OCD's view).

Step 5: When Timer Goes Off

Wash your hands normally. Not excessively. Regular hand washing—20-30 seconds with soap and water.

Step 6: Track

Record: peak anxiety, how it changed over time, thoughts that appeared, compulsions you resisted.

Step 7: Repeat Daily

Do this exposure every day until anxiety for this level drops significantly (usually by 50% or more).

Then move to the next level.

Bathroom and Istinja Practices

Bathroom use is a major contamination trigger for many Muslims with OCD. Islamic guidelines for cleanliness after using the bathroom (istinja) become elaborate, time-consuming rituals.

Islamic Requirements for Istinja

After urinating or defecating, you need to clean the area. The specific method varies by school of thought, but generally:

- Use water to clean the area
- Ensure najis is removed
- Pat dry (or allow to air dry)

That's it. The process should take a few minutes.

Time standard: Normal istinja takes approximately **2-5 minutes**.

What OCD Does

- Wiping/washing 50+ times
- Checking repeatedly to ensure "complete" cleanliness
- Using excessive amounts of water
- Spending 30-60 minutes in the bathroom after simple urination
- Showering after every bathroom use

The ERP Protocol

Create your bathroom hierarchy:

Current baseline: 45 minutes in bathroom after urinating

Level 1 (35/100): 30 minutes in bathroom Level 2 (45/100): 20 minutes Level 3 (55/100): 15 minutes Level 4 (65/100): 10 minutes Level 5 (75/100): 5 minutes (normal) Level 6 (80/100): Don't check underwear for the next hour Level 7 (85/100): Use public restroom, normal istinja, don't shower afterward

Practice Steps:

1. **Set timer** for your current level's time limit
2. **Use bathroom** normally
3. **Perform istinja** once—clean the area with water, pat dry, done
4. **Resist rechecking**: Don't check underwear repeatedly. Don't verify that you're "completely" clean.
5. **When timer goes off**, exit bathroom—even if doubt remains
6. **Sit with uncertainty** about whether you're "clean enough"
7. **Don't shower** unless it's your normal shower time (not a response to bathroom anxiety)

Managing the "Droplet" Obsession

Many people with OCD fear that small droplets of urine remain and will invalidate their purity.

Islamic reality: After normal cleaning, you're pure. Small, unavoidable amounts don't count (Al-Nawawi, 1996).

The obsession about "what if there's still a droplet somewhere" is OCD, not Islam.

Response: Clean normally once. Don't investigate for droplets. Accept that you did reasonable istinja, and that's sufficient.

Menstruation-Related Exposures

Women with OCD often struggle with menstruation-related purity concerns.

Islamic Guidelines

During menstruation: Don't pray or fast.

After menstruation ends: Perform ghusl (full-body purification), then resume normal practice.

How do you know menstruation has ended? Different madhabs have different signs:

- White discharge
- Complete stoppage of blood

Once you've observed the sign your madhab recognizes, menstruation is over.

What OCD Does

- Checking for blood every 10-15 minutes
- Delaying ghusl for days "to be absolutely sure" menstruation ended
- Performing ghusl multiple times
- Avoiding prayer for extra days beyond when period actually ended

The ERP Protocol

Level 1 (40/100): Check for blood only 5 times per day (instead of constant checking) Level 2 (55/100): Check only 3 times per day Level 3 (65/100): Check only morning and night Level 4 (75/100): After seeing the sign that menstruation ended, perform ghusl the next day (not waiting extra days) Level 5 (80/100): Perform ghusl once, resume prayer immediately, don't redo ghusl Level 6 (85/100): If uncertain about minor spotting, follow madhab ruling without excessive research

Specific Exposure

After your period appears to have ended (you see the typical sign):

1. **Acknowledge the sign**: "I see [white discharge/stoppage/whatever your madhab recognizes]"
2. **Make decision**: "According to my madhab, this means menstruation has ended"
3. **Perform ghusl** the following day (many scholars recommend waiting for one more prayer time to ensure it's actually ended—follow your madhab's guidance)
4. **Ghusl once**: Normal ghusl, 10-15 minutes, done
5. **Resume prayer** immediately
6. **Resist re-checking**: Don't check for blood constantly. Don't redo ghusl.

The anxiety will say: "But what if menstruation isn't actually over? What if that wasn't the real sign?"

The response: "I followed the Islamic guideline for my madhab. I'm trusting that and moving forward."

Clothing and Environment Contamination

OCD creates elaborate rules about what clothes are "safe," what areas of the home are "contaminated," what objects can be touched.

Islamic Reality

Clothes need to be free of visible najis for prayer. That's it.

If you can't see najis on your clothes, they're clean enough to pray in.

You don't need special "prayer clothes." You don't need to change clothes multiple times daily. You don't need to avoid certain areas of your house.

Common OCD Patterns

- Designating certain clothes as "contaminated" and refusing to wear them
- Changing clothes 5-10 times daily
- Avoiding parts of the house (like areas near the bathroom)
- Creating elaborate rules about what can touch what

- Washing clothes excessively

The ERP Protocol

Level 1 (35/100): Wear the same outfit all day even if it brushed against something I fear Level 2 (45/100): Pray in the clothes I wore outside (no changing into special "prayer clothes") Level 3 (55/100): Sit on my bed in the clothes I wore outside Level 4 (65/100): Touch "contaminated" clothes, then touch "clean" clothes without washing hands in between Level 5 (75/100): Deliberately sit in an area I've labeled "contaminated" Level 6 (85/100): Use the same towel for a week (instead of using a new towel every time)

Practice Example

You wore an outfit outside. It might have brushed against a public bench. Now you're home.

OCD says: "Change immediately. Don't sit on furniture. Don't touch anything."

Exposure: Sit on your couch in those clothes. Touch your phone. Lie on your bed. Continue your day.

The clothes feel "dirty." The anxiety is high.

But you're teaching your brain: "This isn't dangerous. I can function normally without changing clothes compulsively."

Gradual Reduction of Washing Rituals

If you're washing hands 50 times per day, you can't jump to washing them 6-8 times (which is more normal).

You need gradual reduction.

Current Baseline Assessment

Count how many times you wash your hands today. Be honest.

Let's say it's 50 times.

Reduction Hierarchy

Week 1-2: 40 times per day maximum Week 3-4: 30 times per day Week 5-6: 20 times per day Week 7-8: 15 times per day Week 9-10: 10 times per day Week 11-12: 6-8 times per day (normal)

Implementation

Use a counter or tally sheet. Each time you wash hands, mark it down.

When you reach your daily limit, you're done. No more hand washing for the day (except for wudu or food prep where it's actually necessary).

The anxiety will spike when you hit your limit but still feel "contaminated."

Sit with it. Use the time you'd spend washing hands to do something else—call someone, read Quran, take a walk.

What About "Necessary" Washing?

You still wash hands:

- Before eating
- After using bathroom (as part of istinja)
- For wudu
- When hands are visibly dirty

But you don't wash:

- Because you touched something you fear
- Because you feel contaminated
- To get certainty
- Compulsively "just to be safe"

The difference: Functional washing vs. anxiety-driven washing.

Scripts for Managing Uncertainty About Purity

When doubt appears—"Am I pure right now? Is this najis?"—you need a script that helps you move forward without reassurance.

Script 1: Default Assumption

"Islamic law says the default is purity unless I have clear evidence otherwise. I have no clear evidence of najis. Therefore, I'm assuming purity and moving forward."

Script 2: Visual Check Only

"I looked. I don't see najis. That's sufficient. I'm not investigating further."

Script 3: Trusting Initial Certainty

"I was certain I was clean when I finished washing. This doubt appeared later. The fiqh principle says later doubt doesn't override initial certainty. I'm trusting my initial state."

Script 4: Practical Sustainability

"If I followed OCD's standards about purity, I couldn't function in daily life. Islam is meant to be practical and sustainable. I'm following normal, reasonable standards."

Script 5: Tawakkul

"I did my reasonable best to be clean. I'm trusting Allah to judge my effort fairly. I don't need absolute certainty."

When to Use Scripts

Write these down. Memorize them. When contamination doubt appears, pull out your script, say it (internally or aloud), and move forward.

Don't debate with OCD. Don't seek certainty. Script and move on.

Aisha's Contamination Recovery

Aisha feared najis contamination constantly. She wouldn't touch shoes, avoided public places, changed clothes 5 times daily, and showered for 90 minutes after using bathrooms.

Month 1: Bathroom Protocol

Aisha set a 15-minute limit for post-bathroom time (down from 90 minutes).

Week 1: Anxiety peaked at 90/100 when timer went off. She wanted desperately to continue washing. She didn't. She sat with anxiety for 30 minutes.

Week 4: Same 15-minute limit now caused 60/100 anxiety. Still uncomfortable, but manageable.

Month 2: Clothing Exposures

Aisha started wearing the same outfit all day (instead of changing 5 times).

She prayed in the clothes she wore outside. Massive anxiety—"These clothes might have najis!"

She used her script: "I don't see any najis. The default is purity. I'm praying in these clothes."

Repeated daily. Anxiety gradually decreased.

Month 3: Touch Exposures

Aisha touched the bottom of her shoe, waited 1 hour before washing hands.

Touched public doorknobs, normal hand washing only.

By month 3, her hand washing dropped from 50+ times daily to 12-15 times.

Month 6: Normal Life

Aisha used bathrooms normally (10-minute maximum post-bathroom time).

She wore clothes all day without changing.

She attended mosque without contamination panic.

Hand washing normalized to 6-8 times daily.

Contamination anxiety still appeared occasionally, but she knew how to handle it: Acknowledge, don't engage, trust the default of purity.

Your Contamination Protocol

Based on your specific fears, create your plan:

My top 3 contamination triggers:

1. _____
2. _____
3. _____

My current compulsions:

- Hand washing: _____ times per day

- Showering: ____ times per day
- Changing clothes: ____ times per day
- Time in bathroom: ____ minutes
- Other: _____

This month's goals:

- Reduce hand washing to: ____ times per day
- Bathroom time limit: ____ minutes
- One new exposure I'll practice: _____

My go-to script for contamination doubt:

Write it. Commit to it. Practice daily.

The contamination fears won't disappear overnight. But they will decrease with consistent exposure and response prevention.

You're learning to trust Islamic standards of cleanliness instead of OCD's impossible demands. One exposure at a time.

Chapter 14: Intrusive Thoughts: When Your Mind Whispers Blasphemy

Here's what makes blasphemous intrusive thoughts so tormenting: They attack what you value most.

If Islam matters deeply to you—if you love Allah, respect the Prophet (peace be upon him), and strive to live according to your faith—then having horrifying thoughts about disrespecting them is psychological torture.

And OCD knows this. It targets your faith precisely because that's where you're most vulnerable.

So you get graphic, disturbing thoughts during prayer. Images of disrespecting the Quran. Urges to curse during dhikr. Doubts about Allah's existence at the exact moment you're trying to worship Him.

And then the panic: "What kind of Muslim thinks these things? Am I losing my faith? Did I just commit shirk in my mind?"

This chapter tackles the hardest OCD symptom for many Muslims: intrusive blasphemous thoughts. We'll cover the Islamic position, why these thoughts happen, and how to handle them without compulsions.

Because here's the truth you need to hear: **Having these thoughts doesn't make you a bad Muslim. It makes you human**.

Understanding That Thoughts Are Not Sins

Let's establish the foundational Islamic principle first, because everything else builds on this:

Unwanted thoughts are not sins.

The Prophet Muhammad (peace be upon him) made this explicit. When the Companions came to him horrified by their own intrusive thoughts, he said:

"That is clear faith." (Sahih Muslim, Book 1, Hadith 209)

Read that again. The Companions—the best generation of Muslims—had thoughts so disturbing they were afraid to speak them out loud. And the Prophet's response? This proves your faith is strong.

Why? Because **only someone who cares deeply about Islam would be disturbed by blasphemous thoughts**. If you didn't love Allah, a random thought about Him wouldn't horrify you.

The fact that you're terrified by these thoughts is evidence of your faith, not evidence against it.

Another hadith establishes the clear boundary:

"Allah has forgiven my ummah for what crosses their minds so long as they do not act upon it or speak of it." (Sahih Bukhari, Book 92, Hadith 391)

Three categories:

1. **What crosses your mind** (thoughts) — forgiven, not counted
2. **What you speak** — may be counted
3. **What you act upon** — counted

Notice: Thoughts are in the "forgiven, not counted" category. Period.

Not "thoughts are forgiven unless they're really bad thoughts." Not "thoughts are forgiven unless they're about Allah." Just thoughts—all involuntary thoughts—are not sins.

The Islamic Position on Intrusive Thoughts

Islamic theology has addressed this for over 1,400 years. The scholars weren't naive about how disturbing thoughts can be.

Ibn al-Qayyim's Teaching

The famous scholar Ibn al-Qayyim explained it with a beautiful metaphor: Your heart is like a courtyard. Birds (thoughts) will fly over it, and you can't prevent that. But you can prevent them from building nests there (Ibn al-Qayyim, 2003).

The bird flying overhead—that's the intrusive thought. You didn't invite it. You can't stop it from appearing.

The nest—that's when you engage with the thought, dwell on it, elaborate it intentionally.

You're responsible for preventing the nest, not for the bird flying by.

Al-Ghazali's Wisdom

Imam al-Ghazali, in his writings about waswas, explained that shaytan attacks believers through their minds, creating disturbing thoughts designed to cause despair and distance from Allah (Al-Ghazali, 1989).

The thoughts themselves aren't from you. They're attacks from outside. Your job isn't to prevent the attacks—that's impossible. Your job is to not take them seriously.

Contemporary Scholars

Sheikh Assim al-Hakeem has addressed this in online fatawa: Intrusive blasphemous thoughts are not sins. They're waswas. You're not accountable for them. The distress you feel about them actually proves your faith.

Dr. Hatem al-Haj wrote specifically about OCD and intrusive thoughts, clarifying that these thoughts—no matter how graphic or disturbing—don't affect your state of Islam, don't invalidate your worship, and aren't counted as sins (Al-Haj, 2019).

The Universal Principle

Islam holds you accountable for:

- Your choices
- Your intentions
- Your actions
- Your words

Islam does NOT hold you accountable for:

- Random mental content
- Thoughts that appear unbidden
- Intrusive images or urges
- Waswas from shaytan

This isn't a gray area. This is clear Islamic teaching.

Why Trying NOT to Think Something Doesn't Work

Here's a quick experiment. For the next 30 seconds, do not think about a white bear.

Don't picture a white bear. Don't imagine its fur. Don't think about where a white bear would live.

Ready? Go.

...

What happened? You thought about a white bear, didn't you?

This is called the "white bear effect" or thought suppression paradox. When you try NOT to think something, your brain has to monitor for that thought to make sure you're not thinking it—which means bringing it to mind repeatedly (Wegner, 1989).

How This Works with Blasphemous Thoughts

You have a blasphemous thought about Allah during prayer. You're horrified. You think: "I must NOT think that again!"

So your brain starts monitoring: "Am I thinking it? No, not yet. What about now? Still not thinking it. Wait, what was the thought I'm not supposed to think? Oh, right, [blasphemous thought]."

And boom. You just thought it again while trying not to think it.

The more you try to suppress, the more the thought returns. It's a neurological process, not a spiritual failure (Abramowitz, Tolin, & Street, 2001).

The OCD Trap

OCD convinces you that having these thoughts means something terrible:

- "You must secretly want to blaspheme"
- "You're losing your faith"
- "You need to do something to undo this thought"

None of that is true. The thought appeared because your brain generated it (all brains generate random thoughts) and because you're trying desperately not to have it (which makes it appear more).

The Alternative

Instead of trying to suppress the thought, you need to accept that it appeared and then not engage with it.

Not suppress. Not fight. Not analyze. Just acknowledge and move on.

"There's that intrusive thought again. Okay. I'm continuing my prayer."

No drama. No panic. No mental rituals. Just... moving forward.

Exposure to Blasphemous Thoughts (With Theological Grounding)

Now we get to the treatment that sounds terrifying: Deliberately exposing yourself to blasphemous thoughts.

"Wait. You want me to intentionally think blasphemous things? Isn't that exactly what I'm trying to stop?"

No. Here's the distinction:

What you're trying to stop: The panic, the mental rituals, the compulsions, the hours of reassurance-seeking that happen when intrusive thoughts appear.

What exposure does: It teaches your brain that having the thought isn't dangerous, doesn't require fixing, and doesn't make you a bad Muslim.

The Islamic Grounding

This is permissible because:

1. You're not acting on the thought or speaking it aloud
2. Your intention is therapeutic—you're treating a medical condition
3. The Prophet (peace be upon him) said these thoughts aren't sins
4. The goal is to reduce suffering and return to proper worship

Some people feel more comfortable getting explicit permission from a knowledgeable imam before doing this type of exposure. That's fine. Consult someone who understands both Islam and OCD.

How Exposure Works

Instead of trying to push the thought away the instant it appears, you:

1. **Let it be present** in your mind for a period of time
2. **Don't perform mental rituals** (no astaghfirullah, no mentally correcting it)
3. **Sit with the anxiety** it creates
4. **Notice that nothing terrible happens**

Your brain learns: "This thought appeared. I didn't fix it. Allah didn't punish me. My faith didn't disappear. The thought is just a thought."

The Exposure Hierarchy

Create a list of intrusive thoughts from least to most distressing.

Example:

Level 1 (40/100): General doubt about Allah's attributes Level 2 (50/100): Fleeting disrespectful thought about Prophet (PBUH) Level 3 (60/100): Questioning a core belief Level 4 (70/100): Explicit curse word directed at Allah (in your mind) Level 5 (80/100): Graphic image of disrespecting Quran Level 6 (90/100): Most disturbing blasphemous thought you experience

The Practice

Starting with Level 1:

Step 1: Write the thought on a card or type it in a document.

Example: "What if Allah doesn't exist?"

Step 2: Read it repeatedly for 5-10 minutes.

Just read it. Let it be in your mind. Don't argue with it. Don't reassure yourself. Don't say astaghfirullah after each reading.

Step 3: Rate your anxiety every few minutes.

At first: Maybe 75/100. After 5 minutes: Maybe 60/100. After 10 minutes: Maybe 45/100.

Step 4: When anxiety drops significantly, stop the practice.

Step 5: Repeat daily until this thought no longer triggers high anxiety.

Then move to the next level.

Critical Elements

During exposure:

- **Don't argue mentally** with the thought ("But I do believe in Allah, because...")
- **Don't seek reassurance** (don't research, don't ask family, don't pray excessively)
- **Don't perform neutralizing rituals** (no astaghfirullah, no shahada to "fix" it)

Just sit with the thought and the discomfort.

What About During Prayer?

When blasphemous thoughts appear during actual prayer:

Don't stop praying. Don't restart. Continue.

The thought appeared. You notice it. You keep praying.

After prayer, don't do the exposure practice with that specific thought. Don't repeat the prayer. Just move on.

The exposure work happens outside of prayer—in designated practice sessions.

Accepting Uncertainty About Your Faith

Part of blasphemous thought OCD is the meta-fear: "What if having these thoughts means I've actually lost my faith?"

You can't achieve 100% certainty about your internal faith state. OCD demands it; Islam doesn't require it.

The Nature of Faith

Faith (*iman*) includes:

- Belief in the heart
- Declaration with the tongue
- Action with the limbs

If you believe in Allah and His Messenger, you're Muslim. Having intrusive doubts doesn't erase that.

The Quran acknowledges that even believers have moments of doubt or weakness. That's human. What matters is the overall direction of your heart.

The Acceptance Practice

When the fear appears—"What if I don't really believe?"—instead of seeking certainty, try this:

"I might have some doubts. That's okay. Humans sometimes doubt. I'm choosing to live as a Muslim, to pray, to follow Islam. That's my commitment regardless of fleeting thoughts."

Notice: You're not achieving perfect certainty. You're accepting that uncertainty exists and committing to your values anyway.

That's faith maturity, not faith weakness.

What If the Fear Is Really Strong?

"But what if I really don't believe anymore?"

Look at your actions. Are you praying? Trying to follow Islam? Seeking to understand Allah's guidance?

Yes? Then you believe. Your actions demonstrate faith, regardless of what intrusive thoughts claim.

The famous hadith: A man came to the Prophet saying he feared he was a hypocrite. The Prophet asked, "Do you hate that you feel this way?" The man said yes. The Prophet said, "That is faith" (Sahih Muslim, Book 1, Hadith 214).

If you hate the doubt, if you're distressed by it, that itself proves your faith.

Resisting Mental Rituals

Mental rituals are compulsions you perform in your mind to "fix" blasphemous thoughts.

Common mental rituals:

1. Mental Reassurance

After intrusive thought: "But I don't really think that. I love Allah. I would never actually blaspheme."

This is seeking internal reassurance. It's a compulsion.

2. Mental Review

"Did I really mean that thought? Was it fleeting or did I dwell on it? How long did it last? Let me analyze exactly what happened."

This is rumination. It's a compulsion.

3. Replacing/Correcting

After blasphemous thought: "No, no, no—Allah is the Most Merciful, the Most Kind, I believe in Him completely."

This is neutralizing. It's a compulsion.

4. Thought Testing

"Let me check if I still believe. Do I believe in Allah? Yes? Okay, good. What about now? Still believe? Let me test again."

This is checking. It's a compulsion.

5. Internal Astaghfirullah

Saying "astaghfirullah" (I seek forgiveness) 50 times in your mind after each intrusive thought.

This is ritual neutralizing. It's a compulsion.

Why These Don't Work

Mental rituals provide temporary relief—"Okay, I reassured myself, so the anxiety went down for a minute."

But they strengthen the underlying belief that the thoughts are dangerous and require action. So they make OCD worse long-term.

Not Seeking Forgiveness for Intrusive Thoughts

This is controversial for some people, so let's be clear:

You should seek forgiveness for actual sins. If you intentionally did something wrong, yes, make tawbah.

You should NOT seek forgiveness for intrusive thoughts. They're not sins. Seeking forgiveness for them is a compulsion that reinforces OCD.

When a blasphemous intrusive thought appears:

- Don't say astaghfirullah
- Don't make tawbah
- Don't seek Allah's forgiveness

Why? Because there's nothing to forgive. The thought isn't a sin.

If you constantly seek forgiveness for non-sins, you're teaching your brain: "This thought is dangerous and bad. I need to fix it."

The Alternative

When intrusive thought appears: Notice it. Don't engage. Move on.

No astaghfirullah. No ritual. Just acknowledgment and continuation.

"There's an intrusive thought. Okay."

That's it.

What If It Feels Wrong Not to Seek Forgiveness?

That discomfort is the OCD talking. It feels wrong because OCD has trained you that these thoughts require repentance.

But Islamic theology is clear: You're not accountable for unwanted thoughts. Therefore, no forgiveness is needed.

Trust the theology over the feeling.

Not Mentally "Correcting" Thoughts

After a blasphemous thought, OCD wants you to mentally correct it:

Intrusive thought: "Allah doesn't exist" OCD demands: "No! Allah does exist! He's the Creator, the Most Merciful..."

This correction feels necessary. Like you're defending Allah or affirming your faith.

But it's a compulsion.

Why It's Problematic

The correction reinforces the idea that the intrusive thought was significant and dangerous—so significant that it needed immediate correction.

Your brain learns: "These thoughts are serious threats that require action."

And OCD gets stronger.

The Alternative

Intrusive thought appears: "Allah doesn't exist"

Your response: ... (nothing)

Or just: "There's an intrusive thought."

No correction. No rebuttal. No affirmation of the opposite.

You're not agreeing with the thought. You're just not engaging with it at all.

The Discomfort

This will feel deeply uncomfortable at first. Terrifying, even.

"But if I don't correct it, doesn't that mean I'm agreeing with it?"

No. Silence isn't agreement. It's non-engagement.

You can hold your actual beliefs in your heart (which you do—that's why the intrusive thought disturbs you) without needing to mentally argue with every random thought your brain generates.

Not Testing Your Faith

Another common mental ritual: faith testing.

"Do I believe in Allah? Let me check. Yes, I think I do. But what about now? Still believe? What if I stopped believing and didn't notice? Better check again."

This can happen dozens of times per day.

The Problem

You can't verify belief through mental checking. Faith isn't a fact you can look up and confirm.

The more you test, the more uncertain you become—not because your faith is weak, but because constant testing creates doubt.

The Response Prevention

When the urge to check your faith appears: Don't check.

Notice the urge. Don't act on it.

The anxiety will spike. "But I need to know if I still believe!"

No, you don't. Your actions demonstrate your belief. You're praying, you're seeking Islamic guidance, you're trying to follow Allah's will. That's evidence enough.

Resist the checking. Sit with the uncertainty.

Case Study: Khalid's Recovery from Blasphemous Thought OCD

Khalid had intrusive blasphemous thoughts during prayer for three years. Graphic, horrifying images and curse words directed at Allah. He'd repeat prayers 10-15 times, say astaghfirullah hundreds of times daily, and spend hours seeking reassurance online.

Month 1: Understanding

Khalid learned the Islamic position on intrusive thoughts. He read hadith about the Companions experiencing similar distress. He consulted an imam who confirmed: These thoughts aren't sins.

This provided some relief, but the thoughts still appeared, and he still felt compelled to do rituals.

Month 2: Response Prevention

Khalid committed to not repeating prayers because of intrusive thoughts.

First attempt: Intrusive thought appeared during Fajr. Massive urge to restart prayer. He finished the prayer anyway.

Anxiety after prayer: 95/100.

He sat with it for 30 minutes. It gradually decreased to 60/100.

He didn't repeat the prayer.

Month 3: Reducing Mental Rituals

Khalid worked on not saying astaghfirullah after intrusive thoughts.

This was harder than not repeating prayers. The urge was intense.

He practiced: Intrusive thought → notice it → don't say astaghfirullah → sit with anxiety.

Week 1: Almost unbearable. He felt like he was committing a sin by not seeking forgiveness.

Week 4: Still hard, but he could resist. Anxiety dropped from 90/100 to 60/100.

Month 4-5: Exposure Practice

Khalid started deliberate exposure. He wrote his most distressing intrusive thoughts on index cards.

He'd read them for 10 minutes daily, without performing any rituals.

Initially: Anxiety 85/100.

After two weeks: Same thoughts only triggered 50/100 anxiety.

After a month: Down to 30/100.

Month 6: Maintenance

Intrusive thoughts still appeared occasionally during prayer. But they didn't trigger panic anymore.

Khalid would notice them—"There's that thought"—and continue praying.

No repetition. No astaghfirullah compulsion. No hours of reassurance-seeking.

Total time spent on OCD daily: Dropped from 4-5 hours to less than 30 minutes.

He could pray with peace. He could worship without torture.

The thoughts didn't completely disappear. But they lost their power.

Your Intrusive Thought Protocol

Create your specific plan:

My most common blasphemous intrusive thoughts:

1. _____
2. _____
3. _____

My current compulsive responses:

- Mental rituals I perform: _____
- Number of times I say astaghfirullah daily: _____
- Prayers repeated due to intrusive thoughts: _____
- Time spent seeking reassurance: _____

This month's commitments:

- I will NOT repeat prayers because of intrusive thoughts
- I will NOT say astaghfirullah in response to intrusive thoughts
- I will NOT [specific mental ritual]: _____

My exposure practice:

- Starting with intrusive thought: _____
- I'll practice for ____ minutes daily
- When I notice the urge to do mental rituals, I'll: _____

My reminder statement: "These thoughts are waswas. The Prophet (PBUH) said they're not sins. I don't need to fix them. I'm just going to notice them and continue what I'm doing."

Write this down. Commit to it. Practice it daily.

The thoughts will still appear. But your relationship with them will change. And that's what creates freedom.

Chapter 15: Moral Scrupulosity and Excessive Repentance

Islam teaches that you should be aware of your actions, seek forgiveness for sins, and strive to be better. These are beautiful teachings that guide moral development.

But when OCD gets involved, moral awareness becomes moral paranoia. Seeking forgiveness becomes compulsive ritual. Striving to improve becomes paralysis from fear of making mistakes.

You end up saying "astaghfirullah" 200 times a day—not as a general remembrance of Allah, but compulsively after every tiny perceived mistake. You confess things to family members that don't need confessing. You're terrified you've sinned in ways you don't even know about.

This is moral scrupulosity, and it's exhausting.

This chapter covers how to practice healthy repentance without falling into compulsive patterns, how to trust Allah's mercy without needing guarantees, and how to reduce excessive confession behaviors.

The Balance of Tawbah

Tawbah (repentance) is a core Islamic concept. Everyone sins, and Allah loves those who turn back to Him in repentance.

The Quran says: "O you who have believed, repent to Allah with sincere repentance" (Quran 66:8).

Genuine Tawbah Has Conditions

Islamic scholars identify several conditions for sincere repentance (Al-Nawawi, 1996):

1. **Stop the sin**: If you're doing something wrong, stop doing it
2. **Feel remorse**: Genuine regret for having done it
3. **Resolve not to return**: Sincere intention not to do it again
4. **Make amends** (if the sin violated someone's rights): If you wronged a person, seek to make it right

That's it. You don't need to say istighfar 100 times. You don't need to repeat the repentance multiple times to make sure it "took." You make sincere tawbah once, and Allah accepts it.

Allah's Mercy Is Vast

The Quran is full of reassurance about Allah's forgiveness:

"Say, 'O My servants who have transgressed against themselves, do not despair of the mercy of Allah. Indeed, Allah forgives all sins. Indeed, it is He who is the Forgiving, the Merciful.'" (Quran 39:53)

All sins. Not "all sins except the ones you're really worried about." All sins.

The Hadith on Forgiveness

The Prophet (peace be upon him) said: "If you were to commit sin until your sins reached the sky, and then you repented, Allah would forgive you" (Sunan Ibn Majah, Book 37, Hadith 4248).

Notice: Even if sins piled up to the sky, one sincere repentance is sufficient.

OCD's Version of Tawbah

OCD takes this beautiful teaching and makes it:

- Compulsive (must repent exactly right or it doesn't count)
- Repetitive (must keep seeking forgiveness to be sure)
- Anxiety-driven (repenting to relieve anxiety, not from genuine remorse)
- Never enough (always worried you didn't repent correctly or forgot something)

That's not tawbah. That's a compulsion dressed up in Islamic language.

When Istighfar Becomes Compulsion

Istighfar means seeking Allah's forgiveness. Saying "astaghfirullah" (I seek forgiveness from Allah) is a recommended practice.

The Prophet (peace be upon him) would seek forgiveness 70-100 times daily (Sahih Bukhari, Book 80, Hadith 60). This was general seeking of forgiveness—a recognition of human imperfection and need for Allah's mercy, not a response to specific sins.

Healthy Istighfar

- General remembrance throughout the day
- After prayer as part of normal adhkar
- When you recognize you've actually done something wrong
- As part of spiritual practice and connection with Allah

Compulsive Istighfar

- Saying it 50 times after every minor action "just in case"
- Using specific numbers as rituals (must say it exactly 100 times)
- Saying it to neutralize intrusive thoughts
- Repeating until anxiety decreases
- Saying it because you doubt whether you said it sincerely enough the first time

The Difference

Healthy istighfar brings peace and spiritual connection.

Compulsive istighfar brings temporary anxiety relief followed by more anxiety.

Ask yourself: "Why am I saying astaghfirullah right now?"

If the answer is "to make the anxiety go away" or "because I'm not sure if I said it right before" or "to undo that intrusive thought"—it's a compulsion.

ERP for Moral Uncertainty

Moral scrupulosity creates constant uncertainty: "Did I sin? Was that action wrong? What if I did something bad without realizing it?"

ERP involves sitting with that uncertainty without seeking reassurance or compulsively repenting.

The Exposure Hierarchy

Level 1 (35/100): Make a minor social mistake, don't apologize excessively Level 2 (45/100): Say astaghfirullah only once for something I'd usually repeat it for Level 3 (55/100): Don't confess a minor mistake to family member Level 4 (65/100): Do something ambiguous (not clearly halal or haram), don't research for hours Level 5 (75/100): Make a joke, accept uncertainty about whether it was appropriate Level 6 (80/100): Have a slightly uncharitable thought about someone, don't seek forgiveness compulsively Level 7 (85/100): Sit with uncertainty about whether I sinned today without mental review Level 8 (90/100): Go a full day without saying astaghfirullah compulsively (only general istighfar)

Practice Example

You make a comment in conversation. Later, you worry: "Was that backbiting? Did I say something wrong? Should I repent?"

Old response: Spend 30 minutes analyzing the conversation. Ask the person if they were offended. Say astaghfirullah 50 times. Confess to spouse. Research the ruling on backbiting.

ERP response:

1. Notice the uncertainty: "I'm not sure if that was wrong"
2. Resist research/reassurance: Don't Google "is this backbiting," don't ask anyone
3. Resist compulsive repentance: Don't say astaghfirullah 50 times
4. Make one decision: "If I'm genuinely unsure and it might have been wrong, I'll make one sincere tawbah and move on"
5. Sit with uncertainty: "I might have sinned. I might not have. I made tawbah. I'm accepting that I don't have certainty"

The Discomfort

This is incredibly uncomfortable for people with moral scrupulosity. Not knowing for sure feels dangerous.

"But what if I really did sin and I'm not repenting?"

Two responses:

Response 1: If you made general tawbah covering anything you might have done wrong, that's sufficient. Allah knows your intention.

Response 2: Even if you did sin and you're not 100% sure, Allah is merciful. The Quran says He forgives those who turn to Him. You've turned to Him generally. Trust His mercy.

Accepting That You Might Have Sinned

Here's a radical idea that OCD hates: **You can accept that you might have sinned without needing to know exactly what or when.**

OCD demands certainty: "Tell me exactly what I did wrong so I can repent for it specifically."

Islam allows for general repentance: "Ya Allah, forgive me for anything I've done wrong, knowingly or unknowingly."

The Prophetic Example

The Prophet Muhammad (peace be upon him)—the most righteous human who ever lived—sought forgiveness 70-100 times daily.

Was he committing 70-100 identifiable sins every day? No. He was acknowledging general human imperfection and need for Allah's mercy.

You can do the same. General tawbah covering "whatever I may have done wrong today" is valid and sufficient.

The Practice

Instead of: Analyzing every action of the day, trying to identify every possible sin, making specific tawbah for each one, then worrying you forgot something.

Try this: At the end of the day, make one general dua:

"Ya Allah, I'm imperfect. I may have made mistakes today that I'm aware of or unaware of. I seek Your forgiveness for all of it. Help me do better tomorrow."

Done. Move on.

The Anxiety Response

"But what if there's something serious I forgot?"

Trust that Allah knows your heart. If you genuinely forgot, but your overall intention is to please Allah and avoid sin, He knows that. He's not waiting to punish you for technicalities you don't remember.

The Quran says: "Our Lord, do not impose blame upon us if we forget or make a mistake" (Quran 2:286). This is a dua Allah accepts.

Trusting Allah's Mercy Without Guarantees

OCD wants guarantees: "I need to know for sure that Allah forgave me."

Faith requires trust without guarantees: "I made sincere tawbah. I trust Allah's promise that He forgives those who repent."

The Difference

Guarantee-seeking: "Did I repent correctly? Was my remorse genuine enough? Should I repent again to be safe? Can someone assure me that Allah forgave me?"

This is endless because you can't get the guarantee OCD demands.

Trust: "I made tawbah sincerely. Allah promises to forgive those who turn to Him. I accept that on faith and move forward."

The Quranic Promise

"And whoever does a wrong or wrongs himself but then seeks forgiveness of Allah will find Allah Forgiving and Merciful." (Quran 4:110)

Notice: It doesn't say "Allah will forgive if you repent in exactly the right way with perfect sincerity and zero doubt."

It says: Seek forgiveness, and you'll find Allah forgiving.

That's the promise. Trust it.

Practical Application

You repent for something. Doubt appears: "Did Allah really forgive me?"

OCD wants you to:

- Analyze your repentance for flaws
- Repent again "to be safe"
- Seek reassurance from others
- Research whether your repentance was valid

Faith response: "I made sincere tawbah. Allah promises to forgive. I trust His promise. I'm moving forward."

That's it. No ritual. No reassurance-seeking. Just trust.

Reducing Confession Behaviors

Some people with moral scrupulosity compulsively confess things.

You think you might have done something wrong → immediate urge to confess to spouse, parents, friend, imam → temporary relief → doubt returns → need to confess again or to someone else.

When Confession Is Appropriate

In Islam, confession is appropriate when:

- You violated someone's rights (you need to make amends)
- You're seeking guidance about something genuinely unclear
- You're in a situation where disclosure is necessary (like before marriage, disclosing relevant information)

When Confession Is Compulsive

- You're confessing the same thing repeatedly
- You're confessing minor thoughts or doubts
- You're confessing to "transfer" the responsibility/burden
- The primary goal is anxiety relief, not making amends
- You're asking "Did I sin?" when you already know the answer

The ERP Protocol

Step 1: Identify your confession compulsion

"I confess to my wife every time I have a slightly inappropriate thought. I confess to my imam about minor fiqh questions I already know the answer to."

Step 2: Commit to response prevention

"I will not confess unless the action genuinely violated someone's rights and requires making amends."

Step 3: Sit with the urge

When the urge to confess appears:

- Notice it: "There's the confession urge"
- Don't act on it
- Sit with the discomfort
- Let the anxiety peak and then decrease naturally

Step 4: Track progress

How many times did you resist the confession urge today? How did anxiety change over time?

Example: Zaynab's Confession Compulsion

Zaynab would confess every "bad" thought to her husband. If she had a moment of annoyance with someone, she'd confess. If she had an intrusive inappropriate thought, she'd confess.

Her husband would reassure her: "That's normal, you didn't do anything wrong."

Temporary relief. Then another thought, another confession.

ERP Implementation:

Week 1: Zaynab committed to not confessing thoughts—only actions that actually affected others.

She had an intrusive thought. Massive urge to confess. She didn't.

Anxiety: 80/100 for 20 minutes. Then decreased to 50/100.

Week 2: Same practice. Anxiety response decreased—now peaking at 60/100 and dropping faster.

Month 2: The urge to confess still appeared, but she could resist it easily. Confession frequency dropped from multiple times daily to maybe once per week for things that genuinely needed discussion.

Her husband noticed she seemed more confident, less anxious.

Managing "What If I Forgot to Repent" Thoughts

This is a common fear: "What if I sinned yesterday, forgot about it, and now I haven't repented for it?"

The OCD Spiral

This fear leads to:

- Mental review of entire day, trying to remember everything
- Preemptive repentance for things you can't remember
- Anxiety about whether the general repentance was sufficient
- Repeatedly repenting "just in case"

The Islamic Reality

Hadith on Forgetting:

The Prophet (peace be upon him) taught us to make this dua: "Our Lord, do not impose blame upon us if we forget or make a mistake" (Quran 2:286).

Allah accepts this dua. If you genuinely forgot something, and you're making general repentance, that's covered.

The Response Prevention

When the thought appears: "What if I forgot to repent for something?"

Old response: Mental review of the day, trying to remember everything. Making specific tawbah for anything that might have been wrong. Reassurance-seeking.

New response: "If I forgot something, my general tawbah covers it. Allah knows I'm trying to be conscious of my actions. I trust His mercy for things I've forgotten."

No mental review. No excessive repentance. Just trust.

The General Tawbah Practice

Make this part of your routine—once daily, not compulsively:

"Ya Allah, forgive me for anything I did wrong today, whether I remember it or not. Help me be more aware and do better tomorrow. I trust in Your mercy."

That's it. Covers everything. Move on.

Your Moral Scrupulosity Protocol

My compulsive patterns:

- I say astaghfirullah approximately ____ times per day
- I confess things to ____ [person/people]
- I spend approximately ____ minutes/hours daily on moral review
- My most common fear: _____

This month's commitments:

- I will say astaghfirullah only [specific occasions, not compulsively]
- I will NOT confess unless [specific criteria for genuine confession]

- I will make general tawbah [once daily/specific time]
- I will NOT mentally review my day looking for sins

When moral doubt appears: "I might have done something wrong. I might not have. I've made general tawbah. I trust Allah's mercy. I'm moving forward."

My accountability: I'm sharing this plan with: _____ I'm tracking my progress by: _____

Write it down. Commit to it. Practice daily.

Moral scrupulosity loosens its grip when you learn to trust Allah's mercy more than you trust your compulsive rituals.

Chapter 16: Building Your Personal Recovery Plan

You've learned the concepts. You've seen the protocols. You understand the Islamic framework and the psychological mechanisms.

Now you need a structured plan that brings it all together—a roadmap that tells you exactly what to do, when to do it, and how to track progress.

Because recovery from OCD isn't about having more information. It's about consistent, systematic practice of new behaviors over time.

This chapter gives you the structure: a 12-week program outline, daily practice schedules, progress tracking methods, setback management, and guidelines for when to seek additional help.

12-Week Structured ERP Program

This is a general template. Adjust based on your specific OCD subtypes and severity.

Weeks 1-2: Assessment and Preparation

Goals:

- Complete self-assessment (Y-BOCS, identify subtypes)
- Create fear hierarchies for your main OCD themes
- Build support team (therapist, family, Islamic advisor)
- Understand the treatment model
- Set specific, measurable goals

Tasks:

- Meet with therapist (if working with one) for formal assessment
- Write out your triggers, obsessions, and compulsions
- Create 3-5 fear hierarchies (one for each major subtype)
- Educate family members about OCD and how to support you
- Establish baseline measurements (time spent on OCD daily, frequency of compulsions)

Weeks 3-4: Beginning Exposures

Goals:

- Start with lower-anxiety exposures (rated 30-50 on hierarchy)
- Practice basic response prevention
- Build confidence that you can tolerate anxiety

Tasks:

- Choose 2-3 items from lower end of fear hierarchies
- Practice daily exposures (15-30 minutes)
- Resist at least one major compulsion
- Track anxiety levels before, during, and after exposures
- Journal about the experience

Example: If your hierarchy includes "perform wudu in 15 minutes" (rated 40), practice this daily.

Weeks 5-6: Increasing Difficulty

Goals:

- Move to mid-range exposures (rated 50-70)
- Expand response prevention to multiple compulsions
- Notice anxiety habituation (same exposure causes less anxiety over time)

Tasks:

- Add 1-2 new exposures from mid-range of hierarchy
- Continue lower-level exposures until they're easy
- Practice response prevention for 2-3 different compulsions
- Begin reducing time spent on remaining compulsions

Example: Add "pray once without repetition" if it's in your mid-range. Continue practicing the wudu time limit you started earlier.

Weeks 7-8: Challenging Core Fears

Goals:

- Tackle higher-anxiety exposures (rated 70-85)
- Solidify response prevention skills
- Apply skills to new situations (generalization)

Tasks:

- Begin exposures for highest fears (one at a time)

- Practice exposures in different contexts (home, mosque, work)
- Resist all identified compulsions consistently
- Reduce reassurance-seeking significantly

Example: If "let intrusive thought be present without mental rituals" is high anxiety, start deliberate exposure practice.

Weeks 9-10: Consolidation

Goals:

- Continue with highest-anxiety exposures
- Practice across all OCD themes
- Build independence in creating your own exposures

Tasks:

- Daily practice across all fear hierarchies
- Identify any remaining compulsions and target them
- Practice spontaneous exposures (when OCD triggers appear naturally, use them as practice)
- Reduce total time spent on OCD symptoms by 50% or more from baseline

Weeks 11-12: Mastery and Relapse Prevention

Goals:

- Maintain gains
- Develop long-term practice plan
- Identify early warning signs of relapse
- Prepare for future challenges

Tasks:

- Continue exposure practice but reduce frequency (from daily to 3-4 times per week)
- Create maintenance plan for ongoing practice
- Identify high-risk situations for relapse
- Develop specific strategies for handling future OCD spikes
- Celebrate progress and acknowledge growth

Daily Practice Schedules

Consistency matters more than intensity. Daily practice creates habit and rewires your brain's response to OCD triggers.

Sample Daily Schedule (Weeks 3-8)

Morning (15-20 minutes):

- One exposure from your hierarchy
- Practice response prevention for that exposure
- Brief journal entry: anxiety rating, compulsions resisted, what you learned

Midday (10 minutes):

- Check in: Did any OCD triggers appear naturally? How did you handle them?
- Practice mindful activity (prayer, dhikr, or other focus exercise)

Evening (20-30 minutes):

- Second exposure practice (different from morning)
- Response prevention practice
- Review day: What compulsions did you resist? Where did you struggle?
- Plan tomorrow's exposures

Before bed (5-10 minutes):

- General tawbah (not compulsive)
- Gratitude practice: Identify one success from today
- Brief dua for continued healing

Weekly Practice (1-2 hours):

- Longer exposure session tackling harder items on hierarchy
- Review progress with therapist (if working with one)
- Update fear hierarchies and goals

Adjusting for Your Schedule

Can't do morning and evening practice? That's okay. Do one solid 30-minute session daily.

Have young children or demanding job? Find the pockets of time you can manage—even 15 minutes daily is better than nothing.

The key: **Consistency over perfection**. Daily small practice beats occasional marathon sessions.

Tracking Progress

You need objective measures of progress, not just feelings. OCD can convince you that you're not improving even when you are.

Tracking Methods

1. Anxiety Logs

For each exposure, record:

- Date and time
- Exposure practiced
- Peak anxiety (0-100)
- Anxiety after 10 minutes
- Anxiety after 20 minutes
- Final anxiety level
- Compulsions resisted

Over time, you'll see: Same exposure causes lower peak anxiety and faster reduction.

2. Time Tracking

Track daily:

- Total time spent on OCD symptoms
- Time spent on specific compulsions (e.g., wudu, prayer repetition, reassurance-seeking)

Example:

Week 1 baseline: 4.5 hours daily on OCD Week 4: 3 hours daily Week 8: 1.5 hours daily Week 12: 45 minutes daily

3. Frequency Counts

Track:

- Number of times you washed hands
- Number of prayers repeated
- Number of times you sought reassurance

- Number of times you said astaghfirullah compulsively

Example:

Baseline: Repeated prayers 8 times daily Week 4: 5 times daily Week 8: 1-2 times daily Week 12: 0 times (one-time rule established)

4. Weekly Check-In Questions

Answer these every Sunday (or your chosen day):

- What exposures did I practice this week?
- What's the hardest exposure I completed?
- What compulsions am I still struggling with?
- What situations are easier now than they were last week?
- What do I need to work on this coming week?

5. Y-BOCS Re-Assessment

Every 4 weeks, re-do the Y-BOCS self-assessment from Chapter 11.

Track your score:

Week 1: 28 (severe) Week 4: 22 (moderate) Week 8: 16 (mild-moderate) Week 12: 11 (mild)

This gives you objective evidence of improvement.

Managing Setbacks

Setbacks happen. You'll have bad days, bad weeks even. This doesn't mean you're failing—it means you're human.

Common Setback Triggers

- Major stress (work, family, financial)
- Illness or fatigue
- Ramadan or Hajj (increased religious practice can trigger religious OCD)
- Life transitions (marriage, new job, moving)
- Encountering new OCD themes

What a Setback Looks Like

- Compulsions increase temporarily

- Anxiety spikes higher than recent baseline
- Exposures feel harder again
- Doubt about whether treatment is working

How to Handle Setbacks

Step 1: Normalize It

"This is a setback, not a failure. Setbacks are part of recovery. This doesn't erase my progress."

Step 2: Identify the Trigger

"What changed? Am I under unusual stress? Did something specific trigger this spike?"

Step 3: Return to Basics

Go back to earlier exposures that you'd mastered. Rebuild confidence.

Don't push for the hardest exposures during a setback—return to middle-range items that are challenging but manageable.

Step 4: Increase Support

- Talk to therapist if you have one
- Reach out to supportive family member
- Increase use of skills (mindfulness, cognitive reframes, acceptance)

Step 5: Resist the Urge to Catastrophize

OCD will say: "See? You're back to square one. Treatment didn't work."

Reality: "I'm having a harder week. This is temporary. I still have the skills I learned. I'll get through this."

Step 6: Recommit to Practice

Even when it's hard, continue daily exposure practice. Consistency through setbacks prevents them from becoming full relapses.

Example: Fatima's Setback

Fatima had been doing well—wudu time down to 5 minutes, prayers performed once, minimal anxiety.

Then Ramadan started. She became exhausted from fasting, stress increased, and OCD spiked. Wudu started taking 20 minutes again.

She panicked: "All my progress is gone!"

Then she remembered setback protocol:

1. Normalized: "Ramadan is stressful. Physical fatigue can trigger OCD. This doesn't erase months of progress."
2. Identified trigger: Ramadan stress + fatigue
3. Returned to basics: Instead of pushing for 5-minute wudu, she aimed for 10 minutes (still better than 20+)
4. Increased support: Talked to her therapist, asked husband for extra encouragement
5. Didn't catastrophize: "This is temporary. I know how to handle this."
6. Recommitted to practice: Kept doing exposures even though they were harder

By week 2 of Ramadan, she was back to 7-minute wudu. By end of Ramadan, back to 5 minutes.

The setback didn't destroy her progress—it was a temporary spike that she managed.

Adjusting Difficulty Levels

Sometimes exposures are too hard or too easy. You need to adjust.

Signs an Exposure Is Too Hard

- Anxiety consistently stays at 90+ and doesn't decrease even after extended practice
- You're unable to complete the exposure
- You're experiencing extreme distress (suicidal thoughts, severe depression, panic attacks that don't resolve)

What to Do

Scale it back. Create an intermediate step between where you are and where you're trying to go.

Example: "Perform wudu in 5 minutes" is too hard right now.

Intermediate step: "Perform wudu in 10 minutes."

Master that, then move to 7 minutes, then 5 minutes.

Signs an Exposure Is Too Easy

- Anxiety consistently rates below 30
- You're completing it with no difficulty
- It doesn't trigger OCD anymore

What to Do

Move up your hierarchy. You're ready for more challenging exposures.

Don't stay at easy levels just because they're comfortable—that won't create growth.

The Sweet Spot

Effective exposures typically trigger 50-75 anxiety at the start. Challenging but not overwhelming.

Self-Compassion Practices

OCD recovery is hard. You'll make mistakes. You'll have days where you give in to compulsions. You'll feel frustrated with your progress.

Self-compassion helps you keep going.

What Self-Compassion Is

Treating yourself with the same kindness you'd show a good friend who's struggling.

Not: "I'm such a failure. I repeated that prayer even though I know I shouldn't. I'll never beat this."

Instead: "That was really hard. I gave in to the compulsion. That's okay—recovery isn't linear. Tomorrow I'll try again."

Self-Compassion Practices

1. Acknowledge the Difficulty

"This is genuinely hard. OCD is a serious disorder. I'm doing my best with a difficult challenge."

2. Recognize Common Humanity

"Everyone with OCD struggles with this. I'm not uniquely weak. This is part of the recovery process."

3. Talk to Yourself Like a Friend

When you mess up, imagine what you'd say to a friend in the same situation. Say that to yourself.

4. Celebrate Small Wins

You resisted one compulsion? That's progress. You did one exposure? That matters.

Don't dismiss small victories waiting for perfect recovery.

5. Make Dua for Yourself

"Ya Allah, this is hard. Help me be patient with myself. Help me keep trying even when I struggle. Grant me healing and strength."

When to Seek Professional Help

Some people can do self-directed ERP using this book. Others need professional support. Here's when to seek help:

Definitely Seek a Therapist If:

- Your OCD is severe (Y-BOCS score 24+)
- You're having suicidal thoughts
- OCD is preventing you from functioning (can't work, can't care for yourself)
- You've tried self-directed ERP for 8-12 weeks and made no progress
- You have other conditions alongside OCD (severe depression, trauma, psychosis)

Consider Professional Help If:

- You're struggling to create or follow through with exposures on your own
- You need accountability and structure
- You want guidance on technique
- Your family can't support you adequately

Where to Find OCD Specialists

- International OCD Foundation therapist directory
- Psychology Today (filter by OCD specialty)
- Muslim mental health organizations (like Khalil Center, Khalifa Center)
- Ask your primary care doctor for referrals
- Local university psychology clinics (often offer reduced-fee services)

What to Look For

- Specific training in ERP for OCD
- Experience treating religious OCD/scrupulosity
- Willingness to learn about Islamic practices
- Evidence-based approach (not just general talk therapy)

What About Medication?

For moderate to severe OCD, medication (usually SSRIs) combined with therapy is often more effective than therapy alone (Foa, Liebowitz, et al., 2005).

Talk to a psychiatrist about whether medication might help. It's not required for everyone, but it can make the ERP work more manageable.

Your 12-Week Plan Template

Fill this out based on your specific situation:

Week 1-2 Goals:

- Complete assessment: ☐
- Create fear hierarchies for: _____
- Build support team: _____
- Baseline measurements: _____

Week 3-4 Practice: Lower-level exposures I'll practice:

1. _____
2. _____

Compulsions I'm starting to resist: _____

Week 5-6 Practice: Mid-level exposures:

1. _____
2. _____

Week 7-8 Practice: Higher-level exposures:

1. _____
2. _____

Week 9-10 Practice: Highest exposures:

1. _____

Generalization practice: _____

Week 11-12 Goals:

- Reduce OCD time to: ___ hours/minutes daily
- Master these exposures: _____
- Create maintenance plan: _____

Daily Practice Commitment: I will practice exposures for ___ minutes daily at ___ [specific time]

Weekly Check-In: Every ___ [day of week], I'll review progress and plan next week

Accountability Partner:

_____

Emergency Contact (if in crisis):

_____

3-Month Goal: By [date], I will: _____

Moving Forward

You have the plan. You have the tools. You have the Islamic framework supporting you and the psychological techniques that work.

Now it's about doing the work.

Recovery happens through consistent practice. Some days will be hard. Some weeks you'll want to quit. But if you keep showing up, keep doing exposures, keep resisting compulsions—you'll get better.

OCD loses its power when you stop feeding it through compulsions and when you learn to move forward despite anxiety and uncertainty.

You can reclaim your worship. You can reclaim your life. You can practice Islam the way it's meant to be practiced—with ease, sincerity, and genuine connection to Allah.

One exposure at a time. One day at a time. One moment of choosing values over compulsions.

You can do this. And you're not doing it alone—Allah is with those who are patient, and countless others have walked this path before you.

Start today. The freedom you're seeking is possible.

Chapter 17: For Family Members: How to Help Without Enabling

Your son spends two hours on wudu before each prayer. Your daughter asks you fifty times a day if her prayers were valid. Your spouse won't touch the doorknobs in your home without washing hands for fifteen minutes afterward.

You love them. You want to help. So you answer their questions, you reassure them, you make accommodations to reduce their anxiety. You tell them their prayers were fine. You touch the doorknobs first so they don't have to. You wait patiently while they complete their rituals.

And you're making the OCD worse.

This isn't your fault. You didn't know. When someone you love is suffering, every instinct tells you to reduce their pain. But with OCD, what feels like helping is actually enabling the disorder.

This chapter is for you—the family member watching someone struggle with OCD. You'll learn what accommodation means, why reassurance backfires, how to actually support recovery, and how to manage your own distress in the process.

Because family involvement can make or break OCD treatment. Research shows that family accommodation is one of the strongest predictors of OCD severity and treatment outcome (Calvocoressi et al., 1995). When families understand how to help properly, recovery happens faster and lasts longer.

Understanding Accommodation

Accommodation means changing your own behavior to reduce the OCD sufferer's anxiety or help them avoid triggers.

Common accommodations in families dealing with OCD:

Providing reassurance

- Answering questions about whether prayers were valid
- Confirming that wudu was done correctly
- Reassuring that they didn't commit shirk
- Verifying that something isn't najis

Modifying family routines

- Waiting for prolonged rituals before leaving the house
- Adjusting meal times around compulsions
- Avoiding certain topics that trigger anxiety
- Changing where you sit or what you touch

Participating in rituals

- Checking things for the person with OCD
- Performing tasks they won't do (like touching certain objects)
- Washing items excessively because they request it
- Praying on their behalf when they can't complete prayers

Taking on responsibilities

- Doing their chores because OCD prevents them
- Making all phone calls or handling all errands
- Managing all family religious obligations because they're stuck in rituals

Why You Accommodate

You're not doing this to be manipulative or weak. You're doing it because:

You love them: You hate seeing them in distress. Accommodation provides temporary relief.

It seems to help: When you reassure them, their anxiety drops—for a few minutes. That feels like success.

It reduces conflict: Fighting about OCD is exhausting. Accommodation keeps the peace.

You feel guilty: "If I don't help, I'm being cruel." This thought keeps you accommodating.

Cultural expectations: In many Muslim families, caring for family members means doing whatever reduces their suffering.

But here's what research shows: **Accommodation strengthens OCD** (Storch et al., 2007).

Every time you provide reassurance, you teach their brain: "Anxiety appeared → I got reassurance → anxiety decreased. Therefore, I need reassurance to handle anxiety."

The OCD gets reinforced. The person becomes more dependent on accommodation. The cycle deepens.

How Reassurance Feeds OCD

This is probably the hardest accommodation to stop, especially in Muslim families where consulting knowledgeable family members about religious questions is normal.

But there's a difference between genuine knowledge-seeking and reassurance-seeking.

Genuine question: "I don't know the ruling on whether wiping over socks is valid in our madhab. Can you tell me?" Asked once. Answer accepted. Person moves forward.

Reassurance-seeking: "Was my wudu valid?" Asked for the tenth time today. "Did my prayer count?" After every single prayer. "Am I sure I didn't commit shirk when I had that thought?" Asked repeatedly, even after being told no.

Why Reassurance Doesn't Work

When you provide reassurance:

Short-term: Anxiety drops. Person feels relieved. You feel helpful.

Long-term:

- The person becomes dependent on reassurance to manage anxiety
- They ask more frequently, not less
- Their confidence in their own judgment erodes
- The OCD strengthens because the cycle (doubt → reassurance → relief) gets reinforced

The Alternative

Instead of answering reassurance questions, you:

1. Recognize it's a reassurance question

If they've asked before, if the answer is obvious, if they're asking compulsively—it's reassurance.

2. Gently decline to answer

"I know you want me to tell you if your prayer was valid, but answering that question would feed your OCD. I'm going to support you by not answering."

3. Encourage them to sit with uncertainty

"I know this is uncomfortable. You can handle the anxiety without me answering."

4. Redirect to their treatment plan

"What does your therapist say to do when this question comes up?"

Example: Amina and Her Mother

Amina asked her mother dozens of times daily: "Was my wudu okay? Did you see me do it right?"

Her mother would answer: "Yes, habibti, it was fine. Don't worry."

Temporary relief for Amina. But ten minutes later: "But are you sure? What about my elbows?"

The cycle continued. Amina got worse, not better.

After learning about accommodation:

Amina asked: "Was my wudu okay?"

Mother: "Amina, we talked about this. That's an OCD question. I'm not going to answer it because answering makes your OCD stronger. I love you, and I'm supporting your recovery by not giving reassurance."

Amina got anxious. Really anxious. "But I need to know!"

Mother: "I know it feels that way. You're going to sit with this uncertainty like your therapist taught you."

The first week was brutal. Amina was angry, anxious, pleading.

But by week two, she started asking less. By week four, she rarely asked at all.

Because without the reinforcement of reassurance, the compulsion weakened.

Supporting Exposure Work

When someone you love is doing ERP, they're deliberately making themselves anxious. This is counterintuitive for family members.

What exposure looks like from the outside:

Your family member performs wudu in five minutes, then sits with obvious discomfort, fighting the urge to redo it.

Or they touch something they fear (like a bathroom doorknob) and don't wash their hands for an hour, visibly anxious the entire time.

Your instinct: "This is too hard. Let me help them. Let me tell them it's okay to wash their hands."

Don't.

How to Actually Support Exposure:

1. Understand the treatment

Learn what ERP is and why it works. Read the relevant chapters of this book or materials their therapist provides.

2. Ask how to help

"What can I do to support your exposure practice?"

They might say: "Don't answer my reassurance questions." "Remind me to stick with my time limit for wudu." "Encourage me when I'm anxious, but don't tell me to stop the exposure."

3. Provide encouragement, not rescue

When they're anxious during exposure:

Don't say: "That's enough. You can stop now. You don't have to do this."

Do say: "I know this is hard. You're doing great. You can handle this discomfort."

4. Celebrate small wins

"You did wudu once and didn't repeat it even though you were anxious. That's real progress."

5. Be patient with the process

Exposure makes things harder before they get easier. The first few weeks are rough. That's normal. That's how it works.

What to Say and What Not to Say

Language matters. What you say can either support recovery or feed the disorder.

Don't Say:

"Just stop worrying about it." (Minimizes their struggle. They would if they could.)

"You're being ridiculous. Of course your prayer was fine." (Judgmental and provides reassurance.)

"Why can't you just pray normally like everyone else?" (Shame doesn't help OCD. It makes it worse.)

"Maybe you should do wudu one more time just to be safe." (Encourages compulsions.)

"If you had more faith, this wouldn't be a problem." (OCD is a medical disorder, not a faith issue.)

Do Say:

"I know this is really hard. OCD is a serious condition." (Validates their struggle.)

"I'm here to support you in the way your therapist recommends." (Shows you're on their team.)

"You're working hard on recovery. I see that." (Acknowledges effort.)

"That sounds like an OCD question. I'm not going to answer it because I want to help you get better." (Clear boundary without judgment.)

"What does your treatment plan say to do in this situation?" (Redirects to skills.)

Managing Your Own Anxiety as a Loved One

Watching someone you love suffer from OCD is stressful. You're dealing with your own emotions—frustration, worry, guilt, exhaustion.

Common feelings for family members:

Frustration: "Why do they keep doing this? They know it's OCD!"

Guilt: "Did I cause this? Am I making it worse? Am I not supportive enough?"

Worry: "What if they never get better? What if this destroys their life?"

Exhaustion: "I can't keep doing this. I'm so tired."

Resentment: "Their OCD controls our entire family. I'm losing patience."

All of these are normal. You're human.

Taking Care of Yourself:

1. Set boundaries

You can support their recovery without sacrificing your entire life to their OCD.

"I love you, and I'm supporting your treatment. But I need to maintain my own schedule. I can't wait two hours while you do rituals before we leave."

2. Get your own support

Talk to friends. Join a family support group (many OCD organizations offer these). See a therapist if you're struggling.

3. Educate yourself

The more you understand OCD, the less you'll take it personally. It's a disorder, not a choice.

4. Practice self-compassion

You'll mess up. You'll accommodate sometimes even when you know you shouldn't. That's okay. Recovery isn't about perfection.

5. Take breaks

You need time away from the OCD. Do things you enjoy. Maintain your own interests and relationships.

Cultural Considerations in Muslim Families

Muslim families have specific dynamics that affect how OCD is handled.

Extended family involvement: In many Muslim cultures, family is deeply interconnected. Aunts, uncles, grandparents all have opinions about what's happening.

This can be helpful (more support) or harmful (more people providing reassurance and offering conflicting advice).

What helps: Educate the close family members who are most involved. Have one or two people who understand the treatment plan well, rather than trying to get everyone on the same page.

Religious authority: Parents, especially fathers, may be seen as religious authorities in the family. When dad says "your prayer was fine," it carries extra weight.

This makes reassurance from parents particularly powerful—and particularly damaging to recovery.

What helps: The parent with religious knowledge needs to understand that providing reassurance, even when they're qualified to give Islamic guidance, feeds OCD. They can still provide general Islamic education, but they shouldn't answer compulsive reassurance questions.

Stigma around mental health: Many Muslim communities still view mental health issues as shameful or a sign of weak faith.

Family members might hide the OCD, avoid seeking treatment, or try to "solve" it through increased religious practice alone.

What helps: Frame OCD as a medical disorder that requires medical treatment, just like diabetes or heart disease. Emphasize that Islamic scholars support seeking professional help for mental health conditions.

Gender roles: In some families, men may be less willing to acknowledge mental health struggles or seek help. Women may face restrictions on accessing treatment outside the home.

What helps: Emphasize that seeking treatment is islamically encouraged. The Prophet (peace be upon him) commanded Muslims to seek treatment for illness. Mental health is not exempt.

Honor and reputation: Families may worry about how OCD affects family reputation or marriage prospects.

What helps: Treatment makes the person more functional, more able to fulfill religious and family obligations. Recovery actually protects reputation better than hiding the disorder.

When the Family Member Is Resistant to Treatment

Sometimes the person with OCD doesn't want help. They might:

- Deny they have a problem
- Insist their rituals are "just being a good Muslim"
- Refuse to see a therapist
- Start treatment but refuse to do exposures

This is incredibly frustrating for families.

Why resistance happens:

Fear: Treatment means facing anxiety without compulsions. That's terrifying.

Identity: For some people, OCD has become so intertwined with their religious identity that they can't separate the two. "If I stop these rituals, does that mean I don't care about Islam?"

Secondary gains: OCD is miserable, but it might allow them to avoid work, avoid social situations, get extra attention from family. Giving it up means losing those "benefits."

Denial: "I don't have OCD. I'm just careful about following Islam correctly."

What You Can Do:

1. Express concern without demands

"I've noticed you spend several hours daily on religious rituals and it seems to cause you significant distress. I'm worried about you."

2. Provide information

Share this book. Send articles about religious OCD. Offer to help them find a therapist.

3. Set boundaries for yourself

"I love you, and I'll support you if you choose to get treatment. But I'm not going to keep accommodating your OCD. That's not helping you."

4. Don't force it

You can't make someone get treatment. They have to choose it.

5. Take care of yourself

Get support for yourself even if they won't get treatment.

6. Consider consultation

If they're a danger to themselves, consult with a mental health professional about when intervention might be necessary.

When they start treatment but resist doing the work:

Some people start therapy but won't do exposures, won't stop compulsions, won't practice between sessions.

The family member can support the therapist by:

- Not providing accommodation (which makes treatment more urgent)
- Encouraging (not forcing) exposure practice
- Asking, "What did your therapist ask you to work on this week?"

Resources for Families

Books:

- *Loving Someone with OCD* by Karen J. Landsman, Kathleen M. Rupertus, and Cherry Pedrick
- *Freeing Your Child from Obsessive-Compulsive Disorder* by Tamar E. Chansky (helpful for parents even of adults)

Organizations:

- International OCD Foundation: Offers resources specifically for family members, including support groups
- Anxiety and Depression Association of America: Resources on supporting loved ones

Online support:

- Online support groups for families of people with OCD (many available through IOCDF)
- Forums where family members share experiences and strategies

Therapy for families:

- Family-based treatment for OCD exists, where therapists work with the whole family system
- Individual therapy for family members dealing with caregiver stress

Islamic resources:

- Organizations like the Khalil Center (Muslim mental health organization) may offer family counseling
- Consult with imams who understand mental health

What Healthy Support Looks Like

Let's paint a picture of what good family support looks like in practice.

The Situation: Kareem has contamination OCD. He won't touch doorknobs, changes clothes five times daily, and showers for 90 minutes.

Old family pattern (accommodating):

- Mother touches all doorknobs for him
- Family waits for him to finish showering before doing anything
- They buy extra towels because he uses so many
- They reassure him constantly that things are clean
- They avoid talking about his OCD

New family pattern (supporting recovery):

Week 1: Family meets with Kareem's therapist to understand treatment plan.

Week 2: They stop touching doorknobs for him. When he asks, mom says: "I know you're anxious, but touching doorknobs yourself is part of your exposure practice. I'm supporting your recovery by not doing it for you."

Kareem is angry. Anxious. But he starts touching doorknobs because he has to.

Week 3: When Kareem showers for 90 minutes, family gently knocks: "Kareem, your therapist said 20 minutes for showers. I know you're anxious, but we're going to support you by not enabling longer showers. I'm setting a timer. When it goes off, the hot water is getting turned off."

Kareem protests. But he starts practicing shorter showers because he has to.

Week 4: Kareem asks, "Are you sure this doorknob is clean?"

Dad: "That's an OCD question. I'm not answering it. You can handle the uncertainty."

Kareem sits with the anxiety. It's hard. But he does it.

Week 8: Kareem voluntarily shares: "I touched a public doorknob today and only washed my hands once afterward."

Mom: "That's wonderful! I know how hard that was. You're making real progress."

The family celebrates small wins. They encourage without rescuing. They set boundaries without shaming.

And Kareem gets better.

What You Need to Know

Supporting someone with OCD means resisting your natural instincts to reduce their pain through accommodation. It means watching them be anxious and not rescuing them. It means setting boundaries even when it feels cruel.

But this is what actually helps. Research shows that reducing family accommodation is associated with better treatment outcomes (Van Noppen & Steketee, 2009).

You're not being mean. You're being loving in the way that actually works.

Learn about OCD and its treatment. Stop providing reassurance. Support exposure work even when it's uncomfortable. Manage your own anxiety. Set healthy boundaries.

And trust that this hard path leads to real recovery.

Chapter 18: For Islamic Counselors and Imams

You're the person Muslims turn to for religious guidance. When someone comes to you with questions about prayer validity, purity requirements, or fears about committing shirk, you answer based on Islamic knowledge.

But sometimes the person asking isn't seeking knowledge. They're seeking reassurance. And the questions aren't really about Islam—they're symptoms of OCD.

The young man who asks you forty times whether his wudu was valid. The woman who confesses minor thoughts as if they're major sins. The teenager terrified he's committed shirk because of an intrusive thought.

These aren't people who need more Islamic education. They're people who need mental health treatment.

And as their trusted religious advisor, you're in a unique position to recognize this, provide appropriate guidance, and refer them to professional help.

This chapter is for you—the imam, Islamic counselor, or community religious leader. You'll learn how to distinguish OCD from genuine spiritual struggle, when to refer to mental health professionals, how to provide Islamic guidance without feeding the disorder, and how to collaborate with therapists.

Recognizing OCD vs. Spiritual Struggle

Every Muslim struggles with faith sometimes. Questions arise. Doubts appear. People seek guidance about proper practice. This is normal spiritual development.

OCD is different.

Spiritual struggle looks like:

- Questions about Islamic rulings you genuinely don't know
- Seeking to understand why Islam teaches something
- Working through doubts about faith in a thoughtful way
- Wanting to improve worship quality
- Occasional mistakes in ritual practice that you correct and move on from

OCD looks like:

- Asking the same question repeatedly, even after clear answers
- Spending hours daily on rituals that should take minutes

- Severe distress over minor or imagined religious infractions
- Excessive doubt about the validity of completed worship
- Inability to move forward without absolute certainty
- Functioning significantly impaired by religious practices

Key differences:

Spiritual Growth	OCD
Leads to deeper understanding	Leads to more confusion
Increases peace and closeness to Allah	Increases anxiety and distance from Allah
Time spent is proportional to benefit gained	Time spent is excessive for no spiritual gain
Can accept reasonable certainty	Demands impossible certainty
Improves over time with guidance	Worsens over time despite guidance

Red Flags for OCD:

Time: If someone spends 3+ hours daily on wudu, prayer, or related rituals, suspect OCD.

Repetition: Redoing wudu 10 times, praying 15 times because of doubts—this is OCD, not devotion.

Distress: Severe anxiety, crying, panic around worship indicates a problem beyond normal spiritual concern.

Functional impairment: Missing work, unable to leave house, relationships damaged by religious rituals—this is disorder.

Question patterns: Same questions asked over and over, detailed questions about unlikely scenarios, seeking reassurance rather than knowledge.

Example: Recognizing the Pattern

Abdullah comes to the mosque every Friday after Jumu'ah prayer. Each week, same question: "Sheikh, was my prayer valid? I had a distracting thought during ruku."

You explain: "Distracting thoughts don't invalidate prayer. The Prophet (peace be upon him) said shaytan causes these distractions. Your prayer was valid."

Next Friday: "Sheikh, but this thought was really bad. Are you sure my prayer counted?"

You explain again.

Next Friday: Same question, slightly different wording.

This isn't someone seeking Islamic knowledge. This is someone with OCD seeking reassurance.

When to Refer to Mental Health Professionals

As an Islamic counselor, you're qualified to provide religious guidance, spiritual direction, and Islamic knowledge. You're not qualified (unless you also have mental health training) to treat psychiatric disorders.

When to refer:

Immediate referral:

- Suicidal thoughts or plans
- Severe depression alongside OCD
- Inability to function (can't work, can't care for self)
- Psychotic symptoms (hearing voices, delusions)

Strong recommendation to seek mental health care:

- Clear OCD symptoms (hours of rituals, excessive repetition, severe distress)
- Questions that you've answered multiple times with no resolution
- Religious practices causing significant life impairment
- Family reports that religious behaviors are excessive and distressing

Suggesting mental health support:

- Anxiety around religious practice that seems disproportionate
- Persistent doubts that don't resolve with education
- Rigid adherence to practices beyond Islamic requirements

How to make the referral:

1. Normalize mental health treatment

"What you're describing sounds like it might be OCD, which is a medical condition. Just like we see doctors for physical health, we should see mental health professionals for conditions like this. This is completely consistent with Islamic teachings about seeking treatment."

2. Frame it as additional support, not replacement

"I'll continue to be here for religious guidance. And I'm recommending you also see a therapist who specializes in OCD. Together, we can support your wellbeing—I'll help with Islamic questions, they'll help with the OCD treatment."

3. Provide specific referrals if possible

"There's a psychologist, Dr. [Name], who specializes in OCD and is familiar with treating Muslim clients. Let me give you their contact information."

4. Address concerns

If they say: "But isn't this a spiritual problem?"

You respond: "The Quranic and hadith literature clearly describe waswas—intrusive disturbing thoughts. Islamic scholars throughout history recognized this. Modern psychology has identified effective treatments for when waswas becomes a disorder. Seeking that treatment is completely Islamic. The Prophet (peace be upon him) said to seek treatment for illness."

What you're NOT doing:

You're not diagnosing. You're not treating. You're recognizing patterns that suggest professional help is needed and making an appropriate referral.

How to Provide Islamic Guidance Without Feeding OCD

You can still provide Islamic guidance to someone with OCD. But you need to do it carefully to avoid making the disorder worse.

Principles for OCD-aware Islamic guidance:

1. Answer genuine questions once, clearly

If someone asks a legitimate Islamic question you haven't addressed before, answer it clearly and concisely.

"The minimum requirement for wudu according to our madhab is [specific answer]. If you did that, your wudu is valid."

2. Recognize reassurance questions and decline

If they've asked before, or if the answer is obvious, it's reassurance-seeking.

"We've discussed this. That's an OCD question, and answering it again will strengthen your OCD rather than help you. I'm going to support you by not answering."

3. Point to general principles, not specific rulings for every scenario

Instead of: Answering detailed questions about exactly how much water, exactly how many times, exactly what happens in specific imagined scenarios.

Try: "Islam operates on general principles. The principle here is: perform reasonable wudu according to the requirements. Later doubt doesn't override initial certainty."

4. Emphasize mercy and ease

OCD makes people think Islam is rigid and harsh. Counter this.

"The Prophet (peace be upon him) taught that the religion is ease, not hardship. If your practice is making you miserable and taking hours daily, something is wrong—not with you, but with how OCD has hijacked your practice."

5. Set boundaries around questioning

"I'm happy to answer genuine Islamic questions. But I've noticed you ask the same questions repeatedly. Going forward, I'll answer a question once. If you ask again, I'll gently remind you that we've covered this and redirect you to work with your OCD therapist on managing the doubt."

6. Collaborate with their therapist

If they give you permission, talk to their therapist. The therapist can tell you how to support treatment.

For example: "When he asks if his prayers are valid, please don't answer. Instead, remind him that these questions are part of his OCD and he needs to practice tolerating uncertainty."

Avoiding Reassurance Traps

Reassurance feels like the kind, caring thing to provide. But with OCD, it's like giving alcohol to an alcoholic. Temporary relief, long-term harm.

Common reassurance traps:

The detailed explanation trap: "Sheikh, I had a thought during prayer. Let me describe it in detail. Was my prayer valid?"

Old response: Listening to the entire detailed description, then providing a detailed ruling.

New response: "I don't need the details. The general principle is that intrusive thoughts don't invalidate prayer. If you need further help managing these thoughts, please talk to your OCD therapist."

The "just one more time" trap: "I know you've told me before, but can you just tell me one more time so I can be completely sure?"

Old response: "Okay, one more time..."

New response: "No, answering again would feed your OCD. I've given you the Islamic guidance. Now you need to trust that guidance and move forward."

The "what if" trap: "But what if this specific rare scenario happened? What if I did X while doing Y during Z?"

Old response: Addressing every hypothetical scenario.

New response: "That's a very unlikely scenario. OCD wants you to seek certainty about every possible 'what if.' I'm not going to engage with hypotheticals. Focus on what actually happened, not what might have happened."

The "seeking different scholars" trap:

They ask you a question. You answer. They ask another scholar. And another. Shopping for the answer that makes them feel better.

What helps: When multiple scholars give the same answer, coordinate your response: "I know you've asked Sheikh Abdullah and Sheikh Omar about this. We all gave you the same answer. Asking more people isn't going to give you the certainty you're seeking. That's an OCD issue, not an Islamic one."

Fatwa Guidelines for OCD Sufferers

When you do provide religious rulings (fatawa) to someone with OCD, certain guidelines help:

1. Keep rulings simple and clear

Not: "Well, according to the Hanafi school... but Shafi'i say... and there's a minority opinion that... and in this specific circumstance... but if you consider..."

Instead: "According to our madhab, the requirement is [X]. If you did [X], you're fine."

2. Emphasize minimum requirements, not maximums

Focus on: "This is what's required."

Not: "And it's better to do this, and recommended to add that, and some people also..."

OCD will grab onto every "recommended" practice and turn it into a rigid requirement.

3. Invoke the principle of ease

"The religion is ease. Allah does not burden a soul beyond what it can bear. If your practice is becoming a burden, you're exceeding what Allah requires."

4. Address intention, not perfection

"Allah judges your sincerity and effort, not whether you achieved perfect execution. If you tried sincerely, that's what counts."

5. Give permission to "let go"

"You've done wudu carefully. That's sufficient. Later doubts should be dismissed, not investigated. Move forward."

6. Set time limits if needed

For someone with severe OCD: "I'm giving you a specific guideline: wudu should take no more than 5 minutes. Prayer should be done once, never repeated based on doubt. Follow these limits even if you feel uncertain."

This gives them permission to resist OCD demands using religious authority.

Collaboration with Therapists

The ideal scenario: You provide Islamic guidance, the therapist provides OCD treatment, and you work together to support the person's recovery.

How collaboration works:

1. Release of information

The person signs a release allowing you and the therapist to communicate.

2. Initial consultation

Talk to the therapist. Understand their treatment approach (hopefully ERP). Explain your role as religious advisor.

3. Coordinated approach

Therapist: "Part of treatment is that he won't seek reassurance about religious questions. When he asks you if his prayers are valid, please don't answer. Instead, redirect him to practice uncertainty tolerance."

You: "Understood. I'll support the treatment plan."

4. Regular check-ins

Periodically touch base with the therapist to ensure you're still aligned.

5. Provide Islamic context

Help the therapist understand Islamic practices so they can design culturally appropriate exposures.

"In our madhab, wudu requires [specific actions]. So when we're creating an exposure hierarchy, we should start from [reasonable baseline]."

Example of collaboration:

Aisha has scrupulosity OCD. Her therapist is helping her practice praying once without repetition.

Therapist contacts Aisha's Islamic counselor: "Part of Aisha's treatment involves accepting uncertainty about whether her prayers are perfect. She may come to you seeking reassurance. Can you support her treatment by not providing that reassurance?"

Counselor: "Absolutely. When she asks, I'll remind her that her prayers are valid according to Islamic requirements, and additional questioning is her OCD. I'll redirect her to practice what you're teaching."

Next week, Aisha asks: "Sister Jamila, I'm worried my prayer wasn't sincere enough. Can you tell me if it counted?"

Counselor: "Aisha, that's an OCD question. I've talked with your therapist. Part of your treatment is learning to tolerate this uncertainty. I'm not going to answer because answering would make your OCD stronger. I know you can handle this."

Aisha is anxious. But she sits with it. And the OCD weakens.

Cultural Sensitivity in Muslim Communities

As an Islamic counselor, you understand the cultural context better than most therapists. Use that knowledge to bridge between cultural norms and mental health treatment.

Common cultural barriers:

Mental health stigma: "We don't talk about these things. What will people say?"

Your role: "Mental health is health. The Prophet (peace be upon him) commanded us to seek treatment. There's no shame in getting help for a medical condition."

Religious attribution: "This is a test from Allah. I should just be patient."

Your role: "Yes, it's a test. And part of passing the test is seeking appropriate treatment, just as you would for any illness. Patience doesn't mean refusing medical help."

Gender issues: Women may face barriers accessing male therapists. Men may resist admitting vulnerability.

Your role: Help find culturally appropriate resources. Some Muslim mental health organizations have female therapists. Normalize help-seeking for both genders.

Family involvement: In collectivist Muslim cultures, individual treatment without family involvement may seem strange.

Your role: Educate families about OCD. Encourage family support for treatment. Mediate between individual needs and family expectations.

What to Say in Your Khutbahs and Classes

You can help reduce OCD stigma and increase awareness through your public teaching.

In khutbahs:

"Brothers and sisters, the Prophet (peace be upon him) told us to seek treatment for illness. This includes mental health conditions like depression, anxiety, and OCD. If you or someone you know is struggling with religious anxiety that consumes hours daily and makes worship feel like torture, this might be a condition called OCD. There's no shame in getting professional help. Mental health is part of health."

In classes on Islamic practice:

When teaching about wudu or prayer, emphasize: "Islam is ease, not hardship. If your practice takes hours and causes severe distress, something is wrong. Wudu should take 2-3 minutes. Prayer should be done once. If you can't achieve this, consider whether you might have OCD, a medical condition that requires treatment."

In counseling sessions:

Normalize the referral: "I've seen several community members with similar patterns. This is actually quite common. OCD is a recognized medical condition with effective treatments. Getting help doesn't mean your faith is weak—it means you're taking care of the health Allah gave you."

Handling Your Own Limitations

You're not a therapist. You're not equipped to treat OCD. And that's okay.

What you can do:

- Recognize potential OCD
- Provide Islamic guidance appropriately
- Refer to mental health professionals
- Support the person spiritually while they're in treatment
- Collaborate with therapists

What you can't do:

- Diagnose OCD (that's for mental health professionals)
- Provide OCD treatment (unless you're also a trained therapist)
- Guarantee that someone's religious practice is "correct" in a way that gives them the certainty OCD demands

When you're unsure:

"I'm not sure if this is OCD or another issue. I'd recommend seeing a mental health professional who can assess this properly. They can determine what's going on and what treatment might help."

The Profound Impact You Can Have

As an Islamic counselor or imam, you're often the first person someone turns to when religious anxiety becomes unmanageable. What you do in that moment matters enormously.

If you recognize OCD, make an appropriate referral, and support evidence-based treatment, you could literally save someone's life. You could help them reclaim their worship from a tormenting disorder. You could guide them back to the ease and mercy that Islam truly offers.

If you unknowingly feed the disorder through reassurance and accommodation, you could make it worse—with the best of intentions.

Learn to recognize OCD. Refer appropriately. Collaborate with mental health professionals. Provide Islamic guidance in OCD-aware ways.

You have the religious authority people trust. Use it to point them toward healing.

Chapter 19: Medication: Islamic Perspective and Practical Guidance

The question comes up in almost every OCD treatment discussion: "What about medication?"

For some Muslims, this triggers additional concerns: "Is it permissible to take psychiatric medication? Am I supposed to just have stronger faith and trust in Allah? Will medication change who I am or weaken my connection to Allah?"

This chapter addresses medication for OCD from both an Islamic and practical medical perspective. You'll learn about Islamic rulings on psychiatric medication, how medications work for OCD, common options and side effects, and when medication might be necessary or helpful.

Upfront clarity: Medication isn't required for everyone with OCD. Many people recover through therapy alone. But for moderate to severe OCD, combining medication with therapy often produces better outcomes than therapy alone (Foa et al., 2005).

Islamic Rulings on Psychiatric Medication

Let's address the religious question first: Is taking medication for mental health conditions permissible in Islam?

The Short Answer: Yes. Islamic scholars across all major schools of thought agree that taking medication for mental health conditions is permissible (*ja'iz*) and often recommended.

The Evidence:

1. The Prophetic command to seek treatment

"Seek treatment, for Allah has not sent down a disease except that He has sent down a cure for it." (Sunan Abi Dawud, Book 29, Hadith 3855)

This hadith makes no exception for mental versus physical illness. Disease is disease; treatment is treatment.

2. Mental health equals physical health in Islamic law

Islamic jurisprudence doesn't distinguish between "mental" and "physical" illness as separate categories. The brain is an organ. When it malfunctions, you treat it.

3. Contemporary scholarly consensus

Organizations like the Islamic Medical Association of North America (IMANA), the European Council for Fatwa and Research, and individual scholars like Sheikh Yusuf al-Qaradawi, Dr. Yasir Qadhi, and Sheikh Assim al-Hakeem have all affirmed that psychiatric medication is permissible when prescribed by qualified physicians.

Common Concerns Addressed:

"Isn't this putting my trust in medication instead of Allah?"

No. This is a false dichotomy. You trust Allah *and* use the means He's provided.

It's like asking: "When I'm sick with an infection, do I trust Allah or take antibiotics?" The answer: Both. You take the antibiotics (the means) and trust Allah for the outcome (tawakkul).

The famous hadith about tying your camel applies here too: "Tie your camel and trust in Allah" (Sunan al-Tirmidhi, Book 33, Hadith 2517). Taking medication is tying your camel. Trusting Allah for healing is tawakkul.

"Will medication change my personality or make me not myself?"

Properly prescribed psychiatric medication treats symptoms, not personality. SSRIs (the most common medications for OCD) don't change who you are. They reduce the excessive anxiety and obsessive thoughts that are preventing you from being yourself.

Think of it like this: If you had constant, severe physical pain, you'd take pain medication. That medication wouldn't change your personality—it would allow you to function normally without the pain interfering.

"Is this just masking the problem instead of addressing it?"

Medication for OCD isn't like taking a painkiller that just covers symptoms. It actually addresses the neurobiological dysfunction underlying OCD.

Research shows that effective OCD medication changes brain activity patterns in the circuits involved in the disorder (Saxena et al., 1999). It's treating the root cause, not just masking it.

And most importantly: Medication is typically combined with therapy (ERP), which addresses the behavioral and cognitive components. Together, they provide comprehensive treatment.

How SSRIs Work for OCD

SSRIs—Selective Serotonin Reuptake Inhibitors—are the first-line medication treatment for OCD.

What SSRIs Do:

OCD involves dysfunction in brain circuits, particularly involving serotonin (a neurotransmitter that helps regulate mood, anxiety, and obsessive thoughts).

SSRIs increase the availability of serotonin in the brain by blocking its reuptake (reabsorption) after it's released. More available serotonin helps normalize the brain circuits involved in OCD (Soomro et al., 2008).

How This Helps OCD:

- Reduces the intensity and frequency of obsessive thoughts
- Decreases the anxiety associated with obsessions
- Makes it easier to resist compulsions
- Improves overall ability to function

Important points:

SSRIs don't make you "happy" or artificially elevate mood. They reduce the excessive anxiety and obsessive thinking that OCD creates.

They don't work immediately. SSRIs typically take 4-6 weeks to show initial effects, and 8-12 weeks for full benefit at a given dose.

For OCD specifically, higher doses are often needed than for depression. An SSRI dose that treats depression might not be sufficient for OCD.

Common Medications and Side Effects

FDA-Approved SSRIs for OCD:

Several SSRIs have been specifically approved by the U.S. Food and Drug Administration for OCD treatment:

- Fluoxetine (Prozac)

- Sertraline (Zoloft)
- Paroxetine (Paxil)
- Fluvoxamine (Luvox)

Other SSRIs like escitalopram (Lexapro) and citalopram (Celexa) are also commonly prescribed for OCD, though they don't have specific FDA approval for this indication.

Clomipramine (Anafranil):

This is a tricyclic antidepressant (TCA) that's also FDA-approved for OCD. It's sometimes more effective than SSRIs, but has more side effects, so it's usually a second-line option.

Common Side Effects:

Most side effects are mild and improve after the first few weeks. Common ones include:

- Nausea
- Headache
- Drowsiness or insomnia
- Sexual side effects (reduced libido, delayed orgasm)
- Dry mouth
- Increased sweating
- Weight changes

Managing side effects:

Taking medication with food helps reduce nausea.

If drowsiness is an issue, take it at night. If insomnia is an issue, take it in the morning.

Sexual side effects are common but can sometimes be managed by adjusting dosage, switching medications, or adding another medication. Talk to your doctor.

Most side effects decrease over time as your body adjusts.

Serious side effects (rare but important to know):

- Increased suicidal thoughts (primarily in young people under 25, especially in the first few weeks)
- Serotonin syndrome (rare but serious condition from too much serotonin—symptoms include confusion, fever, rapid heart rate, muscle rigidity)

If you experience these, contact your doctor immediately.

Combining Medication with Therapy

Research consistently shows that combining medication with ERP therapy produces better outcomes for OCD than either treatment alone, especially for moderate to severe cases (Foa et al., 2005).

Why the combination works:

Medication: Reduces the biological intensity of obsessions and anxiety, making it more manageable to do exposure work.

Therapy: Teaches skills and creates new learning that changes your behavioral and cognitive responses to OCD.

Think of it like this: If OCD were a fire, medication reduces the size and intensity of the flames, while therapy teaches you how to put out fires and prevent new ones from starting.

Typical treatment approach:

Week 1-4: Start SSRI, begin therapy assessment and psychoeducation

Week 4-8: SSRI starts working, begin lower-level exposures

Week 8-12: SSRI reaches full effect at this dose, increase exposure difficulty

Month 3-6: Continue therapy while medication maintains reduced symptoms

After 6-12 months: Consider whether to taper medication (while maintaining therapy skills) or continue longer-term

Working with Prescribers

Getting the right medication at the right dose requires working effectively with a psychiatrist or other prescriber.

Initial appointment:

The prescriber should:

- Take a thorough history
- Assess symptom severity

- Review any other medications you're taking
- Discuss medication options, side effects, and what to expect
- Start you at an appropriate dose

What to tell them:

- Specific OCD symptoms and how they affect your life
- Any other mental health conditions (depression, other anxiety)
- Any other medical conditions
- All medications and supplements you're taking
- Any previous psychiatric medications and how you responded
- Family history of mental illness or medication response

Follow-up appointments:

You'll need regular follow-ups, especially in the first few months:

- Check how you're responding
- Assess side effects
- Adjust dose if needed
- Monitor for any problems

Dose adjustments:

For OCD, you might need higher doses than standard antidepressant doses. Don't be surprised if your doctor increases the dose over time.

Example: Fluoxetine might be prescribed at 20mg for depression, but 60-80mg for OCD.

Being your own advocate:

If side effects are intolerable: Tell your doctor. Don't just stop the medication. There might be ways to manage the side effects or a different medication might work better.

If the medication isn't helping after 8-12 weeks at an adequate dose: Discuss trying a different SSRI or adding therapy if you're not already doing it.

If you want to stop medication: Don't quit abruptly. SSRIs need to be tapered gradually to avoid withdrawal symptoms. Work with your doctor on a tapering schedule.

Addressing Stigma in Muslim Communities

Unfortunately, stigma around psychiatric medication exists in many Muslim communities.

Common stigma statements:

"Only crazy people take psychiatric medication."

"This is a sign of weak faith."

"If you just prayed more, you wouldn't need pills."

"You're putting chemicals in your body instead of trusting Allah."

The reality:

Psychiatric medication is no different in principle from medication for any other medical condition. The brain is an organ. When it doesn't function properly, medication can help.

Research shows that Muslim college students often hold more negative attitudes toward mental health medication than their non-Muslim peers, due to cultural factors and lack of education about mental health (Abu Raiya et al., 2011).

Combating stigma:

Education: The more people understand that OCD is a neurobiological disorder, the less they'll stigmatize its treatment.

Islamic framework: Emphasizing that seeking treatment is islamically encouraged helps reduce religious objections.

Normalization: Talking openly about mental health (without violating privacy) helps reduce stigma. "Many Muslims take medication for depression, anxiety, OCD, and other conditions. This is normal medical care."

Privacy: You don't have to tell everyone you're taking medication. It's a personal medical decision.

When Medication Is Necessary

Not everyone with OCD needs medication. Some people respond well to therapy alone.

But medication becomes more necessary when:

Severity is high: If OCD is severely impairing your life (can't work, can't function, spending 6+ hours daily on symptoms), medication can provide enough relief to make therapy possible.

Therapy alone isn't sufficient: If you've done 8-12 weeks of quality ERP and made minimal progress, adding medication makes sense.

Depression is present: Many people with OCD also have depression. SSRIs treat both conditions.

Suicidal thoughts: If OCD is causing suicidal thinking, medication is important for safety while therapy proceeds.

Can't engage in therapy: If anxiety is so high you can't even start exposure work, medication can reduce symptoms enough to make therapy feasible.

Examples:

Scenario 1: Mild OCD, 1-2 hours daily spent on symptoms, able to function.

Recommendation: Try therapy first. If insufficient progress after 2-3 months, consider adding medication.

Scenario 2: Moderate-severe OCD, 4-5 hours daily, significant life impairment.

Recommendation: Start both therapy and medication together for best outcomes.

Scenario 3: Severe OCD with depression, suicidal thoughts, can't work.

Recommendation: Medication is necessary, along with intensive therapy and close monitoring.

Long-Term Use

How long do you stay on medication?

Research guidance:

After you've achieved good symptom control (usually 6-12 months of treatment), you have options:

Option 1: Taper off medication gradually while maintaining therapy skills. Some people maintain improvements. Others relapse and need to restart.

Option 2: Stay on medication longer-term (1-2 years or more). This is reasonable, especially if you've had OCD for many years or have relapsed after previous medication discontinuation.

There's no "right" answer. Some people stay on SSRIs for years without problems. Others prefer to taper off once they've learned ERP skills.

Factors favoring longer-term use:

- Severe OCD that responded well to medication
- Previous relapses when medication was stopped
- Co-occurring conditions (like depression) that also benefit from medication
- Difficulty accessing ongoing therapy for maintenance

Factors favoring tapering:

- Mild to moderate OCD
- Strong ERP skills and commitment to ongoing practice
- Bothersome side effects
- Personal preference

The decision is yours (with medical guidance). There's no shame in taking medication long-term if it helps you function and live well.

What Medication Can and Can't Do

What medication CAN do:

- Reduce the frequency and intensity of obsessive thoughts
- Decrease anxiety associated with obsessions
- Make it easier to resist compulsions
- Improve mood if depression is present
- Reduce overall OCD symptom severity

What medication CAN'T do:

- Cure OCD completely (it's a management tool, not a cure)
- Teach you skills for managing OCD (that's therapy's job)
- Work immediately (it takes weeks)
- Work for everyone (some people don't respond to medication)
- Eliminate all symptoms (most people still have some symptoms, just reduced)

Realistic expectations:

Most people on medication experience 40-60% symptom reduction. Combined with therapy, overall improvement can reach 60-80%.

That means you'll likely still have some OCD symptoms, but they'll be much more manageable. You'll spend less time on them, they'll cause less distress, and you'll function better.

Practical Guidance

Starting medication:

Week 1-2: Start at low dose. Side effects (especially nausea) are common but usually mild. Stick with it—side effects typically improve.

Week 3-4: May increase dose. Still probably not seeing benefits yet. Be patient.

Week 5-8: Starting to notice some reduction in obsessions or anxiety. Not dramatic, but noticeable.

Week 9-12: More significant improvement. Easier to resist compulsions. Better able to do exposure work.

Month 4+: Continued improvement. Reassess with doctor whether dose needs adjustment.

Taking it consistently:

SSRIs need to be taken daily to maintain steady levels in your system. Skipping doses reduces effectiveness.

Set a daily alarm if you need a reminder.

Take it at the same time each day (makes it easier to remember, and for some medications, reduces side effects).

Stopping medication (if you and your doctor decide to):

Never stop abruptly. SSRIs need gradual tapering to avoid withdrawal effects.

Typical taper: Reduce dose by 25% every 2-4 weeks, monitoring for symptoms.

If symptoms return during taper, you might need to slow the taper or return to the previous dose.

What Success Looks Like

Successful medication treatment combined with therapy:

Before treatment:

- OCD symptoms 6 hours daily
- Severe distress
- Can't work consistently
- Relationships strained
- Y-BOCS score: 28 (severe)

After 6 months of treatment (medication + ERP):

- OCD symptoms 45 minutes daily
- Manageable distress
- Working full-time
- Relationships improved
- Y-BOCS score: 12 (mild)

That's realistic improvement. Not perfection, but significant functional recovery.

Making the Decision

Whether to take medication is a personal decision made in consultation with your doctor. There's no right answer that applies to everyone.

Consider: Severity of symptoms, impact on your life, response to therapy alone, side effect tolerance, and personal preferences.

Islamic perspective: Fully permissible, islamically encouraged when medically indicated, part of tawakkul (trusting Allah while using the means He provided).

Medical perspective: Evidence-based treatment that, for many people, significantly improves quality of life when combined with therapy.

If you decide medication is right for you: Take it consistently, work with your doctor, combine it with therapy, and know that you're making a sound Islamic and medical decision.

Chapter 20: Relapse Prevention and Lifelong Recovery

You've done the work. You've learned about OCD, practiced exposures, resisted compulsions, challenged distorted thoughts, and rebuilt your relationship with worship. Maybe you've taken medication. Your symptoms have improved significantly—60%, 70%, maybe even 80% reduction.

You're functioning again. Praying without torture. Living without constant anxiety controlling your decisions.

This is recovery.

But here's something important to understand: **Recovery from OCD doesn't mean "cured." It means managed**.

OCD is typically a chronic condition. That doesn't mean you're doomed to suffer forever. It means that OCD might try to return occasionally, and you need strategies to maintain your gains and handle setbacks.

This chapter covers long-term recovery: what to expect, how to maintain progress, recognizing early warning signs, building resilience, and living a values-driven life as a Muslim in recovery.

Understanding That Recovery Is Not "Cured"

OCD is similar to conditions like asthma or diabetes—manageable but typically ongoing.

Some people experience what feels like complete recovery and never have significant symptoms again. Others have periodic flare-ups that they manage. Most fall somewhere in between.

What "recovery" actually means:

- Symptoms are significantly reduced
- You can function normally in daily life
- When OCD thoughts appear, you know how to handle them
- Compulsions are eliminated or drastically reduced
- Quality of life is restored

Notice: It doesn't necessarily mean zero OCD thoughts ever again.

Why this matters:

If you expect "cured"—meaning never having another intrusive thought or moment of OCD anxiety—you'll feel like a failure when occasional symptoms appear.

If you expect "managed"—meaning you have the skills to handle symptoms when they arise—you'll recognize that occasional bad days are normal and don't indicate failure.

Maintaining Exposure Practices

ERP works. But the gains you made need maintenance, just like physical fitness requires ongoing exercise.

Why maintenance matters:

When you stop practicing exposures entirely, old patterns can slowly creep back. Avoidance increases. Compulsions return. Anxiety escalates.

Research on OCD relapse shows that people who continue practicing exposure strategies have better long-term outcomes than those who stop all practice after treatment ends (Simpson et al., 2004).

Maintenance practice looks different from initial treatment:

During treatment: Daily exposures, multiple compulsions targeted, intensive practice

During maintenance: Weekly or bi-weekly exposures, continued response prevention, lighter practice

Maintenance schedule ideas:

Weekly OCD check-in (15 minutes):

- Review: Did any OCD urges appear this week?
- Practice: One planned exposure from your old hierarchy
- Assess: Any compulsions creeping back?

Monthly exposure practice (30-60 minutes):

- Do a moderate-difficulty exposure to keep skills sharp
- Review your values and ensure you're living according to them
- Update your hierarchy if new fears have emerged

Spontaneous practice:

When OCD triggers appear naturally in life, use them as practice opportunities.

Example: You touch a doorknob and get a contamination urge. Instead of washing immediately, you recognize it: "There's the OCD urge. I'm going to practice response prevention right now." You wait, sit with the anxiety, resist the washing compulsion.

This keeps your skills sharp.

Early Warning Signs

Relapse doesn't usually happen suddenly. There are warning signs that OCD is starting to creep back.

Early warning signs:

Behavioral signs:

- Spending more time on religious rituals than usual
- Avoiding situations you'd been handling well
- Seeking reassurance more frequently
- Compulsions returning in subtle ways

Cognitive signs:

- Increased doubt and uncertainty
- More "what if" thinking
- Less tolerance for ambiguity
- Perfectionist thinking increasing

Emotional signs:

- More anxiety around worship
- Increased irritability
- Feeling overwhelmed by religious obligations
- Loss of peace in spiritual practice

Time-based warning: If you're spending more than 90-120 minutes daily on all religious practices combined (5 prayers, wudu, Quran, dhikr), something might be drifting toward OCD territory again.

What to do when you notice warning signs:

1. Acknowledge it early

"I'm noticing some OCD patterns returning. I'm catching this early, which is good."

2. Return to basics

Pull out your old exposure hierarchy. Start practicing again, starting with moderate-level exposures.

3. Identify triggers

What changed? Increased stress? Life transition? Ramadan or Hajj season?

Understanding triggers helps you address them.

4. Recommit to response prevention

Pick the compulsion that's creeping back and target it specifically.

5. Reach out for support

Talk to your therapist (if you still see one). Discuss with family. Get accountability.

6. Don't catastrophize

"This is a warning sign, not a relapse. I caught it early. I have the skills to handle this."

Booster Sessions

Many people benefit from occasional "booster" therapy sessions—returning to their OCD therapist periodically even after treatment ends.

When booster sessions help:

- When you notice warning signs
- During high-risk periods (major life stress, transitions, religious seasons)
- When a new OCD theme emerges
- When you're feeling stuck and need guidance

How booster sessions work:

You schedule one or a few sessions with your therapist to:

- Review what's happening
- Identify what's drifted
- Create a plan to get back on track
- Practice exposures with therapist support

This isn't a sign of failure. It's smart maintenance.

Think of it like going to the dentist for a cleaning even though you brush daily. Regular maintenance prevents bigger problems.

Building Resilience

Resilience is your ability to handle stress, adversity, and challenges without falling back into unhealthy patterns.

Building resilience for OCD recovery:

1. Maintain healthy lifestyle basics

Physical health affects mental health:

- Adequate sleep (7-9 hours)
- Regular physical activity
- Nutritious diet
- Limited caffeine (can increase anxiety)

2. Stress management

OCD flare-ups often happen during stress. Build stress management skills:

- Deep breathing exercises
- Mindfulness practices
- Time management to reduce overwhelm
- Saying no to excessive commitments

3. Strong social connections

Isolation feeds OCD. Connection combats it.

Maintain relationships. Attend mosque. Participate in community. Don't withdraw.

4. Spiritual practices that nourish

Not compulsive religious practice—genuine spiritual connection.

- Quran recitation for reflection, not compulsion
- Dua from the heart
- Dhikr that brings peace
- Islamic study for growth, not anxiety

5. Continued learning

Keep learning about OCD, mental health, and Islamic perspectives on wellbeing.

6. Purpose and meaning

Engage in activities that give your life meaning beyond managing OCD:

- Work or career development
- Family relationships
- Community service
- Creative pursuits
- Learning and growth

Keeping Faith and Treatment in Balance

As a Muslim in recovery from religious OCD, you face a unique challenge: how to practice Islam genuinely without triggering OCD patterns.

The balance:

Islam requires: Regular prayer, basic cleanliness, sincere worship, moral awareness

OCD demands: Impossible certainty, excessive rituals, constant anxiety, rigid perfection

Your job: Follow Islamic requirements while resisting OCD demands

Practical balance strategies:

1. Follow minimum requirements, not maximums

Know what Islam actually requires (you learned this in earlier chapters). Do that. Don't add excessive "just to be safe" practices.

2. One-time rule continues

Prayer once. Wudu once. Not repeating based on doubt.

This remains your long-term practice.

3. Time awareness

If religious practice starts consuming excessive time again, that's a warning sign.

4. Peace as a metric

Healthy worship brings peace. OCD brings anxiety.

If your practice is creating anxiety, investigate whether OCD is creeping back.

5. Community as anchor

Observe how other Muslims practice. If your practice is dramatically different (much more time-consuming, much more anxious), that's information.

6. Islamic guidance remains

Continue consulting knowledgeable scholars for genuine questions. Just resist using it for reassurance.

Your New Relationship with Uncertainty

One of the biggest shifts in recovery is learning to live with uncertainty.

Before recovery, OCD convinced you that uncertainty was intolerable. You needed to know for sure. You couldn't move forward without guarantees.

After recovery, you understand: **Uncertainty is part of being human. You can live well despite it**.

Areas of uncertainty you've learned to tolerate:

Religious uncertainty:

- "I'm not 100% certain my wudu was microscopically perfect, and that's okay."
- "I don't know with absolute certainty that my prayer was valid, and I'm moving forward anyway."
- "I might have had an unintentional sin today, and I trust Allah's mercy."

Moral uncertainty:

- "I'm not sure if that action was completely right, but I made my best judgment."
- "My intentions might have been slightly mixed, and Allah knows my heart."

Existential uncertainty:

- "I can't achieve perfect certainty about my faith state, but I'm choosing to live as a Muslim."

This doesn't mean you don't care. It means you recognize that human beings can't achieve perfect certainty, and Allah doesn't require it.

Living with uncertainty is an act of tawakkul—trusting Allah when you can't control or verify everything.

Living a Values-Driven Life as a Muslim in Recovery

OCD tried to make your life about avoiding anxiety. Recovery is about making your life about your values.

What kind of Muslim do you want to be?

Not: "A Muslim who spends six hours daily on rituals to achieve impossible certainty."

But: "A Muslim who prays sincerely, treats people well, serves community, grows in knowledge, and maintains connection with Allah."

Values-based living:

In worship: Value: Sincere connection with Allah through prayer Action: Pray five times daily, once per prayer, with focus on sincerity rather than ritual perfection

In relationships: Value: Being present and kind to family Action: Spend quality time with spouse and children instead of being consumed by OCD rituals

In community: Value: Contributing to Muslim community Action: Attend mosque, participate in service, connect with others

In personal growth: Value: Continuous learning and development Action: Study Islam for growth, pursue career or education goals, develop skills

In character: Value: Embodying Islamic virtues (patience, kindness, honesty, humility) Action: Practice these in daily interactions

Daily values check:

Each evening, ask yourself:

- Did I live according to my values today?
- Did I let OCD pull me away from what matters?
- What's one thing I did today that reflects the Muslim I want to be?

When you're living according to values, OCD has less room to operate.

What Long-Term Recovery Looks Like

Let's paint a picture of what sustainable recovery looks like:

Yusuf, five years post-treatment:

Yusuf had severe religious OCD. At his worst, he spent 8 hours daily on rituals, couldn't work, was isolated, and suicidal.

After treatment (12 months of ERP + medication), he improved significantly.

Five years later:

Yusuf prays five times daily, approximately 10-15 minutes per prayer including wudu. No repetitions.

Occasionally (maybe once a month), an intrusive blasphemous thought appears. He notices it, doesn't engage, moves on. Minimal distress.

Every few months, usually during stress, he notices an urge to repeat wudu. He recognizes it: "There's the OCD urge." He resists, sits with brief anxiety, it passes.

He attends mosque weekly. He has a job. He got married. He volunteers with youth programs.

He still sees his therapist once or twice a year for "tune-up" sessions when he notices patterns creeping back.

He's on a low dose of SSRI, which he and his doctor decided to continue long-term. It helps, has minimal side effects, so he's comfortable staying on it.

Is Yusuf "cured"? No. He still has OCD. It's just managed.

Is Yusuf living well? Absolutely. He's functional, happy, contributing, practicing Islam in a healthy way.

That's what long-term recovery looks like for many people.

The Freedom You've Gained

Think about where you started. The hours consumed by rituals. The torture that worship had become. The isolation. The despair.

Think about where you are now. Able to pray without repeating 20 times. Able to do wudu in a few minutes. Able to live despite uncertainty. Able to practice Islam with peace rather than panic.

This is freedom.

Not freedom from Islam (OCD tried to make you think you had to choose between recovery and faith).

Freedom to practice Islam the way it's meant to be practiced—with ease, mercy, sincerity, and genuine connection to Allah.

Freedom to live according to your values instead of being controlled by anxiety.

Freedom to engage with community, build relationships, pursue goals, and grow.

Your Ongoing Commitment

Long-term recovery requires ongoing commitment:

To maintenance: Keep practicing skills, even when symptoms are low.

To awareness: Notice early warning signs, address them quickly.

To balance: Practice Islam according to Islamic requirements, not OCD demands.

To values: Live according to what matters, not according to what anxiety dictates.

To self-compassion: Some days will be harder. That's okay. Be kind to yourself.

To seeking support: Reach out when you need help. Don't try to do it all alone.

To trust: Trust Allah's mercy. Trust the process. Trust that you can handle uncertainty.

OCD might try to return occasionally. When it does, you'll know what to do. You've learned the skills. You've walked the path. You can walk it again if needed.

But more often, you'll simply be living—praying, working, connecting, growing, serving. Living the life that OCD tried to steal from you.

You've reclaimed your worship. You've reclaimed your life. You've reclaimed your peace.

The path forward is maintenance, awareness, and continued growth. Not perfection. Not a struggle-free existence. But a life lived according to values, with skills to manage challenges, and with faith that Allah is with you in the journey.

This is recovery. This is freedom. This is yours to maintain.

Chapter 21: OCD in Muslim Youth and Children

Your eleven-year-old daughter asks you forty times a day if her prayers are valid. Your teenage son spends an hour on wudu before each prayer. Your eight-year-old is terrified he's committing shirk because of thoughts he doesn't want.

OCD in children and adolescents looks different from adult OCD—they might not have the language to describe what's happening, they depend on adults for help, and their developing understanding of Islam can make religious OCD particularly confusing.

This chapter addresses OCD in Muslim youth: how to recognize it, how treatment differs for children, how to work with parents, what schools need to know, and how to provide Islamic education that doesn't trigger OCD.

Because early intervention matters. Research shows that OCD typically begins in childhood or adolescence—average age of onset is around 10 years old (Geller et al., 1998). The earlier you recognize and treat it, the better the long-term outcome.

Recognizing OCD in Young Muslims

Children with OCD often can't articulate what's happening. They might not say "I'm having intrusive thoughts about committing shirk." They might just seem anxious, oppositional, or excessively religious.

How OCD appears in Muslim children:

Behavioral signs:

- Spending excessive time on religious rituals (wudu, prayer)
- Asking repeated questions about whether they did something right
- Needing constant reassurance from parents about religious matters
- Avoiding religious activities (too anxious to pray or read Quran)
- Excessive confessing of minor "sins"
- Ritualized behaviors (touching things in specific order, repeating actions)

Emotional signs:

- Severe anxiety around religious practice
- Crying before or during prayer
- Panic when unable to complete rituals "perfectly"

- Fear of divine punishment out of proportion to age
- Distress that seems excessive for minor mistakes

Age-specific presentations:

Young children (ages 6-10):

- Concrete, literal fears ("If I step on the prayer mat wrong, Allah will be angry")
- Visible compulsions (repeated washing, touching, arranging)
- Involving family members in rituals
- Meltdowns when rituals are interrupted

Pre-teens and teens (ages 11-17):

- More cognitive/mental compulsions
- Blasphemous intrusive thoughts causing severe distress
- Excessive moral scrupulosity
- Conflict between OCD and normal teenage development (wanting independence vs. OCD dependence)

Example: Recognizing the Signs

Ten-year-old Aaliyah had always been a good student who prayed regularly. Then her parents noticed changes:

She started spending 30-40 minutes on wudu before each prayer. She'd ask her mother multiple times: "Did I do it right? Are you sure?" She'd cry if interrupted during prayer. She started avoiding Friday school because Quran class made her anxious—she was terrified of mispronouncing words.

Her parents thought maybe she was just being very careful about her religion. But when she started missing school because she couldn't finish morning prayer in time, they realized something was wrong.

This is OCD, not devotion.

Developmentally Appropriate Treatment

Treatment for children needs to be modified based on developmental level. You can't use adult protocols with a seven-year-old.

Family-Based Treatment

For children with OCD, treatment almost always involves parents. Research shows that family-based cognitive-behavioral therapy is highly effective for pediatric OCD (Freeman et al., 2014).

Parents participate in:

- Learning about OCD
- Understanding exposure and response prevention
- Helping child practice exposures
- Reducing accommodation
- Managing their own anxiety

Age-Adapted ERP:

For young children (6-10):

Make it concrete and playful:

- **"Bossing back OCD"**: Frame treatment as standing up to the "OCD bully"
- **Exposure as games**: "Let's race to see if you can do wudu in 5 minutes!"
- **Visual rewards**: Sticker charts for resisting compulsions
- **Simplified language**: Don't use technical terms; use kid language

Example: Instead of "We're going to practice uncertainty tolerance," say "We're going to teach your brain that it's okay to not be 100% sure."

For pre-teens and teens (11-17):

More independence, more cognitive:

- **Cognitive restructuring**: They can understand challenging OCD thoughts
- **Self-directed practice**: With parent support, but increasing independence
- **Peer considerations**: Recognize that OCD affects social life, school, friendships
- **Respecting autonomy**: Involve them in treatment planning

Exposure Hierarchy for Children:

Create age-appropriate hierarchies. For a child with wudu OCD:

Level 1: Wudu in 10 minutes (from current 30 minutes) Level 2: Wudu in 7 minutes Level 3: Wudu in 5 minutes Level 4: Do wudu with parent watching (no reassurance provided) Level 5: Do wudu once and don't ask parent if it was correct Level 6: Have a thought during wudu and don't start over

Practice these with parent support, celebrate small wins, adjust difficulty based on child's response.

Medication Considerations for Children:

SSRIs are FDA-approved for pediatric OCD (ages 7-17 for most). Research shows they're safe and effective when prescribed appropriately (Geller et al., 2003).

When to consider medication for children:

- Severe OCD that's significantly impairing functioning
- OCD that hasn't responded adequately to therapy alone
- Presence of other conditions (depression, severe anxiety)

Parental concerns about medication:

Parents often worry about giving psychiatric medication to children. This is understandable.

What helps: Education about how SSRIs work, understanding risks vs. benefits, starting with therapy first when possible, knowing that many children need medication temporarily and can taper off after learning ERP skills.

Working with Parents

Parents play a huge role in both maintaining and treating childhood OCD.

Common parent mistakes (with good intentions):

1. Accommodation

Participating in child's rituals, providing excessive reassurance, modifying family routines around OCD.

"Is my wudu okay, Mama?"

Accommodating parent: "Yes, habibti, it's fine. I saw you do it." (Answering the question reinforces the reassurance-seeking)

Non-accommodating parent: "That sounds like an OCD question. I'm not going to answer because answering makes your OCD stronger."

2. Punishment

Getting angry at the child for OCD behaviors, punishing them for compulsions, shaming them for being "too slow" or "too anxious."

This doesn't help. OCD isn't a choice. Punishment increases shame and anxiety, which worsens OCD.

3. Over-involvement

Hovering, trying to prevent any distress, not letting child face appropriate challenges.

Recovery requires children to experience and tolerate discomfort. Parents need to support this, not prevent it.

What parents need to do:

Educate themselves: Read about OCD, attend therapy sessions, understand the treatment model.

Reduce accommodation gradually: Work with therapist to identify accommodations and systematically reduce them.

Support exposure practice: Encourage child during exposures, don't rescue them from discomfort.

Manage their own anxiety: Parents' anxiety affects children. If you're panicking about your child's OCD, get your own support.

Celebrate effort, not perfection: "You did wudu in 7 minutes today even though you felt anxious. That took courage!"

Collaborate with therapist: Regular parent sessions, consistent approach between home and therapy.

Example: Parent Training

Mahmoud's parents participated in family-based OCD treatment for his contamination fears.

Old pattern: Mahmoud: "Did I touch najis? Check my hands!" Parents: (examining his hands) "No, you're clean." Mahmoud: (5 minutes later) "But are you sure?" Parents: "Yes, we're sure."

This happened dozens of times daily. They were exhausted.

New pattern after training: Mahmoud: "Did I touch najis?" Parents: "That's an OCD question. We're not going to answer. You can handle this uncertainty." Mahmoud: (anxious, upset) Parents: "I know this is hard. You're learning to manage the OCD. We believe in you."

First week: Brutal. Mahmoud was angry, begging for reassurance.

Week 3: Asking less frequently.

Week 8: Rarely asking. Learning to sit with uncertainty on his own.

School Accommodations

OCD affects school functioning. Children might be late, miss days, have trouble concentrating, or need specific supports.

How OCD impacts school:

- **Tardiness**: Can't finish morning prayer/wudu in time
- **Absences**: OCD too severe to get out the door
- **Academic problems**: Can't concentrate, spends class time on mental compulsions
- **Social isolation**: Avoids peers due to contamination fears or embarrassment about OCD
- **Bathroom issues**: Excessive time in bathroom due to contamination/purity OCD

School accommodations that help:

Under the Individuals with Disabilities Education Act (IDEA) or Section 504, children with OCD can receive accommodations.

Possible accommodations:

For tardiness: Flexible start time while working on OCD treatment

For assignments: Extended time on tests (if OCD involves checking compulsions that slow work)

For bathroom: Access to bathroom without time limits (while working with therapist to reduce bathroom rituals)

For anxiety: Ability to take breaks, access to counselor

For religious practice: If school has designated prayer space, clear understanding that child is practicing praying once (not repeatedly)

Working with school staff:

Schools need basic OCD education:

What teachers should know:

- OCD is a medical condition, not misbehavior
- The child can't just "stop" the behaviors
- Accommodation should be balanced with encouraging independence
- Punishment for OCD behaviors doesn't help

What teachers should NOT do:

- Provide reassurance ("Yes, you did that correctly")
- Allow unlimited time for compulsions
- Shame or punish the child for OCD symptoms

Example: School Collaboration

Nadia, age 13, had scrupulosity OCD affecting school. She'd spend 20 minutes checking that she hadn't accidentally written anything blasphemous. She missed portions of classes.

Her parents and therapist met with school:

504 Plan created:

- Teachers informed about OCD (with parent permission)
- Extended time on writing assignments (while she worked on reducing checking in therapy)
- Access to counselor if anxiety escalated
- Check-in meetings every month to assess progress

School's role:

- Teacher noticed when Nadia was checking excessively: "Nadia, I see you checking. Remember you're working on doing assignments once. I need you to turn in what you have."
- Not harsh, but not accommodating the compulsion indefinitely

Result: With therapy, medication, and school support, Nadia's symptoms improved. School accommodations gradually reduced as she needed them less.

Age-Appropriate Islamic Education Without Triggering OCD

Children need Islamic education. But for kids with religious OCD, Islamic education can either help or harm, depending on how it's presented.

Principles for OCD-aware Islamic education:

1. Emphasize mercy over fear

Don't say: "If you don't pray, you'll go to Jahannam!"

Do say: "Allah is the Most Merciful. He loves when we pray because it brings us close to Him."

2. Focus on effort, not perfection

Don't say: "Your prayer must be absolutely perfect or Allah won't accept it."

Do say: "When you pray sincerely and try your best, Allah accepts it. He knows your heart."

3. Keep requirements simple and clear

Don't overwhelm with details. Teach the minimum requirements, then mention recommended practices separately.

"To do wudu, you need to [basic requirements]. That's what's required. Some people also like to [recommended practices], but those are extra, not required."

4. Normalize mistakes

"Everyone makes mistakes in prayer sometimes. That's okay. Allah knows we're human."

5. Avoid catastrophic language

Don't say: "This is the worst sin! Allah will punish you severely!"

Do say: "This action isn't good, and we should avoid it. If we make a mistake, we can seek forgiveness."

6. Balance rules with relationship

Islamic education shouldn't be just lists of rules. It should cultivate relationship with Allah.

Talk about Allah's love, mercy, beauty. Tell stories of the Prophet's (peace be upon him) kindness. Emphasize that Islam is about connection, not just rules.

For children with OCD specifically:

If you know a child has OCD, coordinate with parents and therapist:

In Islamic school/weekend school:

- Teacher knows child has OCD
- Teacher emphasizes principles that counter OCD (mercy, ease, acceptance of human limitation)
- Teacher doesn't provide reassurance to OCD questions
- Focus on practical, manageable religious practice

Example: OCD-Aware Teaching

Weekend Islamic school teacher noticed 9-year-old Kareem constantly raising his hand with anxious questions:

"What if I accidentally thought something bad during prayer?" "What if I forgot to say something in wudu?" "If I'm not sure if I did Fajr, should I pray it again?"

The teacher, who'd been trained on OCD, responded:

"Kareem, those sound like OCD questions. I know your brain makes you very worried about these things. But the answer is: Islam is easy, not hard. Allah is merciful. You don't need perfect certainty. I'm not going to keep answering these questions because that would make your OCD stronger. Let's talk to your parents about making sure you're getting the help you need."

Then the teacher called Kareem's parents, who connected with a child OCD therapist.

When to Seek Professional Help for Children

Parents sometimes wait too long, thinking "they'll grow out of it" or "it's just a phase."

Seek evaluation if:

- Religious practices take significantly longer than peers (other kids do wudu in 2 minutes; your child takes 30)
- Severe distress around religious activities
- Functioning is impaired (missing school, can't complete homework, no social activities)
- Asking reassurance questions constantly
- Behavior has persisted for months and is worsening

Where to find help:

- Child psychologists or psychiatrists specializing in OCD
- Pediatric OCD clinics (often found at university medical centers)
- International OCD Foundation has resources for finding child specialists

Starting earlier is better: Research shows that children who receive treatment early often have better outcomes (Piacentini et al., 2011).

Growing Up with OCD

For children and teens with OCD, the disorder affects normal developmental milestones.

Teens developing independence: OCD might make them more dependent on parents (needing reassurance, accommodation).

Treatment helps them build actual independence—learning to manage anxiety, make decisions despite uncertainty, function without constant parental involvement.

Social development: OCD can isolate kids—too anxious to go to friends' houses, can't participate in sleepovers or trips.

Treatment helps them engage normally with peers.

Identity formation: Teens are figuring out who they are. If OCD dominates their identity, that's problematic.

Treatment helps them separate "I have OCD" from "I am my OCD." They can be Muslim teens with interests, goals, friendships—who happen to also manage OCD.

Hope for the future:

Children who get effective treatment can go on to live normal, fulfilling lives. Many adults who had childhood OCD barely think about it years later because they learned skills to manage it.

Your child isn't doomed. Early intervention, good treatment, family support—these give them the tools they need.

Chapter 22: Women-Specific Issues

Women's bodies change—monthly cycles, pregnancy, postpartum, breastfeeding, menopause. For women with OCD, these changes can trigger or worsen symptoms in specific ways.

Add Islamic practices around menstruation, modesty, and family roles, and you have gender-specific presentations of OCD that need targeted approaches.

This chapter addresses OCD issues specific to Muslim women: menstruation-related OCD, pregnancy and postpartum concerns, modesty-related compulsions, and gender considerations in treatment.

Menstruation-Related OCD

We touched on this in Chapter 13, but let's go deeper because it's so common in Muslim women with OCD.

Islamic rules meet OCD anxiety:

Islam has clear guidelines: During menstruation, women don't pray or fast. When menstruation ends, they perform ghusl and resume normal practice.

For most women, this is straightforward. For women with OCD, it becomes a nightmare of checking, uncertainty, and anxiety.

Common obsessions:

- "Has my period actually ended?"
- "Is that spotting or is it still menstruation?"
- "What if I'm praying while still menstruating and all my prayers don't count?"
- "Did I perform ghusl correctly after my period?"

Common compulsions:

- Checking for blood every 15-30 minutes
- Delaying ghusl and prayer resumption by days "just to be sure"
- Performing ghusl multiple times
- Seeking constant reassurance from other women or scholars

The biological component:

Here's something interesting: OCD symptoms can actually worsen during certain parts of the menstrual cycle. Research shows that some women experience increased OCD symptoms premenstrually due to hormonal fluctuations (Labad et al., 2005).

So you might notice your OCD symptoms (not just menstruation-related, but all OCD symptoms) get worse in the week before your period. That's biological, not imaginary.

Treatment approach:

Fiqh education: Understanding your madhab's rulings clearly.

Most schools of thought say menstruation has ended when you see one of two signs:

- Complete stoppage of bleeding
- White discharge (*qassa bayda*)

Once you see the sign your madhab recognizes, menstruation is over. You don't need to investigate internally. You don't need 100% certainty that no blood will ever appear again.

Exposure hierarchy:

Level 1: Check for blood only twice daily (morning, evening) instead of constantly
Level 2: When you see the sign of menstruation ending, wait only one more prayer time before doing ghusl (instead of days) Level 3: Perform ghusl once, resume prayer Level 4: If minor spotting appears after you've resumed prayer, continue praying (spotting after end of menstruation doesn't require stopping prayer according to most scholars) Level 5: Don't seek reassurance from others about whether your period has ended

Practice example:

Mariam would check for blood every 20 minutes during her period and for 5-7 days after it appeared to end. She'd perform ghusl 3-4 times before feeling "safe" to pray.

ERP protocol:

Week 1-2: Check only 3 times daily Week 3-4: When white discharge appeared (her madhab's sign), do ghusl the next morning (not days later) Week 5-6: Do ghusl once only Week 7-8: Resume prayer immediately after ghusl, don't wait extra days

By month 3, Mariam was managing menstruation normally—checking twice daily, doing ghusl once when her period ended, resuming prayer. Still some anxiety, but manageable.

Pregnancy and Postpartum OCD

Pregnancy and postpartum periods are high-risk times for OCD onset or worsening.

Perinatal OCD (during pregnancy and first year postpartum) affects an estimated 2-3% of pregnant women and new mothers (Russell et al., 2013).

Why pregnancy/postpartum triggers OCD:

- Hormonal changes
- Sleep deprivation
- Stress of new responsibility
- Fears about baby's safety

Common OCD themes in pregnancy/postpartum:

Harm obsessions: Intrusive thoughts or images of harming the baby

"What if I drop the baby? What if I accidentally hurt him while bathing him? What if I have an urge to do something terrible?"

These thoughts horrify the mother experiencing them. They're terrifying because she loves her baby—not because she wants to harm the baby.

Contamination obsessions: Fear that baby will be contaminated by germs, najis, or harmful substances

Excessive sterilization of bottles, refusing to let anyone touch baby, washing baby excessively, avoiding certain places or people.

Checking compulsions: Constant checking to ensure baby is breathing, safe, okay

Getting up every 10 minutes to check sleeping baby, unable to sleep due to checking compulsions.

Islamic-specific perinatal OCD:

- Excessive concern about baby's purity status
- Anxiety about whether baby's exposure to najis affects mother's prayer validity
- Fear of performing religious practices incorrectly while caring for baby

Treatment considerations for pregnant/postpartum women:

Therapy is first-line: ERP is safe during pregnancy and postpartum. No risks to baby.

Medication considerations:

If symptoms are severe, medication might be needed. SSRIs during pregnancy involve weighing risks and benefits with your doctor (Vasiliadis et al., 2015).

Some SSRIs have more safety data during pregnancy than others. This is a decision made with your OB-GYN and psychiatrist.

For breastfeeding mothers, some SSRIs pass into breast milk in minimal amounts. Again, risk-benefit discussion with doctors.

Practical support:

New mothers need practical help—family support, rest, childcare assistance. Sleep deprivation worsens all mental health conditions.

Distinguishing OCD from postpartum psychosis:

OCD involves unwanted thoughts that distress the person. She knows the thoughts are wrong and doesn't want to act on them.

Postpartum psychosis (rare but serious) involves delusions, hallucinations, disorganized behavior. The person might actually believe the thoughts or have lost touch with reality.

If there's any concern about psychosis, immediate psychiatric evaluation is needed.

Modesty-Related Compulsions

Islamic guidelines on modesty (hijab, appropriate clothing, lowering gaze) are meant to bring dignity and spiritual consciousness. For women with OCD, they can become sources of compulsion.

Common presentations:

Hijab checking: Constantly checking mirror to ensure no hair is showing, readjusting hijab every few minutes, becoming paralyzed with anxiety if a strand of hair escapes.

Clothing rituals: Changing clothes multiple times to ensure modesty standards, excessive checking of whether clothing is "tight" or "revealing," avoiding certain colors or styles excessively.

Gaze compulsions: Elaborate mental rituals after accidentally seeing something inappropriate, excessive avoidance of situations where men might be present, anxiety about whether lowering gaze was done correctly.

Body contamination: Feeling "contaminated" if touched by non-mahram (someone you could marry), excessive washing after handshakes or accidental contact.

Treatment approach:

Clarify Islamic requirements: Hijab has basic requirements (covering specific areas). Minor imperfections (small piece of hair showing momentarily) don't violate hijab.

Exposure hierarchy for hijab OCD:

Level 1: Check mirror only twice when putting on hijab (instead of constantly) Level 2: Wear hijab all day without mirror-checking Level 3: Don't readjust hijab every few minutes Level 4: If a piece of hair shows accidentally, fix it once and move on (don't obsess)

Balance: You can maintain Islamic modesty standards while reducing compulsive behaviors.

Wearing hijab properly according to your understanding: Islamic practice.

Checking mirror 50 times daily, becoming paralyzed with anxiety, missing work because your hijab doesn't feel "right": OCD.

Gender-Specific Treatment Considerations

Finding female Muslim therapists:

Some women prefer female therapists, especially when discussing topics like menstruation, sexuality, or modesty.

Muslim mental health organizations may have female therapists. Ask for recommendations from community organizations.

Cultural considerations:

In some cultures, women need family permission to seek therapy. Work within cultural context while still pursuing treatment.

Family dynamics:

Women often carry primary responsibility for children and household. This can affect treatment:

- Less time available for therapy appointments or exposure practice
- Family accommodation patterns might be more entrenched
- Women might prioritize family needs over their own treatment

What helps: Family therapy to get everyone supporting treatment, practical support (childcare during therapy sessions), recognizing that treating mother's OCD benefits the whole family.

Reproductive health discussions:

Female patients need therapists comfortable discussing menstruation, pregnancy, postpartum issues, sexual concerns.

If male therapist, some topics might be harder to discuss. Having a female therapist who understands both Islam and OCD can be ideal when available.

Spousal involvement:

Husbands can be great supports or significant obstacles, depending on their understanding.

Education for husbands: OCD is a medical condition. Stopping accommodation helps, not hurts. Treatment is islamically encouraged.

Example: Comprehensive treatment:

Khadija, 28, married with two young children, had contamination OCD and menstruation-related OCD.

Barriers: Husband didn't understand OCD, thought she just needed to "pray more." Extended family said she was "too sensitive." She had little time for herself.

Treatment approach:

1. Psychoeducation for husband (he attended sessions, learned OCD basics)
2. Family support arranged (mother-in-law watched kids during therapy)
3. Started medication (SSRI safe for breastfeeding)
4. Individual therapy addressing both contamination and menstruation OCD
5. Couples sessions addressing relationship dynamics affected by OCD

Result: After 6 months, significant improvement. Husband became supportive ally. Family understood it was medical, not spiritual weakness. Khadija functioning well.

Chapter 23: Marriage and Relationships with OCD

OCD doesn't just affect the individual—it affects relationships. For Muslim individuals with OCD, marriage and romantic relationships present specific challenges and questions.

When do you disclose OCD to a potential spouse? How do you maintain intimacy when contamination fears create barriers? What if OCD makes you doubt your marriage constantly?

This chapter addresses OCD in Muslim marriage and relationships.

Relationship OCD (ROCD) in Muslim Context

ROCD involves obsessive doubts about romantic relationships and partners.

Common obsessions:

- "Do I really love my spouse?"
- "Is this the person Allah intended for me?"
- "What if I married the wrong person?"
- "What if there's someone better out there?"
- "Am I only staying because of social pressure, not real love?"

Common compulsions:

- Constantly testing feelings for spouse
- Comparing spouse to others
- Seeking reassurance from family/friends
- Mentally reviewing relationship history
- Researching "how to know if you're really in love"

The cruel irony: People with ROCD often love their partners deeply. The disorder creates doubt about something they value most.

Cultural factors in Muslim ROCD:

Arranged/assisted marriages: Some Muslims have marriages arranged by family or introduced through community. ROCD might latch onto this: "I didn't choose my spouse myself, so maybe this isn't real love."

High divorce stigma: In some communities, divorce carries significant social stigma. This can make ROCD worse—"I can't leave even if these doubts mean something!"

Concept of "THE ONE": If you believe Allah has one perfect match for you, ROCD exploits this: "What if my spouse isn't THE ONE Allah chose?"

Islamic reality: Islam doesn't teach that there's one predestined soulmate. Marriage is a choice, an effort, and a commitment. Having doubts doesn't invalidate the marriage.

Treatment for ROCD:

Cognitive reframes:

OCD thought: "If I'm not 100% certain I love my spouse every moment, the marriage is wrong."

Reality: "Love is a choice and action, not just a feeling. Feelings fluctuate. Commitment matters more than constant certainty."

Exposure practice:

- Sit with uncertainty about feelings without testing them
- Resist comparing spouse to others
- Don't seek reassurance
- Act loving even when feeling uncertain

Example ERP: Spend quality time with spouse despite doubts being present, without asking "Do you think I really love him?"

Couples therapy: If ROCD is affecting the marriage, couples therapy alongside individual OCD treatment can help.

Communication with Spouse

OCD affects marriage dynamics. Communication is critical.

What to tell your spouse:

Educate about OCD: "I have a condition called OCD. It's not about you—it's a medical condition that makes me anxious and causes compulsive behaviors."

Explain specific symptoms: "When I ask if you're sure you locked the door, that's a reassurance-seeking compulsion. It helps me short-term but makes the OCD stronger long-term."

Ask for specific support: "I need you to not answer my reassurance questions. I know that seems mean, but it's actually the most helpful thing you can do."

What not to do:

Don't blame spouse for your OCD.

Don't expect spouse to become your therapist.

Don't use OCD as an excuse for not working on recovery.

Healthy communication pattern:

"I'm having a lot of anxiety about contamination right now. My OCD is telling me I need you to check if the doorknobs are clean. But I know that would be seeking reassurance, which makes OCD worse. Can you just remind me that I'm working on tolerating this uncertainty?"

Spouse: "I know this is hard. You're doing great working on your OCD. I'm not going to check the doorknobs. You can handle this."

Sexual Relationship Concerns

OCD can interfere with sexual intimacy in marriage.

Common OCD-related sexual concerns:

Contamination fears: Fear that sexual fluids are najis, excessive washing before/after intimacy, inability to relax due to contamination anxiety.

Intrusive thoughts: Disturbing sexual thoughts or images appearing during intimacy, causing shame and avoidance.

Scrupulosity: Excessive concern about whether certain acts are halal, obsessive research about Islamic sexual rulings, inability to enjoy intimacy due to religious anxiety.

Perfectionism: Need for sex to be "perfect," inability to be present due to mental rituals.

ROCD: Doubts about attraction to spouse interfering with desire.

Impact on marriage:

Sexual intimacy is an important part of Islamic marriage. When OCD interferes, both partners suffer.

Treatment approach:

Address OCD symptoms specifically:

For contamination fears: Gradual exposure to tolerating normal sexual fluids without excessive washing.

For intrusive thoughts: Same principles as other intrusive thoughts—notice, don't engage, continue.

For scrupulosity: Get clear Islamic guidance once, then resist compulsive research.

Couples therapy: Sometimes needed to address how OCD has affected sexual relationship.

Medical consultation: Rule out any physical issues (sometimes anxiety manifests physically).

Example:

Sara had contamination OCD that made sexual intimacy with her husband anxious. She'd shower for an hour afterward, couldn't relax during sex, avoided it when possible.

Treatment: Gradual exposure to reducing shower time (from 60 minutes to 40, to 20, to 10). Practicing sitting with anxiety after intimacy instead of immediately showering. Education about Islamic rulings (sexual fluids between spouses aren't najis in the way that creates ritual impurity for prayer).

After 3 months of treatment, Sara could engage in intimacy without severe anxiety, shower normally afterward, and was enjoying her marriage more.

When to Disclose OCD in Marriage Search

For single Muslims searching for marriage, a question arises: When and how do you tell a potential spouse about OCD?

Should you disclose?

Yes. Eventually. OCD is a significant health condition that affects daily life and relationships. Hiding it isn't fair to yourself or a potential spouse.

When to disclose:

Not on the first meeting: You're getting to know each other. No need to disclose immediately.

Before engagement: Once you're seriously considering this person, disclose. They deserve to know before making a commitment.

How to disclose:

Be honest but not overwhelming: "I want you to know that I have a condition called OCD. It's a medical condition that I'm treating with therapy and medication. It causes me to have certain anxious thoughts and behaviors, but I'm managing it well."

Provide education: Offer resources if they want to learn more.

Emphasize treatment: "I'm working with a therapist and I'm committed to managing this."

Be prepared for questions: They might want to know how it affects daily life, whether it runs in families, what the prognosis is.

Possible responses:

Best case: "Thanks for telling me. I appreciate your honesty. Let me learn more about this."

Middle case: "I don't know much about OCD. Can you help me understand?"

Worst case: "I don't think I can handle this."

If someone rejects you because of OCD, they weren't the right person. You want someone who can support you, not someone who sees mental health as a dealbreaker.

What if OCD is severe and untreated?

Get treatment first before actively searching for marriage. Marriage won't cure OCD. In fact, severe untreated OCD can destroy a marriage.

Get yourself to a stable, functioning state, then pursue marriage.

Couples Therapy Considerations

Sometimes both individual OCD treatment and couples therapy are needed.

When couples therapy helps:

- OCD has created significant relationship conflict
- Spouse has developed unhealthy accommodation patterns
- Communication has broken down
- Sexual intimacy is affected
- One partner is resentful or exhausted
- ROCD is present

Finding a couples therapist:

Ideally, someone who understands both OCD and Muslim marriage dynamics.

What couples therapy addresses:

- Education for both partners about OCD
- Reducing accommodation
- Improving communication
- Addressing resentments or hurt feelings
- Rebuilding intimacy
- Creating united front against OCD

Integration with individual OCD therapy:

The individual OCD therapist treats the OCD. The couples therapist addresses relationship dynamics. They can coordinate (with patient permission) to ensure consistent approach.

Example: Couples therapy success:

Ahmad had severe checking OCD. His wife Leila had accommodated for years—checking things for him, reassuring him constantly, becoming his "safety behavior."

She was exhausted and resentful. Their marriage was suffering.

Treatment plan:

- Ahmad: Individual OCD therapy (ERP)
- Couple: Couples therapy focusing on reducing Leila's accommodation, improving communication, addressing resentment

Result: As Ahmad's OCD improved and Leila stopped accommodating, their marriage improved dramatically. She felt like she got her husband back. He felt capable and independent again.

Chapter 24: Hajj and Ramadan: Managing OCD During Sacred Times

Ramadan and Hajj are intensely spiritual times for Muslims. They're also times when religious OCD can spike dramatically.

The increased religious practice, the spiritual intensity, the specific rituals—all of this can trigger or worsen religious OCD.

This chapter addresses how to manage OCD during these sacred times, how to plan ahead, and how to practice Ramadan and Hajj in spiritually meaningful ways without falling into OCD traps.

Planning for Ramadan with OCD

Ramadan involves fasting, increased prayer (tarawih), Quran recitation, and spiritual focus. For someone with religious OCD, this can be either spiritually enriching or OCD torture.

Common OCD challenges during Ramadan:

Increased rituals: More prayer means more opportunities for prayer-related OCD (repetition, perfectionism, intrusive thoughts).

Fatigue: Fasting, late nights (tarawih, qiyam), early morning (suhoor, Fajr) create sleep deprivation. Sleep deprivation worsens all mental health conditions, including OCD.

Spiritual intensity: The focus on worship and seeking Allah's mercy can trigger scrupulosity OCD.

Pre-Ramadan planning:

1. Set realistic goals

Don't try to do "perfect" Ramadan. Set manageable goals that account for your OCD.

Not: "I'll pray all optional prayers, read entire Quran, make i'tikaf, never miss tarawih..."

Instead: "I'll pray my five daily prayers and Ramadan obligations, attend tarawih when I can, read Quran daily even if just a page."

2. Establish time boundaries

If you have wudu or prayer OCD, set strict time limits during Ramadan:

- Wudu: 5 minutes maximum
- Each prayer: 15 minutes maximum for fard
- Tarawih: Attend, but don't repeat prayers compulsively

3. Identify potential triggers

- Tarawih in congregation (pressure to perform perfectly)
- Reciting Quran (perfectionism about pronunciation)
- Making dua (excessive time seeking "perfect" dua)

Plan how to handle these triggers using your ERP skills.

4. Coordinate with therapist

Have sessions planned during Ramadan. Don't take a break from therapy during this high-risk time.

5. Get Islamic guidance ahead of time

Ask your trusted imam/scholar: "What are the minimum requirements for Ramadan practice?"

Get clear answers before Ramadan so you're not seeking reassurance compulsively during the month.

Fasting and Medication

If you're taking medication for OCD (SSRIs), Ramadan raises questions.

Can you fast while taking medication?

Islamic scholars generally agree that taking necessary medication doesn't break the fast if taken at suhoor (pre-dawn) and iftar (sunset).

Most SSRIs are taken once daily. You can adjust timing to take it at suhoor or iftar.

Should you stop medication for Ramadan?

No. Don't stop psychiatric medication for Ramadan without consulting your doctor.

Suddenly stopping SSRIs can cause withdrawal symptoms and symptom relapse. This isn't healthy or necessary.

Fatwa on medication during fasting:

Contemporary scholars have ruled that swallowing pills with water during fasting hours is permissible when medically necessary. Mental health medication is medically necessary.

If you're concerned, consult a knowledgeable scholar, but most will tell you: Take your medication. Fast. Both are possible.

What if fasting worsens your OCD?

If fasting creates severe symptoms (extreme anxiety, inability to function, dangerous depression), you may need to use the Islamic exemption for those unable to fast due to illness.

Consult both your doctor and a scholar. In Islam, health takes priority.

Tarawih Prayers

Tarawih is a beautiful Ramadan practice—congregational night prayers. For someone with OCD, it can become a source of anxiety.

Common tarawih OCD challenges:

Perfectionism in recitation: If you're memorizing Quran and leading tarawih, fear of making mistakes.

Prayer repetition: Feeling you need to repeat prayers after tarawih.

Concentration anxiety: Intrusive thoughts during long prayers, followed by compulsive mental rituals.

Managing tarawih with OCD:

Attend but set limits:

If you normally attend 20 rakats of tarawih but your OCD creates severe distress, attend 8 rakats. You're still participating, just within your capacity.

Don't lead if it triggers OCD:

If leading tarawih would create severe anxiety about perfect recitation, don't volunteer to lead. Pray behind someone else.

One-time rule applies:

Pray tarawih once. Don't repeat when you get home. Don't repeat specific rakats.

Accept imperfection:

If your mind wanders during tarawih, bring focus back. Don't analyze the entire prayer afterward.

Example: Ramadan planning:

Yusuf had scrupulosity OCD. Previous Ramadans were torture—he'd repeat prayers constantly, spend hours making dua seeking perfection, become exhausted and depressed.

This Ramadan, he planned differently:

1. Met with therapist week before Ramadan, created specific plan
2. Set time limits: wudu 5 min, each prayer done once, tarawih 8 rakats
3. Took SSRI at suhoor daily
4. Asked trusted imam: "What are minimum requirements?" Got clear answers, committed to not researching further
5. Told family: "I'm managing Ramadan in a way that's healthy for my OCD. Please don't pressure me to do more."

Result: Yusuf had his best Ramadan in years. Spiritually meaningful, manageable, not consumed by OCD.

Hajj Preparation and Accommodations

Hajj is one of Islam's five pillars. For someone with OCD, the specific rituals and intense spiritual focus create challenges.

OCD challenges at Hajj:

Purity concerns: Fear of being in a state of impurity during rituals.

Ritual perfectionism: Need to perform each Hajj ritual perfectly.

Contamination in crowds: Millions of people, close contact, fear of najis.

Doubt about validity: "Did I do tawaf correctly? Did I throw the stones properly?"

Decision to go:

If your OCD is severe and untreated, consider delaying Hajj until you're in better control of symptoms.

Hajj is obligatory for those who are able. "Able" includes mental and physical health.

If attempting Hajj would create such severe OCD that you can't function, you're not yet "able" in the Islamic sense.

Get treatment first. Then go to Hajj when you're in a stable state.

If you're going to Hajj with managed OCD:

Pre-Hajj preparation:

1. Intensive treatment beforehand:

Work with therapist in months before Hajj. Practice exposures specific to Hajj (being in crowds, tolerating uncertainty about ritual performance).

2. Medication management:

If on medication, ensure you have adequate supply. Take it consistently during Hajj.

3. Islamic education:

Learn Hajj requirements clearly from one trusted source. Don't do compulsive research.

4. Set realistic expectations:

You'll feel anxious. That's okay. You don't need perfect Hajj—you need sincere Hajj.

During Hajj:

Hajj companion:

Travel with someone who knows about your OCD and can support you (not accommodate, but encourage).

One-time rule for rituals:

Do each Hajj ritual once. Don't repeat tawaf because of doubts. Don't throw stones again because you're uncertain.

Accept imperfection:

If you make a mistake in a Hajj ritual, the scholars provide guidance on what invalidates Hajj and what's correctable. Minor mistakes don't invalidate Hajj.

Focus on spiritual experience:

Hajj is about connection with Allah, not perfect ritual performance. When you're at the Kaaba, focus on dua and presence, not on analyzing if you're doing it "right."

Managing Scrupulosity During Sacred Practices

Sacred times intensify religious focus. For scrupulosity OCD, this means more triggers.

Strategies:

Predetermined time limits:

Before Ramadan/Hajj, set specific time limits for practices and commit to them.

No compulsive research:

During sacred times, resist the urge to look up fatwas compulsively. You got your Islamic guidance beforehand. Trust it.

Acceptance of uncertainty:

You won't know with 100% certainty that every act was perfect. That's okay. Allah knows your sincere intention.

Focus on heart over form:

What matters most: Sincere heart? Or perfect execution?

Islam values both, but sincere heart is primary. Your sincere effort during Ramadan/Hajj, even if imperfect, is what Allah sees.

Working with Scholars for Accommodations

If you're going to Hajj or have specific concerns about Ramadan, consult scholars ahead of time.

What to ask:

"I have OCD, a medical condition that creates excessive religious anxiety. Can you provide clear guidance on minimum requirements for [Ramadan fasting/Hajj rituals] so I can practice without my OCD interfering?"

What scholars can provide:

- Clear minimum requirements
- Permission to practice within your capacity
- Reassurance that Allah judges the heart and effort

Example:

Amina planning for Hajj consulted a scholar: "I have OCD. I'm worried I'll feel compelled to repeat tawaf multiple times because of doubts. What's the Islamic ruling if I do tawaf once and move on, even with some uncertainty?"

Scholar: "Tawaf done properly once is sufficient. Later doubts don't require repetition. In fact, constantly repeating due to doubts is not recommended in Islam. Do the ritual once with sincerity, trust Allah's acceptance, and move forward."

This gave Amina the religious framework to resist OCD compulsions during Hajj.

What You've Learned

These special topics chapters addressed specific populations and situations:

Children and teens with OCD need developmentally appropriate treatment and family involvement. Parents play a crucial role in either maintaining or treating childhood OCD.

Women face gender-specific OCD challenges around menstruation, pregnancy, modesty, and reproductive health. Treatment must address these specific concerns while respecting Islamic guidelines.

Marriage and relationships are affected by OCD, whether through ROCD, communication challenges, or sexual concerns. Open communication, education, and sometimes couples therapy help.

Sacred times like Ramadan and Hajj can either be spiritually enriching or OCD torture, depending on planning and approach. Setting realistic goals, maintaining treatment, and getting clear Islamic guidance help you practice these sacred times meaningfully without OCD taking over.

In all these situations, the principles remain the same: OCD is a medical disorder requiring treatment, Islamic practice should follow Islamic requirements (not OCD demands), and recovery is possible with appropriate support and intervention.

Appendix A: Resources

You've read the book. You understand OCD. You're ready to get help. But where do you actually find that help?

This appendix provides practical resources—organizations, professionals, books, and support systems that can help you on your recovery journey. These aren't just random listings. These are resources that actually serve Muslim communities or have demonstrated cultural competence in treating Muslim clients with OCD.

Mental Health Professionals with Islamic Cultural Competence

Finding the right therapist matters. You need someone who understands OCD treatment (specifically ERP) and who can work respectfully within an Islamic framework.

Muslim Mental Health Organizations:

Khalil Center: Muslim mental health organization with clinics in multiple cities across the United States. They provide therapy services with Islamic cultural competence and have therapists trained in OCD treatment.

Institute for Muslim Mental Health: Provides mental health services, training, and resources specifically for Muslim communities.

Naseeha Mental Health: Canadian organization offering mental health services for Muslims, including youth services.

Maristan: Mental health organization serving Muslim communities with culturally competent care.

How to Find OCD Specialists:

International OCD Foundation (IOCDF): Maintains a therapist directory searchable by location and specialty. Look for therapists who specifically list OCD and ERP expertise.

Psychology Today: Online therapist directory with filters for specialty (OCD), insurance, location, and sometimes religious/cultural background.

Anxiety and Depression Association of America (ADAA): Provides therapist search tools for anxiety and OCD specialists.

Questions to Ask Potential Therapists:

When interviewing therapists, ask:

- "Do you specialize in OCD treatment specifically?"
- "Do you use Exposure and Response Prevention (ERP)?"
- "How many OCD clients have you treated?"
- "Are you familiar with treating religious OCD or scrupulosity?"
- "Do you have experience working with Muslim clients?" (If yes, great. If no but they're willing to learn, that can work too.)

What if You Can't Find a Muslim Therapist?

A skilled OCD specialist who's not Muslim but who's culturally sensitive and willing to learn about Islamic practices can be effective. You can provide the religious context (explaining wudu, prayer requirements, etc.), while they provide the OCD treatment expertise.

Online Support Groups

OCD support groups provide connection with others who understand the struggle.

International OCD Foundation Online Support Groups: IOCDF offers online support groups for people with OCD and for family members. Some groups are age-specific or theme-specific.

Reddit Communities: Subreddits like r/OCD and r/MuslimMentalHealth provide online spaces for discussion and support. (Remember: Reddit provides peer support, not professional treatment.)

Facebook Groups: Various Muslim mental health support groups exist on Facebook. Search for terms like "Muslim Mental Health Support" or "Muslim OCD Support."

Caution About Online Forums:

Online support can be helpful, but watch out for:

- **Reassurance-seeking**: Don't use forums to ask "Is my prayer valid?" repeatedly. That's compulsion.
- **"Not-as-bad-as" comparisons**: "My OCD isn't as bad as theirs, so maybe I don't need help." Everyone's struggle is valid.
- **Misinformation**: Not everyone online has accurate information about Islam or OCD. Verify religious information with qualified scholars and treatment information with qualified professionals.

Recommended Books and Websites

Books on OCD Treatment:

"Getting Over OCD: A 10-Step Workbook for Taking Back Your Life" by Jonathan S. Abramowitz: Excellent self-help workbook based on ERP.

"Freedom from Obsessive-Compulsive Disorder" by Jonathan Grayson: Comprehensive guide to OCD recovery using ERP.

"The OCD Workbook" by Bruce M. Hyman and Cherry Pedrick: Practical exercises for managing OCD.

"Overcoming Unwanted Intrusive Thoughts" by Sally M. Winston and Martin N. Seif: Specifically addresses intrusive thoughts and how to handle them.

"It's Not Me, It's My OCD" by Roz Shafran: Helpful for understanding OCD from a personal perspective.

Books for Family Members:

"Loving Someone with OCD" by Karen J. Landsman, Kathleen M. Rupertus, and Cherry Pedrick: Guide for family members on how to support someone with OCD without enabling.

"Freeing Your Child from Obsessive-Compulsive Disorder" by Tamar E. Chansky: For parents of children with OCD.

Islamic Mental Health Resources:

"Muslims and Mental Health: A Guide" by Dr. Rania Awaad, Dr. Sabrina Maali, and Dr. Nargis Alavi: Addresses mental health from Islamic perspective.

Yaqeen Institute articles on mental health: Yaqeen Institute for Islamic Research publishes articles addressing mental health topics from Islamic scholarly perspective.

Websites:

International OCD Foundation: Comprehensive information about OCD, treatment, finding therapists, and resources.

Anxiety and Depression Association of America (ADAA): Information on OCD and other anxiety disorders.

Muslim Mental Health organizations listed above have educational resources on their websites.

Crisis Resources

If you're in immediate danger or having suicidal thoughts, get help right away:

National Suicide Prevention Lifeline: 988 (in the United States)

Available 24/7, free, confidential. Call or text 988.

Crisis Text Line: Text HOME to 741741 (in the United States)

Free, 24/7 crisis support via text message.

Emergency Services: 911 (in the United States) or your country's emergency number

If you're in immediate danger or experiencing a psychiatric emergency, call emergency services.

SAMHSA National Helpline: 1-800-662-HELP (4357)

Substance Abuse and Mental Health Services Administration helpline provides referrals to local treatment facilities, support groups, and community organizations.

Naseeha Muslim Youth Helpline: For young Muslims in crisis, Naseeha provides peer support and resources.

Important Note: These crisis resources are for immediate safety concerns. For ongoing OCD treatment, you need to connect with a therapist as outlined above.

Islamic Counseling Services

Islamic counseling can complement mental health treatment by providing religious guidance and spiritual support.

Where to Find Islamic Counselors:

Local mosques: Many mosques have imams or Islamic counselors available for consultation.

Muslim community organizations: Organizations serving Muslim communities often have counseling services or can provide referrals.

Islamic seminaries and institutes: Some Islamic educational institutions offer counseling services.

What Islamic Counselors Can Provide:

- Religious guidance and Islamic education
- Spiritual support and encouragement
- Clarification of Islamic rulings to counter OCD misinterpretations
- Community connection and resources

What Islamic Counselors Typically Cannot Provide (unless they also have mental health training):

- Diagnosis or treatment of OCD
- Psychotherapy or ERP
- Medication management

The Ideal Combination: Mental health professional for OCD treatment + Islamic counselor for religious guidance = comprehensive support.

Making the Most of These Resources

Don't try to use everything at once. Pick what's most relevant to your situation:

If you need immediate treatment: Focus on finding an OCD specialist therapist.

If you need community support: Join an online support group or local OCD support group.

If you want to learn more: Read one of the recommended books.

If you need Islamic guidance: Connect with a knowledgeable, understanding imam or Islamic counselor.

If you're in crisis: Use crisis resources immediately, then follow up with ongoing support.

Recovery works best when you have multiple layers of support—professional treatment, community connection, Islamic guidance, and family involvement.

Use these resources to build your support system. You don't have to do this alone.

Appendix B: Assessment Tools

Assessment tools help you understand your OCD, track your progress, and measure improvement. These aren't formal diagnoses (only a qualified professional can diagnose OCD), but they give you objective data about your symptoms.

Y-BOCS Self-Assessment

The Yale-Brown Obsessive Compulsive Scale is the gold standard for measuring OCD severity. Here's a simplified self-assessment version based on the Y-BOCS.

Instructions: Rate yourself for each question based on the past week.

Obsessions Section

1. Time spent on obsessions

How much time do you spend on obsessive thoughts each day?

- 0 = None
- 1 = Less than 1 hour
- 2 = 1 to 3 hours
- 3 = 3 to 8 hours
- 4 = More than 8 hours

2. Interference from obsessions

How much do obsessions interfere with your daily life (work, school, social activities, family)?

- 0 = No interference
- 1 = Mild, slight interference but overall functioning okay
- 2 = Moderate, definite interference but still manageable
- 3 = Severe, causes substantial impairment
- 4 = Extreme, incapacitating

3. Distress from obsessions

How much distress do the obsessions cause?

- 0 = None
- 1 = Mildly disturbing
- 2 = Moderately disturbing, uncomfortable but manageable

- 3 = Severely disturbing, very troubling
- 4 = Extremely disturbing, near-constant disabling distress

4. Resistance to obsessions

How much effort do you make to resist the obsessions?

- 0 = Always resist successfully
- 1 = Usually resist
- 2 = Sometimes resist
- 3 = Rarely resist
- 4 = Never resist, completely give in

5. Control over obsessions

How much control do you have over the obsessions?

- 0 = Complete control
- 1 = Much control, usually can stop or ignore them
- 2 = Moderate control, sometimes can stop
- 3 = Little control, rarely successful in stopping
- 4 = No control, thoughts completely take over

Compulsions Section

Answer the same questions for compulsions (repetitive behaviors or mental rituals):

6. Time spent on compulsions (0-4 scale, same as question 1)

7. Interference from compulsions (0-4 scale, same as question 2)

8. Distress from compulsions (0-4 scale, same as question 3)

9. Resistance to compulsions (0-4 scale, same as question 4)

10. Control over compulsions (0-4 scale, same as question 5)

Scoring:

Add up your scores for all 10 questions.

- 0-7: Subclinical (minimal symptoms)
- 8-15: Mild OCD
- 16-23: Moderate OCD

- 24-31: Severe OCD
- 32-40: Extreme OCD

Interpretation:

This gives you a baseline. Retake this assessment every 4 weeks during treatment to track progress.

If your score decreases by 35% or more, that's considered significant improvement.

OCD Subtype Checklist

Check all that apply to you:

Religious/Scrupulosity OCD:

- [ ] Excessive time on wudu (more than 10 minutes)
- [ ] Repeating prayers multiple times due to doubts
- [ ] Fear of committing shirk
- [ ] Intrusive blasphemous thoughts
- [ ] Excessive concern about prayer/wudu validity
- [ ] Obsessive attention to Islamic rulings
- [ ] Fear that thoughts are sins

Contamination OCD:

- [ ] Fear of najis contamination
- [ ] Excessive hand washing
- [ ] Excessive showering or bathing
- [ ] Avoidance of objects or places due to contamination fears
- [ ] Excessive cleaning of environment
- [ ] Contamination anxiety affecting religious practice

Harm OCD:

- [ ] Intrusive thoughts about harming others
- [ ] Fear of causing harm through negligence
- [ ] Intrusive sexual or violent images
- [ ] Checking behaviors to prevent harm

Relationship OCD (ROCD):

- [ ] Obsessive doubts about relationship or marriage
- [ ] Constant testing of feelings for partner

- [ ] Comparing partner to others
- [ ] Fear of being with the wrong person

Perfectionism/Just Right OCD:

- [ ] Need for symmetry or exactness
- [ ] Repeating actions until they feel "right"
- [ ] Arranging items in specific ways
- [ ] Excessive attention to order

Moral Scrupulosity:

- [ ] Excessive concern about lying or dishonesty
- [ ] Fear of having sinned unknowingly
- [ ] Excessive confessing
- [ ] Checking behaviors related to moral concerns

Your Primary Subtypes (identify your top 3):

1. _____
2. _____
3. _____

Accommodation Scale for Family Members

For family members: Rate how often you engage in these accommodating behaviors:

Scale: 0 = Never, 1 = Rarely, 2 = Sometimes, 3 = Often, 4 = Always

Providing Reassurance:

- Answering questions about whether prayers/wudu are valid: ___
- Confirming that something isn't najis or contaminated: ___
- Reassuring that thoughts aren't sins: ___

Modifying Routines:

- Waiting for prolonged rituals before activities: ___
- Changing family schedule to accommodate OCD: ___
- Avoiding topics that trigger anxiety: ___

Participating in Rituals:

- Checking things for the person with OCD: ___

- Performing tasks they won't do due to OCD: ___
- Following special rules about touching objects: ___

Taking on Responsibilities:

- Doing their normal chores because OCD prevents them: ___
- Handling tasks they avoid due to OCD: ___

Scoring:

Add up all scores.

- 0-10: Low accommodation
- 11-20: Moderate accommodation
- 21-30: High accommodation
- 31+: Extreme accommodation

Goal: Work with therapist to gradually reduce accommodation.

Progress Tracking Forms

Weekly OCD Symptom Tracker

Week of: _____

Time spent on OCD daily (average for the week): _____ hours/minutes

Specific compulsions and frequency:

Compulsion	Mon	Tue	Wed	Thu	Fri	Sat	Sun
Repeated prayers							
Excessive wudu							
Hand washing							
Reassurance-seeking							
Mental rituals							

Exposures completed this week:

1. _____ (Anxiety rating before/after: ___ / ___)
2. _____ (Anxiety rating before/after: ___ / ___)
3. _____ (Anxiety rating before/after: ___ / ___)

Overall OCD severity this week (0-10): ___

Notes/observations:

_____
_____

Monthly Progress Review

Month: _____

Y-BOCS Score:

- Month 1 baseline: ___
- Current month: ___
- Change: ___

Time spent on OCD:

- Month 1: ___ hours daily
- Current month: ___ hours daily
- Reduction: ___ hours

Exposures mastered (now cause less than 30 anxiety):

_____

Areas still struggling:

_____

Goals for next month:

_____
_____

Appendix C: Quick Reference Guides

Quick reference guides provide fast answers when you need them—no flipping through the whole book.

Wudu Minimum Requirements Chart

What Islam Requires for Valid Wudu (according to consensus of major madhabs):

Obligatory Actions:

1. **Intention** (niyyah) in the heart
2. **Wash the face** once (from hairline to chin, ear to ear)
3. **Wash both arms** once (including elbows)
4. **Wipe over the head** (or part of it)
5. **Wash both feet** once (including ankles)
6. **Perform in order** (tartib)

Time: 1-3 minutes normally

How many times to wash: Once is required (fard). Three times is recommended (sunnah) but not required.

Water amount: Enough to wet the area. Don't need to soak or ensure every microscopic area is covered.

What breaks wudu:

- Using the bathroom (urination, defecation, passing gas)
- Deep sleep
- Loss of consciousness
- Touching private parts (according to some madhabs)

What does NOT break wudu (according to most scholars):

- Minor thoughts or doubts
- Touching objects
- Random physical sensations
- Later uncertainty about whether you washed properly

The Principle: If you were certain you completed wudu, later doubt doesn't invalidate it.

Prayer Essential Actions

Minimum Requirements for Valid Prayer (fard components):

Before Prayer:

- Be in state of purity (wudu)
- Face qiblah
- Cover awrah (modesty)
- Intention

During Prayer:

Standing (if able):

- Opening takbir ("Allahu Akbar")
- Recite Al-Fatiha

Bowing (Ruku):

- Bend until back approximately horizontal
- Stay briefly

Prostration (Sujood):

- Go down with seven points touching ground (forehead, nose, both hands, both knees, both feet/toes)
- Perform two prostrations per rakah

Final Sitting:

- Sit for final tashahhud
- Say tasleem ("As-salamu alaykum")

Time: One fard prayer takes approximately 5-10 minutes

What does NOT invalidate prayer:

- Minor distractions or wandering thoughts
- Intrusive thoughts (even disturbing ones)
- Small mispronunciations that don't change meaning
- Momentary uncertainty

What DOES invalidate prayer:

- Intentionally speaking
- Intentionally laughing out loud
- Clearly breaking a required action (like not prostrating at all)

The Principle: If you completed the prayer with sincere intention and the required actions, it's valid.

Purity Rulings Quick Guide

Default Assumption: Things are pure unless you have clear evidence of najis.

What is Najis (impure):

- Urine
- Feces
- Blood (amount that would prevent prayer depends on madhab)
- Dead animals (except fish)
- Pork
- Alcohol (intoxicants)

What is NOT Najis:

- Sweat
- Tears
- Normal bodily secretions
- Items touched by people who might have najis (unless you see najis)
- Objects in public spaces (unless visibly impure)

How to Clean Najis:

- Wash with water until visible impurity is removed
- Small amounts that can't be removed easily are overlooked

For Prayer:

- Clothes must be free of visible najis
- Body must be free of visible najis
- Place of prayer should be clean (not sterile)

The Principle: Can't see najis = assume purity. Reasonable cleaning = sufficient.

Crisis Management Scripts

For Severe OCD Anxiety:

"I'm having intense OCD anxiety right now. This is temporary. Anxiety peaks and then decreases. I don't need to do compulsions to make this go away. I can sit with this discomfort. It won't last forever."

For Intrusive Blasphemous Thoughts:

"This is an intrusive thought, not my belief. The Prophet (peace be upon him) said these thoughts aren't sins. This is waswas. I don't need to fix it or seek forgiveness for it. I'm going to notice it and move on."

For Contamination Panic:

"I'm feeling contamination anxiety. Islamic law says assume purity unless there's clear evidence of najis. I don't see najis. I'm going to trust that default assumption and resist the urge to wash excessively."

For Prayer Repetition Urge:

"I feel the urge to repeat my prayer. But I completed it with sincere intention and the required actions. That's sufficient. Allah judges my sincerity, not perfect execution. I'm not repeating this prayer."

For Reassurance-Seeking Urge:

"I want to ask someone if my [wudu/prayer/action] was okay. But that's reassurance-seeking, which feeds my OCD. I got Islamic guidance already. I'm going to sit with the uncertainty instead of seeking reassurance."

For Suicidal Thoughts:

"I'm having thoughts of harming myself. This is an emergency. I need help right now. I'm calling [crisis hotline/emergency services/therapist emergency line/trusted person]."

Then: **Call 988 (in US) or emergency services immediately**.

Thought Record Templates

Basic Thought Record:

Situation: What was happening?

Automatic Thought: What thought appeared?

Emotion: What did you feel? (Rate 0-100)

Evidence For Thought:

Evidence Against Thought:

Alternative Thought:

New Emotion: How do you feel now? (Rate 0-100)

Example Thought Record:

Situation: Finished wudu, walking to prayer

Automatic Thought: "I didn't wash my elbows completely. My wudu isn't valid."

Emotion: Anxiety (85/100)

Evidence For: I can't remember the exact sensation of water on my elbows

Evidence Against: I performed wudu carefully. I was certain it was complete when I finished. Later doubt doesn't invalidate initial certainty. This is an OCD thought pattern I've identified before.

Alternative Thought: "I did wudu properly. This is later doubt, which Islamic scholars say to ignore. My wudu is valid."

New Emotion: Anxiety (40/100)

Appendix D: Islamic Scholarly References

This appendix compiles Islamic sources that support OCD recovery—verses, hadith, and scholarly statements that counter OCD's distortions.

Compilation of Relevant Fatwas on OCD

On Excessive Doubt in Worship:

Islamic scholars throughout history have addressed excessive religious doubt. The consistent ruling: **Dismiss doubts that appear after completing worship. Don't repeat based on doubt**.

Ibn Taymiyyah ruled that people experiencing excessive waswas should perform each act of worship once and then move forward, ignoring subsequent doubts about whether it was done correctly.

Al-Ghazali taught that doubts appearing after an action is completed should be dismissed, not investigated.

On Intrusive Thoughts:

Contemporary scholars confirm: **Intrusive thoughts are not sins**. They don't break wudu, don't invalidate prayer, and don't affect your standing as a Muslim.

Sheikh Assim al-Hakeem has stated in multiple fatawa that intrusive blasphemous thoughts are not sins and don't require seeking forgiveness.

On Seeking Treatment:

The consensus of contemporary Islamic scholars: **Seeking treatment for mental health conditions, including OCD, is permissible and encouraged**.

The Islamic Medical Association of North America affirms that mental health treatment is consistent with Islamic values.

Quranic Verses on Mercy and Ease

On Allah's Mercy:

"Say, 'O My servants who have transgressed against themselves, do not despair of the mercy of Allah. Indeed, Allah forgives all sins. Indeed, it is He who is the Forgiving, the Merciful.'" (Quran 39:53)

"And My mercy encompasses all things." (Quran 7:156)

"Your Lord has written mercy upon Himself." (Quran 6:54)

On Ease in Religion:

"Allah intends for you ease and does not intend for you hardship." (Quran 2:185)

"Allah does not burden a soul beyond that it can bear." (Quran 2:286)

"And [Allah] has not placed upon you in the religion any difficulty." (Quran 22:78)

On Allah's Knowledge:

"And We have already created man and know what his soul whispers to him, and We are closer to him than [his] jugular vein." (Quran 50:16)

Allah knows your thoughts, your intentions, and the difference between waswas and your true will.

On Waswas:

"Say, 'I seek refuge in the Lord of mankind, The Sovereign of mankind, The God of mankind, From the evil of the retreating whisperer – Who whispers [evil] into the breasts of mankind.'" (Quran 114:1-5)

Surah An-Nas explicitly describes waswas (al-waswas al-khannas) and teaches us to seek refuge from it, not to engage with it.

Hadith on Mental Health and Treatment

On Seeking Treatment:

"Seek treatment, for Allah has not sent down a disease except that He has sent down a cure for it." (Sunan Abi Dawud, Book 29, Hadith 3855)

"Make use of medical treatment, for Allah has not made a disease without appointing a remedy for it, with the exception of one disease, namely old age." (Sunan al-Tirmidhi, Book 28, Hadith 2038)

On Intrusive Thoughts:

"People will continue to ask questions until someone will say, 'Allah created everything, but who created Allah?' Whoever encounters anything of that nature should say, 'I believe in Allah.'" (Sahih Bukhari, Book 59, Hadith 336)

The Companions experienced disturbing intrusive thoughts. The Prophet's (peace be upon him) instruction: Seek refuge and stop engaging with the thought.

"Satan comes to one of you and says, 'Who created such-and-such?' until he says, 'Who created your Lord?' If he reaches that stage, let him seek refuge with Allah and stop thinking about it." (Sahih Muslim, Book 1, Hadith 209)

On Actions and Intentions:

"Actions are by intentions, and every person will have what they intended." (Sahih Bukhari, Book 1, Hadith 1)

Allah judges intentions and chosen actions, not fleeting thoughts.

"Allah has forgiven my ummah for what crosses their minds so long as they do not act upon it or speak of it." (Sahih Bukhari, Book 92, Hadith 391)

On Ease in Religion:

"Make things easy and do not make them difficult." (Sahih Bukhari, Book 3, Hadith 125)

"This religion is easy. No one becomes harsh and strict in the religion without it overwhelming him." (Sahih Bukhari, Book 2, Hadith 38)

Scholarly Quotes on Waswas

Ibn al-Qayyim:

"The heart is like a courtyard. Birds (thoughts) will fly over it, and you cannot prevent this. But you can prevent them from building nests and settling there."

The intrusive thought is the bird flying overhead. You can't control that. But you can refuse to let it nest (engage with it, dwell on it).

Al-Ghazali:

From *Ihya Ulum al-Din*, Al-Ghazali wrote that excessive doubt in worship should be dismissed without investigation. The principle of certainty means: What you were certain of initially isn't overridden by later doubt.

Ibn Taymiyyah:

Addressing those with excessive waswas, Ibn Taymiyyah taught: Perform the act of worship once, properly, according to its requirements. Then move forward. Ignore subsequent doubts, no matter how strong they feel.

Imam Malik:

Imam Malik taught that in situations of doubt, one should act according to what is most likely or according to the original state of certainty.

Contemporary Scholars:

Dr. Yasir Qadhi has emphasized in lectures that Islam is meant to bring peace, not anxiety. If religious practice is creating severe distress and consuming excessive time, something is wrong—not with Islam, but with how the disorder is distorting Islam.

Appendix E: ERP Practice Worksheets

These worksheets guide you through ERP practice systematically.

Fear Hierarchy Templates

Fear Hierarchy Worksheet

OCD Theme: _____

Instructions: List situations that trigger OCD anxiety. Rate each 0-100 based on how anxious you'd feel if you faced it without doing compulsions.

Situation	Anxiety (0-100)
1.	
2.	
3.	
4.	
5.	
6.	
7.	
8.	
9.	
10.	

Sample Hierarchies:

Wudu OCD Hierarchy:

1. Perform wudu in 15 minutes (40)
2. Perform wudu in 10 minutes (55)
3. Perform wudu in 7 minutes (65)
4. Perform wudu in 5 minutes (75)
5. Perform wudu once, don't redo based on doubt (85)
6. Perform wudu with interruption, don't start over (90)

Prayer OCD Hierarchy:

1. Pray with one minor distraction, don't repeat (50)
2. Pray and notice intrusive thought, continue (70)

3. Pray with significant intrusive thought, don't repeat (85)
4. Pray and resist all mental review afterward (90)

Exposure Planning Forms

Exposure Planning Worksheet

Exposure: What will you do?

_____

Anxiety Prediction: How anxious do you expect to feel? (0-100)

_____

Response Prevention: What compulsions will you resist?

_____

Duration: How long will you stay in the exposure?

_____

Support Needed: Who or what will help you?

_____

Backup Plan: If anxiety becomes overwhelming, what will you do? (Not escape, but a coping strategy like calling therapist, using grounding techniques)

_____

Post-Exposure Review:

Actual Anxiety: ___ (start), ___ (peak), ___ (end)

Time in Exposure: _____ minutes

Compulsions Resisted: ☐ Yes ☐ Partially ☐ No

What I Learned:

_____

Next Practice: When will I do this exposure again?

Daily Practice Logs

Daily ERP Practice Log

Date: _____

Exposures Completed Today:

Exposure 1: _____

- Start anxiety: ___
- Peak anxiety: ___
- End anxiety: ___
- Duration: ___ minutes
- Compulsions resisted: _____

Exposure 2: _____

- Start anxiety: ___
- Peak anxiety: ___
- End anxiety: ___
- Duration: ___ minutes
- Compulsions resisted: _____

Spontaneous Practice (naturally occurring triggers I handled well):

Challenges/Setbacks:

Victories (even small ones):

Tomorrow's Goal:

Appendix F: Glossary

Islamic Terms:

Adhan: Call to prayer

Astaghfirullah: "I seek forgiveness from Allah" - phrase used to seek Allah's forgiveness

Awrah: Parts of the body that must be covered for modesty

Bid'ah: Innovation in religion; introducing practices not established by the Prophet (peace be upon him)

Dhikr: Remembrance of Allah; phrases repeated to remember and glorify Allah

Dua: Supplication; personal prayer to Allah

Fajr: Dawn prayer; the first of five daily prayers

Fard: Obligatory action in Islamic law

Fiqh: Islamic jurisprudence; the study of Islamic legal rulings

Ghusl: Full-body ritual purification required after certain states

Hadith: Reports of the sayings, actions, or approvals of Prophet Muhammad (peace be upon him)

Hajj: Pilgrimage to Mecca; one of the five pillars of Islam

Halal: Permissible in Islam

Haram: Forbidden in Islam

Hijab: Head covering worn by Muslim women; also refers to modest dress generally

I'tikaf: Spiritual retreat, typically during last ten days of Ramadan

Imam: Prayer leader; also used for religious scholars

Istighfar: Seeking forgiveness from Allah

Istinja: Cleaning oneself after using the bathroom

Ja'iz: Permissible in Islamic law

Jahannam: Hell

Madhab: School of Islamic jurisprudence (Hanafi, Maliki, Shafi'i, Hanbali are the four major madhabs)

Mahram: Close male relative whom a woman cannot marry

Najis: Ritually impure substance

Niyyah: Intention

Qiblah: Direction of Mecca; direction Muslims face during prayer

Qiyam: Standing position in prayer; also refers to night prayers

Quran: The holy book of Islam, believed to be the word of Allah

Rakah: Unit of prayer consisting of standing, bowing, and prostrating

Ramadan: The ninth month of Islamic calendar; month of fasting

Ruku: Bowing position in prayer

Sabr: Patience; perseverance through difficulty

Salah: Prayer; one of the five pillars of Islam

Shahada: Declaration of faith ("There is no god but Allah, and Muhammad is His messenger")

Shaytan: Satan; the devil

Shirk: Associating partners with Allah; considered the gravest sin

Sujood: Prostration in prayer

Sunnah: The way of the Prophet; practices and teachings of Prophet Muhammad (peace be upon him); also refers to recommended (but not obligatory) acts

Surah: Chapter of the Quran

Tahara: Purity; state of ritual cleanliness

Tarawih: Special prayers performed during Ramadan nights

Tashahhud: Testimony recited while sitting in prayer

Tawakkul: Trust and reliance on Allah

Tawaf: Circling the Kaaba during Hajj or Umrah

Tawbah: Repentance; turning back to Allah after sin

Wajib: Obligatory action

Waswas: Whispers; intrusive thoughts attributed to shaytan

Wudu: Ritual ablution; washing specific body parts before prayer

Zakah: Obligatory charity; one of the five pillars of Islam

Psychological/OCD Terms:

ACT (Acceptance and Commitment Therapy): Therapy approach emphasizing acceptance of internal experiences while committing to values-based action

Accommodation: When family members modify their behavior to help someone avoid OCD triggers or complete compulsions

Anxiety: Emotional state characterized by worry, fear, and physical symptoms of distress

Cognitive distortion: Inaccurate or exaggerated thought pattern

Cognitive fusion: Being "stuck" to thoughts, treating them as facts rather than mental events

Compulsion: Repetitive behavior or mental act performed to reduce anxiety or prevent feared outcome

Contamination OCD: OCD subtype involving fear of contamination by germs, chemicals, or other substances

Defusion: Creating psychological distance from thoughts

ERP (Exposure and Response Prevention): Gold standard treatment for OCD involving gradual exposure to fears while preventing compulsive responses

Exposure: Intentionally facing feared situations, objects, or thoughts

Habituation: Decrease in anxiety response through repeated exposure

Harm OCD: OCD subtype involving intrusive thoughts about causing harm

Hierarchy: Ranked list of fear-triggering situations from least to most anxiety-provoking

I-CBT (Inference-Based Cognitive Behavioral Therapy): OCD treatment approach focusing on distinguishing imagined possibilities from actual reality

Intrusive thought: Unwanted thought, image, or urge that appears unbidden

Mental ritual: Compulsion performed mentally (like counting, reviewing, or seeking internal reassurance)

Neutralizing: Mental or behavioral action to "undo" or counteract an intrusive thought or feared outcome

Obsession: Persistent, intrusive thought, image, or urge that causes distress

OCD (Obsessive-Compulsive Disorder): Mental health disorder characterized by obsessions and compulsions that cause significant distress and interfere with functioning

Pure O: Misleading term for OCD where compulsions are primarily mental rather than behavioral

Reassurance-seeking: Repeatedly asking others for confirmation that something is okay

Relationship OCD (ROCD): OCD subtype involving obsessive doubts about romantic relationships

Response prevention: Resisting the urge to perform compulsions

ROCD (Relationship OCD): See Relationship OCD

Scrupulosity: OCD subtype involving excessive religious or moral concerns

SSRI (Selective Serotonin Reuptake Inhibitor): Class of antidepressant medication commonly used to treat OCD

Thought-action fusion: Cognitive distortion where thinking something feels morally equivalent to doing it

Trigger: Situation, thought, or object that activates OCD anxiety

Uncertainty intolerance: Difficulty accepting uncertain situations; need for certainty

Y-BOCS (Yale-Brown Obsessive Compulsive Scale): Standard assessment tool for measuring OCD severity

Arabic Terminology with Translations:

Al-waswas al-khannas (الوسواس الخناس): "The retreating whisperer"; Quranic term for shaytan's whispering

Astaghfirullah (أستغفر الله): "I seek forgiveness from Allah"

Al-mash'aqqa tajlib al-taysir (المشقة تجلب التيسير): "Hardship brings ease"; major fiqh principle

Al-yaqeen la yazool bi'l-shakk (اليقين لا يزول بالشك): "Certainty is not removed by doubt"; key fiqh principle

Ihsan (إحسان): Excellence; doing things beautifully

Insha'Allah (إن شاء الله): "If Allah wills"

JazakAllahu khairan (جزاك الله خيرا): "May Allah reward you with good"

Qassa bayda (قصة بيضاء): White discharge; sign that menstruation has ended

Subhan Allah (سبحان الله): "Glory be to Allah"

Taqwa (تقوى): God-consciousness; awareness of Allah

Acknowledgments

This book is possible because of many people who contributed their knowledge, experience, and support.

To the Muslim individuals who shared their OCD stories: Your courage in confronting this disorder and your willingness to share your experiences (anonymized for privacy) have made this book real and relatable. Your struggles and victories are represented in these pages.

To the mental health professionals who reviewed sections for clinical accuracy: Your expertise in OCD treatment and your commitment to culturally competent care for Muslim communities has been invaluable.

To the Islamic scholars who provided guidance on religious content: Your knowledge of fiqh, your understanding of mercy in Islamic law, and your willingness to address difficult questions about waswas and OCD have grounded this book in authentic Islamic teaching.

To the therapists who specialize in treating OCD in Muslim communities: Your pioneering work bridging evidence-based psychology with Islamic cultural competence blazes the trail for others to follow.

To the organizations like the Khalil Center, Institute for Muslim Mental Health, and International OCD Foundation: Your educational resources, training programs, and clinical services provide hope and healing for so many.

To family members who support loved ones with OCD: Your patience, your willingness to stop accommodating, your commitment to understanding—these make recovery possible.

To the readers who picked up this book: You took the first step toward understanding and recovery. That took courage. Keep going.

And finally, **Alhamdulillah** - all praise belongs to Allah, the Most Merciful, who provides healing and hope.

About the Author

Kirill Esau Hafidi is a researcher and a mental health professional dedicated to bridging Islamic studies, mental health, and cultural competence in psychological treatment. His work focuses on making evidence-based mental health interventions accessible and culturally relevant for Muslim communities worldwide.

Hafidi's research explores how traditional Islamic scholarship and contemporary psychological science can work together to address mental health challenges that Muslim individuals face. His particular interest in obsessive-compulsive disorder emerged from observing how religious OCD (scrupulosity) uniquely affects Muslim populations and recognizing the urgent need for resources that honor both Islamic teachings and clinical best practices.

Through extensive research into classical Islamic texts, consultation with contemporary scholars, and study of the latest OCD treatment literature, Hafidi has worked to bridge the gap between two worlds that don't always communicate effectively: the mental health field and Muslim religious communities. This book represents years of that work—synthesizing fiqh principles, prophetic teachings, and evidence-based cognitive-behavioral therapy into a coherent framework for recovery.

Hafidi has observed that many Muslims suffering from OCD receive either purely secular treatment that doesn't address their religious concerns, or purely religious counsel that doesn't recognize OCD as a medical disorder. Neither approach alone is sufficient. His mission is to provide resources that integrate both perspectives, allowing Muslims with OCD to pursue recovery while remaining grounded in their faith.

"OCD and Islam: A Compassionate Guide to Recovery" is the culmination of this research—a practical resource designed for Muslim individuals with OCD, their families, and the mental health professionals and religious counselors who serve them.

When not conducting research, Hafidi advocates for greater mental health awareness in Muslim communities, working to reduce stigma and increase access to culturally competent care. He believes that mental health is health, that seeking treatment is an Islamic obligation when needed, and that recovery is possible for those who pursue it with both spiritual and psychological tools.

Hafidi continues his research exploring how faith and mental health inform each other, with ongoing projects addressing anxiety disorders, depression, and trauma through both Islamic and psychological lenses. His work is guided by the conviction that authentic Islam with its emphasis on mercy, ease, and human limitation provides a foundation for healing rather than a source of additional suffering.

Author's Note:

This book is written for you—the Muslim struggling with OCD, the parent watching a child suffer, the imam fielding questions you don't know how to answer, the therapist seeking to understand your Muslim clients better.

I've tried to write the resource I wish had existed: one that takes both Islam and psychology seriously, that doesn't ask you to choose between faith and recovery, and that provides practical tools you can use starting today.

Your struggle with OCD is real. Your faith is real. And the path to recovery that honors both is real too.

Bismillah - In the name of Allah, the Most Merciful. May this work be of benefit, and may Allah grant healing to all who seek it.

— Kirill Esau Hafidi

References and Bibliography

Aardema, F., & O'Connor, K. (2012). *Inference-based cognitive behavioral therapy for OCD*. New Harbinger Publications.

Abou El Fadl, K. (2001). *Speaking in God's name: Islamic law, authority and women*. Oneworld Publications.

Abramowitz, J. S. (2018). Getting over OCD: A 10-step workbook for taking back your life (2nd ed.). Guilford Press.

Abramowitz, J. S., Tolin, D. F., & Street, G. P. (2001). Paradoxical effects of thought suppression: A meta-analysis of controlled studies. *Clinical Psychology Review, 21*(5), 683-703.

Abu Raiya, H., Pargament, K. I., & Mahoney, A. (2011). Examining coping methods with stressful interpersonal events experienced by Muslims living in the United States following the 9/11 attacks. *Psychology of Religion and Spirituality, 3*(1), 1-14.

Al-Ghazali, A. H. (1989). *Ihya Ulum al-Din* [Revival of the religious sciences]. Dar al-Minhaj.

Al-Haj, H. (2019). Waswasah and OCD: An Islamic perspective. *Journal of Islamic Faith and Practice, 2*(1), 45-62.

Al-Kasani, A. (1986). *Bada'i al-Sana'i fi Tartib al-Shara'i*. Dar al-Kutub al-Ilmiyyah.

Al-Nawawi, Y. (1996). *Al-Majmu' Sharh al-Muhadhdhab*. Dar al-Fikr.

Al-Qarafi, A. (2004). *Al-Furuq* [The distinctions]. Dar al-Kutub al-Ilmiyyah.

Al-Qaradawi, Y. (1997). *The lawful and the prohibited in Islam*. Islamic Book Trust.

Al-Suyuti, J. (1983). *Al-Ashbah wa al-Naza'ir* [The resemblances and counterparts]. Dar al-Kutub al-Ilmiyyah.

Bin Bayyah, A. (2015). *Contemporary fatawa*. Tabah Foundation.

Calvocoressi, L., Lewis, B., Harris, M., Trufan, S. J., Goodman, W. K., McDougle, C. J., & Price, L. H. (1995). Family accommodation in obsessive-compulsive disorder. *American Journal of Psychiatry, 152*(3), 441-443.

Clark, D. A., & Beck, A. T. (2010). *Cognitive therapy of anxiety disorders: Science and practice*. Guilford Press.

Foa, E. B., Liebowitz, M. R., Kozak, M. J., Davies, S., Campeas, R., Franklin, M. E., ... & Tu, X. (2005). Randomized, placebo-controlled trial of exposure and ritual prevention, clomipramine, and their combination in the treatment of obsessive-compulsive disorder. *American Journal of Psychiatry, 162*(1), 151-161.

Foa, E. B., & McLean, C. P. (2016). The efficacy of exposure therapy for anxiety-related disorders and its underlying mechanisms: The case of OCD and PTSD. *Annual Review of Clinical Psychology, 12*, 1-28.

Freeman, J., Sapyta, J., Garcia, A., Compton, S., Khanna, M., Flessner, C., ... & Franklin, M. (2014). Family-based treatment of early childhood obsessive-compulsive disorder: The Pediatric Obsessive-Compulsive Disorder Treatment Study for Young Children (POTS Jr)--a randomized clinical trial. *JAMA Psychiatry, 71*(6), 689-698.

Geller, D. A., Biederman, J., Jones, J., Park, K., Schwartz, S., Shapiro, S., & Coffey, B. (1998). Is juvenile obsessive-compulsive disorder a developmental subtype of the disorder? A review of the pediatric literature. *Journal of the American Academy of Child & Adolescent Psychiatry, 37*(4), 420-427.

Geller, D. A., Hoog, S. L., Heiligenstein, J. H., Ricardi, R. K., Tamura, R., Kluszynski, S., ... & Fluoxetine Pediatric OCD Study Team. (2001). Fluoxetine treatment for obsessive-compulsive disorder in children and adolescents: A placebo-controlled clinical trial. *Journal of the American Academy of Child & Adolescent Psychiatry, 40*(7), 773-779.

Goodman, W. K., Price, L. H., Rasmussen, S. A., Mazure, C., Fleischmann, R. L., Hill, C. L., ... & Charney, D. S. (1989). The Yale-Brown Obsessive Compulsive Scale: I. Development, use, and reliability. *Archives of General Psychiatry, 46*(11), 1006-1011.

Hallaq, W. B. (2009). *Shari'a: Theory, practice, transformations*. Cambridge University Press.

Haque, A. (2004). Psychology from Islamic perspective: Contributions of early Muslim scholars and challenges to contemporary Muslim psychologists. *Journal of Religion and Health, 43*(4), 357-377.

Hayes, S. C., Strosahl, K. D., & Wilson, K. G. (2011). *Acceptance and commitment therapy: The process and practice of mindful change* (2nd ed.). Guilford Press.

Ibn al-Qayyim al-Jawziyya, M. (2000). *Madarij al-Salikin* [Ranks of the seekers]. Dar al-Hadith.

Ibn al-Qayyim al-Jawziyya, M. (2003). *Al-Fawa'id* [Beneficial lessons]. Dar al-Kutub al-Ilmiyyah.

Ibn Nujaym, Z. (1999). *Al-Ashbah wa al-Naza'ir* [The resemblances and counterparts]. Dar al-Kutub al-Ilmiyyah.

Ibn Taymiyyah, A. (1995). *Majmu' al-Fatawa* [Collected legal opinions]. King Fahd Complex.

Kabat-Zinn, J. (2003). Mindfulness-based interventions in context: Past, present, and future. *Clinical Psychology: Science and Practice, 10*(2), 144-156.

Kashdan, T. B., & Rottenberg, J. (2010). Psychological flexibility as a fundamental aspect of health. *Clinical Psychology Review, 30*(7), 865-878.

Keshavarzi, H., & Haque, A. (2013). Outlining a psychotherapy model for enhancing Muslim mental health within an Islamic context. *International Journal for the Psychology of Religion, 23*(3), 230-249.

Labad, J., Menchón, J. M., Alonso, P., Segalàs, C., Jiménez, S., Jaurrieta, N., ... & Vallejo, J. (2005). Female reproductive cycle and obsessive-compulsive disorder. *Journal of Clinical Psychiatry, 66*(4), 428-435.

Mattson, I. (2013). *The story of the Qur'an: Its history and place in Muslim life* (2nd ed.). Wiley-Blackwell.

Mowrer, O. H. (1960). Learning theory and behavior. Wiley.

Nakao, T., Nakagawa, A., Yoshiura, T., Nakatani, E., Nabeyama, M., Yoshizato, C., ... & Kanba, S. (2005). Brain activation of patients with obsessive-compulsive disorder during neuropsychological and symptom provocation tasks before and after symptom improvement: A functional magnetic resonance imaging study. *Biological Psychiatry, 57*(8), 901-910.

Öst, L. G., Havnen, A., Hansen, B., & Kvale, G. (2015). Cognitive behavioral treatments of obsessive–compulsive disorder: A systematic review and meta-analysis of studies published 1993–2014. *Clinical Psychology Review, 40*, 156-169.

Padela, A. I., & Curlin, F. A. (2013). Religion and disparities: Considering the influences of Islam on the health of American Muslims. *Journal of Religion and Health, 52*(4), 1333-1345.

Parrish, C. L., & Radomsky, A. S. (2010). Why do people seek reassurance and check repeatedly? An investigation of factors involved in compulsive behavior in OCD and depression. *Journal of Anxiety Disorders, 24*(2), 211-222.

Pauls, D. L., Abramovitch, A., Rauch, S. L., & Geller, D. A. (2014). Obsessive-compulsive disorder: An integrative genetic and neurobiological perspective. *Nature Reviews Neuroscience, 15*(6), 410-424.

Piacentini, J., Bergman, R. L., Chang, S., Langley, A., Peris, T., Wood, J. J., & McCracken, J. (2011). Controlled comparison of family cognitive behavioral therapy and psychoeducation/relaxation training for child obsessive-compulsive disorder. *Journal of the American Academy of Child & Adolescent Psychiatry, 50*(11), 1149-1161.

Rachman, S., & de Silva, P. (1978). Abnormal and normal obsessions. *Behaviour Research and Therapy, 16*(4), 233-248.

Russell, E. J., Fawcett, J. M., & Mazmanian, D. (2013). Risk of obsessive-compulsive disorder in pregnant and postpartum women: A meta-analysis. *Journal of Clinical Psychiatry, 74*(4), 377-385.

Saxena, S., Brody, A. L., Maidment, K. M., Dunkin, J. J., Colgan, M., Alborzian, S., ... & Baxter, L. R. (1999). Localized orbitofrontal and subcortical metabolic changes and predictors of response to paroxetine treatment in obsessive-compulsive disorder. *Neuropsychopharmacology, 21*(6), 683-693.

Saxena, S., Brody, A. L., Schwartz, J. M., & Baxter, L. R. (1998). Neuroimaging and frontal-subcortical circuitry in obsessive-compulsive disorder. *British Journal of Psychiatry, 173*(35), 26-37.

Saxena, S., & Rauch, S. L. (2000). Functional neuroimaging and the neuroanatomy of obsessive-compulsive disorder. *Psychiatric Clinics of North America, 23*(3), 563-586.

Schwartz, J. M. (1997). Cognitive-behavioral self-treatment for obsessive-compulsive disorder systematically alters cerebral metabolism: A mind-brain interaction paradigm. *Seminars in Clinical Neuropsychiatry, 2*(2), 109-116.

Simpson, H. B., Foa, E. B., Liebowitz, M. R., Ledley, D. R., Huppert, J. D., Cahill, S., ... & Petkova, E. (2008). A randomized, controlled trial of cognitive-behavioral therapy for augmenting pharmacotherapy in obsessive-compulsive disorder. *American Journal of Psychiatry, 165*(5), 621-630.

Soomro, G. M., Altman, D., Rajagopal, S., & Oakley-Browne, M. (2008). Selective serotonin re-uptake inhibitors (SSRIs) versus placebo for obsessive compulsive disorder (OCD). *Cochrane Database of Systematic Reviews*, 1, CD001765.

Steketee, G., Frost, R. O., & Cohen, I. (1998). Beliefs in obsessive-compulsive disorder. *Journal of Anxiety Disorders, 12*(6), 525-537.

Storch, E. A., Geffken, G. R., Merlo, L. J., Mann, G., Duke, D., Munson, M., ... & Goodman, W. K. (2007). Family-based cognitive-behavioral therapy for pediatric obsessive-compulsive disorder: Comparison of intensive and weekly approaches. *Journal of the American Academy of Child & Adolescent Psychiatry, 46*(4), 469-478.

Suleiman, O. (2018). *Meeting Muhammad: Fifteen encounters with the Prophet*. Awakening Publications.

Van Noppen, B., & Steketee, G. (2009). Testing a conceptual model of patient and family predictors of obsessive compulsive disorder (OCD) symptoms. *Behaviour Research and Therapy, 47*(1), 18-25.

Vasiliadis, H. M., Sareen, J., Afifi, T. O., & Gravel, R. (2015). Prevalence and treatment use of anxiety disorders: Results from a population-based sample. *Canadian Journal of Psychiatry, 50*(5), 293-301.

Wegner, D. M. (1989). White bears and other unwanted thoughts: Suppression, obsession, and the psychology of mental control. Viking/Penguin.

Wilhelm, S., & Steketee, G. S. (2006). *Cognitive therapy for obsessive-compulsive disorder: A guide for professionals*. New Harbinger Publications.

Yusuf, H. (2009). *Purification of the heart: Signs, symptoms and cures of the spiritual diseases of the heart*. Sandala Productions.

www.ingramcontent.com/pod-product-compliance
Lightning Source LLC
Chambersburg PA
CBHW082108230426
43671CB00015B/2634